What is VAK?

YOU CAN APPROACH the topic of learning styles with a simple and powerful system—one that focuses on just three ways of perceiving through your senses:

- Seeing, or *visual learning*
- Hearing, or *auditory learning*
- Movement, or *kinesthetic learning*

To recall this system, remember the letters VAK, which stand for **v**isual, **a**uditory, and **k**inesthetic. The theory is that each of us prefers to learn through one of these sense channels. To reflect on your VAK preferences, answer the following questions. Circle the answer that best describes how you would respond. This is not a formal inventory—just a way to prompt some self-discovery.

When you have problems spelling a word, you prefer to

1. Look it up in the dictionary.
2. Say the word out loud several times before you write it down.
3. Write out the word with several different spellings and then choose one.

You enjoy courses the most when you get to

1. View slides, videos, and readings with plenty of charts, tables, and illustrations.
2. Ask questions, engage in small-group discussions, and listen to guest speakers.
3. Take field trips, participate in lab sessions, or apply the course content while working as a volunteer or intern.

When giving someone directions on how to drive to a destination, you prefer to

1. Pull out a piece of paper and sketch a map.
2. Give verbal instructions.
3. Say, "I'm driving to a place near there, so just follow me."

When planning an extended vacation to a new destination, you prefer to

1. Read colorful, illustrated brochures or articles about that place.
2. Talk directly to someone who's been there.
3. Spend time at that destination on a work-related trip before vacationing there.

You've made a commitment to learn to play the guitar. The first thing you do is

1. Go to a library or music store and find an instruction book with plenty of diagrams and chord charts.
2. Listen closely to some recorded guitar solos and see whether you can sing along with them.
3. Buy a guitar, pluck the strings, and ask someone to show you a few chords.

You've saved up enough money to lease a car. When choosing from among several new models, the most important factor in your decision is

1. The car's appearance.
2. The information you get by talking to people who own the cars you're considering.
3. The overall impression you get by taking each car on a test drive.

You've just bought a new computer system. When setting up the system, the first thing you do is

1. Skim through the printed instructions that come with the equipment.
2. Call up someone with a similar system and ask her for directions.
3. Assemble the components as best as you can, see if everything works, and consult the instructions only as a last resort.

You get a scholarship to study abroad next semester in a Spanish-speaking country. To learn as much Spanish as you can before you depart, you

1. Buy a video-based language course on DVD.
2. Download audio podcasts that guarantee basic fluency in just 30 days.
3. Sign up for a short immersion course in which you speak only Spanish.

Name <u>Elliot McElroy</u> Date <u> </u>

Now take a few minutes to reflect on the meaning of your responses. The number of each answer corresponds to a learning style preference.

1 = visual   **2 = auditory**   **3 = kinesthetic**

	Visual	Auditory	Kinesthetic
My totals			

My dominant Learning Style(s): _____

_____

Do you see a pattern in your own answers? A pattern indicates that you prefer learning through one sense channel over the others. Or you might find that your preferences are fairly balanced.

Whether you have a defined preference or not, you can increase your options for success by learning through *all* your sense channels. For example, you can enhance visual learning by leaving room in your class notes to add your own charts, diagrams, tables, and other visuals later. You can also key your handwritten notes into a computer file and use software that allows you to add colorful fonts and illustrations.

To enhance auditory learning, reinforce your memory of key ideas by talking about them. When studying, stop often to summarize key points and add examples in your own words. After doing this several times, dictate your summaries into a voice recorder and transfer the files to an iPod or similar device. Listen to these files while walking to class or standing in line at the store.

For kinesthetic learning, you've got plenty of options as well. Look for ways to translate course content into three-dimensional models that you can build. While studying grammar, for example, create a model of a sentence using different colors of clay to represent different parts of speech. Whenever possible, supplement lectures with real-world audio and video input and experiences, field trips to Spanish-speaking neighborhoods, and other opportunities for hands-on activity. Also recite key concepts from your courses while you walk or exercise.

These are just a few examples. In your path to mastery of learning styles, you can create many more of your own.

VOLUME 1

CUADROS
INTRODUCTORY SPANISH

Sheri Spaine Long
University of Alabama at Birmingham

María Carreira
California State University at Long Beach

Sylvia Madrigal Velasco

Kristin Swanson

HEINLE
CENGAGE Learning™

Australia • Brazil • Japan • Korea • Mexico • Singapore • Spain • United Kingdom • United States

HEINLE
CENGAGE Learning™

Cuadros
Sheri Spaine Long, María Carreira,
Sylvia Madrigal Velasco, and
Kristin Swanson

Vice President, Editorial Director:
  PJ Boardman

Publisher: Beth Kramer

Senior Acquisitions Editor:
  Heather Bradley Cole

Senior Development Editor: Kim Beuttler

Assistant Editor: Sara Dyer

Editorial Assistant: Claire Kaplan

Senior Media Editor: Morgen Murphy

Senior Marketing Manager: Ben Rivera

Marketing Coordinator: Claire Fleming

Marketing Communications Manager:
  Glenn McGibbon

Senior Content Project Manager:
  Aileen Mason

Senior Art Director: Linda Jurras

Senior Manufacturing Planner:
  Betsy Donaghey

Rights Acquisition Specialist:
  Mandy Grozsko

Production Service: PreMediaGlobal

Text Designers: Carol Maglitta, Susan Gilday

Cover Designer: Harold Burch

Cover Image: ©Marc Le Fèvre/Photolibrary

Compositor: PreMediaGlobal

For product information and technology assistance, contact us at
Cengage Learning Customer & Sales Support, 1-800-354-9706

For permission to use material from this text or product,
submit all requests online at **www.cengage.com/permissions**
Further permissions questions can be emailed to
permissionrequest@cengage.com

Library of Congress Control Number: 2011937474

ISBN-13: 978-1-111-34114-5

ISBN-10: 1-111-34114-1

Heinle
20 Channel Center Street
Boston, MA 02210
USA

Cengage Learning is a leading provider of customized learning solutions with office locations around the globe, including Singapore, the United Kingdom, Australia, Mexico, Brazil, and Japan. Locate your local office at **www.cengage.com/global**

Cengage Learning products are represented in Canada by Nelson Education, Ltd.

To learn more about Heinle, visit **www.cengage.com/heinle**

Purchase any of our products at your local college store or at our preferred online store **www.cengagebrain.com**

Instructors: Please visit **login.cengage.com** and log in to access instructor-specific resources.

Printed in Canada
3 4 5 6 7 16 15 14 13 12

To the Student

¡Bienvenidos! Welcome to the *Cuadros* introductory Spanish program. Spanish is one of the most useful languages you can learn; it is spoken by nearly 500 million people across the globe, including over 50 million Hispanics in the United States alone—one out of every six Americans. It is the most spoken language in the world after Mandarin Chinese and English. As you undertake your study of the Spanish language with *Cuadros*, keep in mind the following:

- We strive to present the Spanish-speaking world in all its diversity, with particular attention to Indigenous and African-Hispanic populations, as well as European and Latin American immigrant populations.

- We guide you to make cross-cultural comparisons between the cultures you learn about and your own. Too often, the emphasis has been on the differences among cultures, when what may be surprising is the number of things we have in common with Spanish speakers around the world.

- We encourage you to look at your own community and to meet and interact with the Spanish speakers you encounter in both local and global communities. Spanish is all around you—just keep your eyes and ears open for it!

- *Cuadros* is designed to enrich your language-learning experience—while you are learning another language, you are also gathering information *about* the people who speak it and the countries where it is spoken. At first, you may think that you are unable to read or understand much Spanish, but in *Cuadros*, the focus is on getting the main ideas, and the tasks expected of you are limited to what you have already learned or what you can safely deduce from context. You will be surprised to see that you can comprehend more than you think you can!

- *Cuadros* features a variety of resources to help you achieve your language-learning goals more easily. Media icons at relevant points throughout the print book tell you exactly which component to use for additional practice or support. Or, work right from the eBook for direct access to all of the program's resources, including audio recordings of key vocabulary and grammar terms, instant activity feedback, and online chat and commenting functionality.

- Learning a language is easier if you relax and have fun. Keeping this in mind, we've included humorous and contemporary content with the goal of making language learning enjoyable and interesting.

We hope you enjoy your introduction to the Spanish language and its many peoples and cultures. Learning a language sets you on a course of life-long learning. It is one of the most valuable and exciting things you can do to prepare yourself to be a global citizen of the twenty-first century.

—The Authors

Student Components

Student Text

Your **Student Text** contains all the information and activities you need for in-class use. Volumes 1 and 2 each contain a preliminary chapter followed by five regular chapters that contain vocabulary presentations and activities, grammar presentations and activities, video-related practice, cultural information, reading selections, and writing practice. There are also valuable reference sections at the back of each book, including Spanish-English and English-Spanish glossaries and verb charts. In addition, Volume 2 contains an appendix that reviews all of the grammar presented in Volume 1.

Student Activities Manual (SAM): Workbook / Lab Manual / Video Manual

The **Student Activities Manual (SAM)** includes out-of-class practice of the material presented in the Student Text. Volumes 1 and 2 of the SAM are each divided into a Workbook **(Cuaderno de práctica)**, which focuses on written vocabulary and grammar practice, reading, and writing; a Lab Manual **(Manual de laboratorio)**, which focuses on pronunciation and listening comprehension; and a Video Manual **(Manual de video),** which offers extra practice of the storyline and **Voces del mundo hispano** segments.

iLrn™ Heinle Learning Center

An all-in-one online learning environment, including an audio- and video-enhanced interactive eBook, assignable textbook activities, companion videos, assignable voice-recorded activities, an online workbook and lab manual with audio, interactive enrichment activities, a chapter- and volume-level diagnostic study tool for better exam preparation, and now, media sharing and commenting capability through Share It! The iLrn: Heinle Learning Center is offered separately for Volumes 1 and 2.

Premium Website

You will find a wealth of resources and practice on the *Cuadros* **Premium Website**, accessible for Volumes 1 and 2 at **www.cengagebrain.com.** The **Premium Website** assets should be used as you work through each chapter and as you review for quizzes and exams.

To get access, visit CengageBrain.com

- It provides access to the text audio program, Web activities and links, Google Earth™ coordinates, and an iTunes™ playlist.
- The premium password-protected resources include the SAM audio program, the video program, grammar and pronunciation podcasts, grammar tutorial videos, auto-graded quizzes, and more!
- The web quizzes focus on vocabulary and grammar and provide automatic feedback, which helps you understand errors and pinpoints areas for review.
- The web activities offer the opportunity to explore authentic Spanish-language websites. Cultural web links relate to the **Voces de la comunidad, ¡Fíjate!,** and **¿Quieres saber más?** activities as well as **Tú en el mundo hispano,** which covers volunteer, study abroad, and internship opportunities throughout the Hispanic world and **Ritmos del mundo hispano**, a section that explores traditional and contemporary Hispanic music through music and video links.

Acknowledgments

Reviewers and Contributors

We would like to acknowledge the helpful suggestions and useful ideas of our reviewers, whose commentary was invaluable to us in shaping *Cuadros*.

Many thanks go to the following professors, each of whom offered valuable suggestions through their participation in live and virtual focus groups:

ACTFL: Introductory Spanish Focus Group
Aleta Anderson, *Grand Rapids Community College*
Yolanda González, *Valencia Community College*
Monica Montalvo, *University of Central Florida*
Renee Wooten, *Vernon College*

Pasadena Focus Group
Esther Castro, *San Diego State University*
Mercedes Limón, *Chaffey College*
Ofelia McQueen, *Los Angeles City College*
Markus Muller, *California State University, Long Beach*
Rosalinda Nericcio, *San Diego State University*
Yelgy Parada, *Los Angeles City College*
Victoria Tirado, *Chaffey College*

Philadelphia Focus Group
Norma Corrales-Martin, *Temple University*
Judith R. Downing, *Rutgers University – Camden*
April Jacobs, *Temple University*
Maríadelaluz Matus-Mendoza, *Drexel University*
Patricia Moore-Martinez, *Temple University*
Eva Recio-Gonzalez, *University of Pennsylvania*
Kimberly Ann Vega, *Temple University*

Development Reviews
Karen Berg, *College of Charleston*
Genevieve Breedon, *Darton College*
Matt Carpenter, *Yuba College, Clear Lake Campus*
John Catlett, *Cabrini College*
Daria Cohen, *Rider University*
Carmen García, *Valencia Community College*
Martha García, *University of Central Florida*
Diego Emilio Gómez
Yolanda González, *Valencia Community College*
Laurie Huffman, *Los Medanos College / Florida State College*
Isabel Killough, *Norfolk State University*
Lori Lammert, *Chattanooga State Community College*

Jill Loney, *Urbana University*
Richard McCallister, *Delaware State University*
Meghan Mehlos, *University of Wisconsin – Eau Claire*
Deanna Mihaly, *Eastern Michigan University*
Dianne Moneypenny
Lisa Nalbone, *University of Central Florida*
Janet Norden, *Baylor University*
Catherine Ortíz, *University of Texas at Arlington*
Sieglinde Poelzler-Kamatali, *Ohio Northern University*
Rosalea Postma-Carttar, *University of Kansas*
Laura Ruiz-Scott, *Scottsdale Community College*
Lester Edgardo Sandres Rapalo, *Valencia Community College*
Erika Sutherland, *Muhlenberg College*
David Tate, *Brevard Community College*
Wendy Westmoreland, *Cleveland Community College*
Sandra Wise, *University of Texas at Arlington*

Testing Program Consultants
Bárbara Ávila-Shah, *University at Buffalo, The State University of New York*
Patrick Brady, *Tidewater Community College*
Marta Nunn, *Virginia Commonwealth University*
Helga Winkler, *Ventura County Community College District – Moorpark College*

We would like to extend our gratitude to the Graduate Teaching Assistant and Adjunct Faculty Focus Group, which discussed the tools needed to ensure a successful transition to a new edition and successful use over the course of the semester.

Graduate Teaching Assistant / Adjunct Faculty Focus Group
Alison Atkins, *Boston University*
Alison Carberry, *Boston University*
Alejandra Cornejo, *Boston University*
Daniela Dorfman, *Boston University*
Megan Gibbons, *Boston University*
Rebeca Hey-Colón, *Harvard University*
Magdalena Malinowska, *Boston University*
Glenda Quiñónez, *Harvard University*

Finally, special thanks go to the following professors and writers, who have written the outstanding supplements to accompany this program:

Meghan Allen, *Babson College – Volume-level diagnostics and Web assets*

Flavia Belpoliti, *University of Houston – Bridge chapter teaching suggestions*

María Colina – *Lesson plans*

Juan De Urda, *SUNY Fredonia – Web quizzes*

Karen Haller Beer – *Testing program*

Maribel Lárraga, *Our Lady of the Lake University – Testing program and audio script*

Sarah Link – *PowerPoint presentations*

Jeff Longwell, *New Mexico State University – Volume-level oral assessments*

Nina Patrizio-Quiñones, *Our Lady of the Lake University – Testing program and audioscript*

Joshua Pope, *University of Wisconsin – Madison – Information gap activities*

Nidia Schuhmacher, *Brown University – Web searches*

Sierra Turner, *University of Alabama – Activity worksheets*

A hearty thanks to our fine VAK system, Learning Style worksheet writers: **Carlos Abaunza, Rebeca Hey-Colón** from **Harvard University** and **Magdalena Malinowska** from **Boston University**. Through creativity, hard work, and proactive communication, these writers took full ownership of the project from its incipient stages to create a comprehensive set of intuitive and valuable tools for visual, auditory, and kinesthetic learners.

We would also like to thank the World Languages Group at Heinle Cengage Learning for their ongoing support of this project and for guiding us along the long and sometimes difficult path to its completion! Many thanks especially to Beth Kramer and Heather Bradley for their professional guidance and outstanding support. We would also like to thank Kim Beuttler, our development editor, for her enthusiastic support and dedication to the project, her unflagging energy and enthusiasm, and her unerring eye for detail, Sara Dyer for her creative and focused work on the supplements that support *Cuadros*, and Morgen Murphy for her dedication to the quality of the media package. Thanks also to Aileen Mason, our production editor, for her meticulous care, and for her cheerful and good-humored tenacity in keeping the production side of things moving efficiently, and to Katy Gabel for her excellent project management work. We would like to extend our appreciation to Lindsey Richardson, Marketing Director, and Ben Rivera, Senior Marketing Manager, for their outstanding creative vision and hard work on campus, and to Glenn McGibbon, Senior Marketing Communications Manager, for his phenomenal work on marketing and promotional materials. We would like to acknowledge our copyeditor Janet Gokay, our proofreaders Pilar Acevedo and Jonathan Jucker, our art director, Linda Jurras, for her inspired design work, our illustrators JHS Illustration Studio and Fian Arroyo, Hilary Hudgens for his creative design contributions, and the many other design, art, and production staff and freelancers who contributed to the creation of this program.

¡Mil gracias a todos!

To my inspirational students, who helped shape *Cuadros*, and to *mi querida familia*, John, Morgan, and John, who have accompanied me on my life's magical journey as a Hispanist. *Gracias por el apoyo infinito.*
—S. S. L.

I am particularly appreciative of the help and encouragement of my husband, Bartlett Mel, my father, Domingo Carreira, and my colleagues Ana Roca, Najib Redouane, and Irene Marchegiani Jones.
—M. C.

I would like to thank my parents, Dulce and Óscar Madrigal, for bequeathing to me their language, their culture, their heritage, their passion for life, and their *orgullo* in *México, lindo y querido.*
—S. M. V.

A special thanks to Mac Prichard and to Shirley and Bill Swanson for their constant support and encouragement, both personal and professional.
—K. S.

Scope and Sequence

Volume 1

	TEMAS	COMUNICACIÓN	VOCABULARIO ÚTIL
capítulo 4 ¿Te interesa la tecnología? 120	Conexiones virtuales y personales España	▪ talk about computers and technology ▪ identify colors ▪ talk about likes and dislikes ▪ describe people, emotions, and conditions ▪ talk about current activities ▪ say how something is done	1. Technology, computers, and colors **122–123** 2. Emotions, electronics **126** 3. On the Internet **128**
capítulo 5 ¿Qué tal la familia? 160	Relaciones familiares El Salvador y Honduras	▪ talk about and describe your family ▪ talk about professions ▪ describe daily routines ▪ indicate ongoing actions	1. The family **162** 2. Professions and careers **164** 3. Personal care items **168**

Volume 2

	COMUNICACIÓN
capítulo preliminar 2 Mi identidad P2-2	▪ **identity:** personal information, greetings, introductions, phone calls ▪ **likes and dislikes:** interests, activities, personal and physical descriptions ▪ **studies:** classes, schedules, time and dates ▪ **technology:** hardware, software, Internet, electronics, emotions ▪ **family:** family members, professions, daily routines, personal care items

Reference Materials

GRAMÁTICA ÚTIL	CULTURA	SKILLS
1. Talking about what you used to do: The imperfect tense **318** 2. Talking about the past: Choosing between the preterite and the imperfect tenses **321** 3. Avoiding repetition: Double object pronouns **325** 4. Indicating for whom actions are done and what is done routinely: The uses of **se 329**	**Opener** Comparative facts about Bolivia and Paraguay **307** **¡Fíjate!** The metric system **311** **Voces de la comunidad 317** *Voces del mundo hispano* video Aarón Sánchez, specialist in Pan-Latin food **¡Explora y exprésate! 332** ▪ facts about Bolivia and Paraguay ▪ **quinua**, a special food from Bolivia ▪ **tereré**, a social tea tradition from Paraguay ▪ some ancient and modern sites in Bolivia and Paraguay	**A ver ▪ Estrategia** Using visuals to aid comprehension **316** **A leer ▪ Estrategia** Setting a time limit **336** **Lectura** *Botijlaca: El pueblo se abre al turismo gracias a la trucha* **337** **A escribir ▪ Estrategia** Writing—Writing a paragraph **340** **Composición** A personal anecdote **341** **Repaso y preparación 344**
1. Emphasizing ownership: Stressed possessives **358** 2. Expressing ongoing events and duration of time: **Hace / Hacía** with time expressions **360** 3. Expressing yourself correctly: Choosing between **por** and **para 363**	**Opener** Comparative facts about Guatemala and Nicaragua **347** **¡Fíjate!** Proverbs from the Spanish-speaking world **355** **Voces de la comunidad 357** *Voces del mundo hispano* video César and Rafael Pelli, architects **¡Explora y exprésate! 366** ▪ facts about Guatemala and Nicaragua ▪ Ethnic diversity in Guatemala and Nicaragua ▪ Some ancient and modern sites in Guatemala and Nicaragua ▪ A unique recycling program in Guatemala ▪ Alter Eco: "green" furniture and decorations for your home	**A ver ▪ Estrategia** Listening to tone of voice **356** **A leer ▪ Estrategia** Understanding poetry **370** **Lectura** Poems by Nicaraguan poets José Coronel Urtecho and Rubén Darío **371** **A escribir ▪ Estrategia** Writing—Adding transitions between paragraphs **372** **Composición** Description of a favorite place **373** **Repaso y preparación 376**

¡Bienvenidos a la clase de español!

The Spanish alphabet has 29 characters—the same as the English alphabet, plus the extra letters **ch, ll**, and **ñ**. When using a Spanish dictionary to look up words that begin with **ch** and **ll**, note that they do not have a separate listing, but are instead listed alphabetically under the letters **c** and **l**.

In 2010, the **Real Academia de la Lengua Española** updated the Spanish names of some letters. **Ve** and **doble ve** are now **uve** and **doble uve**, and **i griega** has been shortened to **ye**, but the adoption of these names is not universal among Spanish speakers. In addition, **ch** and **ll** have not been considered independent letters since 1994.

Go to the **Pronunciación** section of the preliminary chapter in the *Student Activities Manual* or *eSAM* and practice the sounds of the alphabet.

The purpose of these pages is to introduce you to some of the "nuts and bolts" of Spanish you'll need right away. Familiarize yourself with these words and expressions and do the activities described. Don't worry about memorizing it all—you'll have many more opportunities to work with these words as you progress through *Cuadros*.

El alfabeto

a	*a*	**A**rgentina		n	*ene*	**N**icaragua
b	*be*	**B**olivia		ñ	*eñe*	Espa**ñ**a
c	*ce*	**C**osta Rica		o	*o*	**O**taval**o**
ch	*che*	**Ch**ichén Itzá		p	*pe*	**P**araguay
d	*de*	**D**inamarca		q	*cu*	**Q**uito
e	*e*	**E**cuador		r	*erre*	Pe**r**ú
f	*efe*	**F**ilipinas		s	*ese*	**S**antiago
g	*ge*	**G**uatemala		t	*te*	**T**oledo
h	*hache*	**H**onduras		u	*u*	C**u**ba
i	*i*	**I**nglaterra		v	*uve*	**V**enezuela
j	*jota*	**J**alisco		w	*doble uve*	Bots**w**ana
k	*ka*	**K**enya		x	*equis*	Mé**x**ico
l	*ele*	**L**os Ángeles		y	*ye*	**Y**ucatán
ll	*elle*	Va**ll**adolid		z	*zeta*	**Z**acatecas
m	*eme*	**M**arruecos				

Los números 1–100

0	*cero*	20	*veinte*	40	*cuarenta*
1	*uno*	21	*veintiuno*	41	*cuarenta y uno*
2	*dos*	22	*veintidós*	42	*cuarenta y dos*
3	*tres*	23	*veintitrés*	43	*cuarenta y tres*
4	*cuatro*	24	*veinticuatro*	44	*cuarenta y cuatro*
5	*cinco*	25	*veinticinco*	45	*cuarenta y cinco*
6	*seis*	26	*veintiséis*	46	*cuarenta y seis*
7	*siete*	27	*veintisiete*	47	*cuarenta y siete*
8	*ocho*	28	*veintiocho*	48	*cuarenta y ocho*
9	*nueve*	29	*veintinueve*	49	*cuarenta y nueve*
10	*diez*	30	*treinta*	50	*cincuenta*
11	*once*	31	*treinta y uno*	51	*cincuenta y uno*
12	*doce*	32	*treinta y dos*	52	*cincuenta y dos*
13	*trece*	33	*treinta y tres*	53	*cincuenta y tres*
14	*catorce*	34	*treinta y cuatro*	54	*cincuenta y cuatro*
15	*quince*	35	*treinta y cinco*	55	*cincuenta y cinco*
16	*dieciséis*	36	*treinta y seis*	56	*cincuenta y seis*
17	*diecisiete*	37	*treinta y siete*	57	*cincuenta y siete*
18	*dieciocho*	38	*treinta y ocho*	58	*cincuenta y ocho*
19	*diecinueve*	39	*treinta y nueve*	59	*cincuenta y nueve*
				60	*sesenta*
				70	*setenta*
				80	*ochenta*
				90	*noventa*
				100	*cien*

Memorize the numbers 1–15.

Notice the pattern for the numbers from 16 to 29: **diez** + **seis** = **dieciséis**; **veinte** + **uno** = **veintiuno**. Notice that 11–15 do not follow that pattern.

Notice the pattern for the numbers over 30: **treinta** + **uno** = **treinta y uno**; **cuarenta** + **dos** = **cuarenta y dos**; **cincuenta** + **tres** = **cincuenta y tres**; etc.

Do not confuse sixty and seventy. Notice that **sesenta** is formed from **seiS**, with an s, and **setenta** is formed from **sieTe**, with a **t**.

With a partner, practice counting in Spanish by taking turns (Student 1: **uno**; Student 2: **dos**, etc.). Or, practice a sequence; for example, multiples of three (Student 1: **tres, seis, nueve**; Student 2: **doce, quince, dieciocho**, etc.).

Las personas

With a partner, name ten people you know. Take turns identifying them first by age and gender and then by their relationship to you: **Marcos Martínez—20 años, hombre, amigo.**

el hombre | la mujer | el muchacho / el chico | la muchacha / la chica | el niño | la niña

el estudiante | el profesor | la instructora | el instructor

la profesora

la estudiante

el compañero de cuarto | la compañera de cuarto | la amiga | el amigo

© Cengage Learning 2013

En el salón de clase

>> **En el libro de texto**

la actividad *activity*
el capítulo *chapter*
el dibujo *drawing*
la foto *photo*
la lección *lesson*
la página *page*

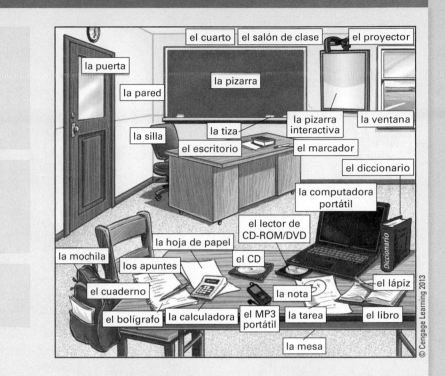

>> **La pregunta** *The question*

¿Cómo se dice... ?
  How do you say . . . ?
¿Qué significa... ?
  What does . . . mean?

>> **La respuesta** *The answer*

Se dice... *It's said . . .*
Significa... *It means . . .*

>> **Mandatos comunes** *Classroom commands*

Abran los libros / libros electrónicos. *Open your books / e-books.*
Adivina. / Adivinen. *Guess.*
Cierren los libros / libros electrónicos. *Close your books / e-books.*
Contesta. / Contesten. *Answer.*
Entreguen la tarea. *Turn in your homework.*
Mándenme la tarea por e-mail. *E-mail me your homework.*
Escriban en sus cuadernos / sus computadoras. *Write in your notebooks / computers.*
Escuchen el audio. *Listen to the audio.*
Estudien las páginas... a... *Study pages . . . to . . .*
Hagan la tarea para mañana. *Do the homework for tomorrow.*
Lean el Capítulo 1. *Read Chapter 1.*
Repitan. *Repeat.*

With a partner, take turns pointing out objects shown in the illustration that you can see in your classroom.

Your instructor will practice the most common classroom commands with the entire class and before you know it, you will know them by heart! Do not worry about memorizing them.

¿Cómo te llamas?

LA IDENTIDAD PERSONAL

As individuals we value our uniqueness while drawing strength from the similarities and experiences we share with others.

How do you define yourself, both as an individual and as a member of different groups?

Communication

By the end of this chapter you will be able to

- exchange addresses, phone numbers, and e-mail addresses
- introduce yourself and others, greet, and say goodbye
- make a phone call
- tell your and others' ages
- address friends informally and acquaintances politely
- write a personal letter

Jeremy Woodhouse/Getty Images

Un viaje por el mundo hispanohablante

1.   Gen Productions/Shutterstock
2.   Jozef Sedmak/Shutterstock
3.   Dmitry Ruhlenko/Shutterstock

¿Qué sabes? *(What do you know?)*

1. Match the names of these famous locations in the Spanish-speaking world with their photos.
    a. la Pirámide del Sol, Teotihuacán, México
    b. las Cataratas de Iguazú, Puerto Iguazú, Argentina
    c. la Catedral de la Sagrada Familia, Barcelona, España

2. There are 21 official Spanish-speaking countries in the world, not including the United States. Can you place them in the correct areas of the world? Use the information below to make a list of the six areas. Then list the countries that you think belong in each one. Save your work to check in the **¡Explora y exprésate!** section on page 33.

Áreas: África, El Caribe, Centroamérica, Europa, Norteamérica, Sudamérica

Países: Argentina, Bolivia, Chile, Colombia, Costa Rica, Cuba, Ecuador, El Salvador, España, Guatemala, Guinea Ecuatorial, Honduras, México, Nicaragua, Panamá, Paraguay, Perú, Puerto Rico, República Dominicana, Uruguay, Venezuela

Lo que sé y lo que quiero aprender Complete the chart in **Appendix A.** Write some facts you *already know* about the Spanish-speaking world in the **Lo que sé** column. Then add some things you *want to learn* about in the **Lo que quiero aprender** column. Save the chart to use again in the **¡Explora y exprésate!** section on page 33.

Cultures

By the end of this chapter you will have explored

- Spanish around the world
- a brief history of the Spanish language
- some statistics about Spanish speakers
- a few comparisons between Spanish and English
- Spanish in the professional world
- Spanish-language telephone conventions

¡Imagínate!

⊙ >> **Vocabulario útil 1**

JAVIER:	¡Hola!
ANILÚ:	Hola, Beto. ¿Cómo te va?
JAVIER:	**Bastante bien,** pero… ¿Beto? Yo no soy Beto.

Spanish has formal and informal means of address: singular formal *(s. form.)*, singular familiar *(s. fam.)*, and plural *(pl.)* for more than one person, formal or informal. You will learn more about how to address people on pages 23–24.

>> **Para saludar** *How to greet*

Hola. *Hello.*
¿Qué tal? *How are things going?*
¿Cómo estás (tú)? *How are you? (s. fam.)*
¿Cómo está (usted)? *How are you? (s. form.)*
¿Cómo están (ustedes)? *How are you? (pl.)*
¿Cómo te va? *How's it going with you? (s. fam.)*
¿Cómo le va? *How's it going with you? (s. form.)*
¿Cómo les va? *How's it going with you? (pl.)*
¿Qué hay de nuevo? *What's new?*
Buenos días. *Good morning.*
Buenas tardes. *Good afternoon.*
Buenas noches. *Good night. Good evening.*

>> **Para responder** *How to respond*

Bien, gracias. *Fine, thank you.*
Bastante bien. *Quite well.*
(No) Muy bien. *(Not) Very well.*
Regular. *So-so.*
¡Terrible! / ¡Fatal! *Terrible! / Awful!*
No mucho. *Not much.*
Nada. *Nothing.*
¿Y tú? *And you? (s. fam.)*
¿Y usted? *And you? (s. form.)*

ACTIVIDADES

1 **Conversaciones** With a classmate, take turns greeting each other and responding. Choose an appropriate response from those provided.

1. Hola, ¿qué tal?
   - a. Buenos días.
   - b. Muy bien, gracias.
   - c. ¿Y tú?

2. Buenas tardes. ¿Qué hay de nuevo?
   - a. No mucho.
   - b. Bastante bien.
   - c. Terrible.

3. Buenas noches. ¿Cómo le va?
   - a. Nada.
   - b. ¿Y usted?
   - c. Fatal.

4. Buenos días. ¿Cómo están?
   - a. Regular.
   - b. Buenas noches.
   - c. No mucho.

5. Hola, ¿cómo está?
   - a. ¿Cómo te va?
   - b. Bien, gracias, ¿y usted?
   - c. Nada.

6. Buenas tardes.
   - a. Terrible.
   - b. Buenas tardes.
     ¿Qué hay de nuevo?
   - c. No muy bien. ¿Y tú?

¿Qué tal?

¡Fatal! ¿Y tú?

© Cengage Learning 2013

2 **Saludos** Exchange greetings with a classmate. Follow the cues.

1. **Greeting:** It is morning, and you want to know how your classmate is doing.

   Response: You had a terrible night and don't feel well.

2. **Greeting:** It is evening, and you run into two classmates; you want to know if anything new has come up.

   Response: Not much has happened since you last saw your friend.

3. **Greeting:** You run into a professor in the afternoon; you want to know how things are going.

   Response: You're doing quite well and want to know how your student is doing.

3 **¿Qué tal?** Have a conversation with one of your friends when you first see him or her that day.

MODELO   Tú: *¡Hola, Adriana! ¿Cómo te va?*
          Compañero(a): *Bien, gracias, Rosa. Y tú, ¿cómo estás?*
          Tú: *Regular.*

© Cengage Learning 2013

ANILÚ: Pues, **¿cómo te llamas?**

JAVIER: ¿Yo? **Soy** Javier de la Cruz. Y yo, ¿con quién hablo?

ANILÚ: **Me llamo** Anilú. Ana Luisa Guzmán. … Pero, **¿cuál es tu número de teléfono?** Yo marqué el 3-39-71-94.

JAVIER: No, ése no es mi número de teléfono. **Mi número es el 3-71-28-12.**

Spanish speakers often ask **¿Cuál es tu / su e-mail?**, using the English term rather than **dirección electrónica**.

In an e-mail address in Spanish, @ is pronounced **arroba** and **.com** is pronounced **punto com**.

>> **Para pedir y dar información personal**
Exchanging personal information

¿Cómo te llamas? *What's your name? (s. fam.)*
¿Cómo se llama? *What's your name? (s. form.)*

Me llamo… *My name is. . .*
(Yo) soy… *I am. . .*

¿Cuál es tu número de teléfono? *What's your phone number? (s. fam.)*
¿Cuál es su número de teléfono? *What's your phone number? (s. form.)*

Mi número de teléfono es el 3-71-28-12. *My phone number is 371-2812.*
Es el 3-71-28-12. *It's 371-2812.*

¿Dónde vives? *Where do you live? (s. fam.)*
¿Dónde vive? *Where do you live? (s. form.)*

Vivo en… *I live in / at / on. . .*
   la avenida… *avenue*
   la calle… *street*
   el barrio… / la colonia… *neighborhood*

¿Cuál es tu dirección? *What's your address? (s. fam.)*
¿Cuál es su dirección? *What's your address? (s. form.)*
Mi dirección es… *My address is. . .*

¿Cuál es tu dirección electrónica? *What's your e-mail address? (s. fam.)*
¿Cuál es su dirección electrónica? *What's your e-mail address? (s. form.)*
Aquí tienes mi dirección electrónica. *Here's my e-mail address. (s. fam.)*
Aquí tiene mi dirección electrónica. *Here's my e-mail address. (s. form.)*

4 **Respuestas** Pick from the second column the correct response to the questions in the first column.

1. ¿Dónde vives?
2. ¿Cuál es su dirección electrónica?
3. ¿Cómo se llama?
4. ¿Cuál es tu número de teléfono?

a. Yo soy Rita Rivera.
b. Es el 4-87-26-91.
c. Es Irene29@yahoo.com.mx.
d. En la colonia Villanueva.

5 **En la reunión** You are at the first meeting of the International Hispanic Student Association at your college. You have been elected secretary and must record in Spanish the name, address, and phone number of every member. With a male and female classmate playing the parts of the members, ask for the information you need. Without looking at the book, listen to their responses and type or write out their personal information. Then ask your partners for their real personal information and record that.

MODELO   Jorge Salinas, avenida B 23, 2-91-66-45
    Tú: *¿Cómo te llamas?*
    Compañero(a): *Me llamo Jorge Salinas.*
    Tú: *¿Dónde vives?*
    Compañero(a): *Vivo en la avenida B, veintitrés.*
    Tú: *¿Cuál es tu número de teléfono?*
    Compañero(a): *Es el dos, noventa y uno, sesenta y seis, cuarenta y cinco.*

1. Amanda Villarreal, calle Montemayor 10, 8-13-02-55
2. Diego Ruiz, Colonia del Valle, calle Iturbide 89, 7-94-71-30
3. Irma Santiago, avenida Flores Verdes 12, 9-52-35-27
4. Baldemar Huerta, calle Otero 39, 7-62-81-03
5. Ingrid Lehmann, avenida Aguas Blancas 62, 4-56-72-93
6. ¿… ?
7. ¿… ?

> Notice in the **MODELO** how, except for the first example, all digits of a telephone number in Spanish are given in pairs. Spanish speakers in the United States might not use this convention.

> Notice that unlike in English, the street name precedes the number in addresses in Spanish: **Calle Iturbide 12** vs. *12 Iturbide Street.*

6 **¡Mucho gusto!** With a classmate, role-play a cell phone conversation in which one of you has reached the wrong number. You are curious about the person you have accidentally reached. Try to get as much information from each other as possible.

MODELO   —Hola. ¿Marcos?
    —No, yo no soy Marcos.
    —Bueno, ¿cómo se llama usted?
    —…

© Cengage Learning 2013

In Spain, a cell phone is called **un móvil**. Can you guess what it means?

¡Fíjate! Los celulares

Cellular phone technology has revolutionized telecommunications throughout the entire world. Cell phones are as popular in Latin America and Spain as they are in the United States. With the advent of the smartphone, cell phones are now routinely used for e-mail, photos, video, text messaging, games, applications, face-to-face phone conversations, GPS directions, and almost anything else you can do online.

Unas chicas usan su celular para hablar con un amigo.

Although customs for speaking on the phone vary from one Spanish-speaking country to another, here are some useful phrases to get you started.

Remember that most Spanish speakers give their phone number by using pairs after the first digit. For example: **Mi número es el dos, treinta y seis, diez, dieciocho.**

Familiar Conversation

—¡Hola!	*Hello?*
—Hola. ¿Qué estás haciendo?	*Hi. What are you doing?*
—Nada, ¿y tú?	*Nothing, and you?*
—¿Quieres hacer algo?	*Do you want to do something?*
—Claro. ¿Nos vemos donde siempre?	*Sure. See you at the usual place?*
—Está bien. Hasta luego.	*OK. See you later.*
—Chau.	*Bye.*

Formal Conversation

—¡Hola! / ¿Aló?	*Hello?*
—Hola. ¿Puedo hablar con… ?	*Hi, may I speak with . . . ?*
—Sí. Aquí está.	*Yes. Here he/she is.*
—Lo siento. No está.	*Sorry. He's/she's not here.*
—Por favor, dígale que llamó (nombre). Mi número es el…	*Please tell him/her that (name) called. My number is . . .*
—Muy bien.	*OK.*
—Muchas gracias.	*Thank you very much.*
—De nada. Adiós.	*You're welcome. Goodbye.*
—Adiós.	*Goodbye.*

Práctica With a partner, role-play two different phone calls, using the expressions provided. In the first call, you dial a friend's cell phone and speak to him or her. In the second call, you dial a friend's home number and speak to his grandmother. In the second case, the person you are trying to reach is not in and you need to leave a message. Don't forget to use the correct level of address (familiar or formal).

▶ >> Vocabulario útil 3

ANILÚ: Beto, **quiero presentarte a** Javier de la Cruz.

BETO: **Mucho gusto**, Javier.

JAVIER: **Encantado**, Beto.

BETO: Aquí está tu celular.

JAVIER: Gracias, Beto. Y aquí está tu celular.

BETO: **Bueno, ¡tengo que irme! Muchas gracias**, Javier. Y gracias a ti también, Anilú.

ANILÚ: Pues, Javier, **mucho gusto en conocerte**.

JAVIER: **El gusto es mío.**

ANILÚ: Pues, entonces, **¡nos vemos!**

JAVIER: ¡Hasta luego! Chau.

>> Para presentar a alguien *Introducing someone*

Soy... *I am . . .*
Me llamo... / Mi nombre es...
   My name is . . .
Quiero presentarte a... *I'd like to introduce you (s. fam.) to . . .*

Quiero presentarle a... *I'd like to introduce you (s. form.) to . . .*
Quiero presentarles a... *I'd like to introduce you (pl.) to . . .*

>> Para responder *How to respond*

Mucho gusto. *My pleasure.*
Mucho gusto en conocerte. *A pleasure to meet you (s. fam.).*
Encantado(a). *Delighted to meet you.*

Igualmente. *Likewise.*
El gusto es mío. *The pleasure is mine.*
Un placer. *My pleasure.*

>> Para despedirse *Saying goodbye*

Adiós. *Goodbye.*
Hasta luego. *See you later.*
Hasta mañana. *See you tomorrow.*
Hasta pronto. *See you soon.*

Nos vemos. *See you later.*
Chau. *Bye.*
Bueno, tengo que irme. *Well / OK, I have to go.*

The word **chau** comes from the Italian word *ciao,* which means both *hello* and *goodbye.* In Spanish, it is only used to say *goodbye.* The spelling has been changed to reflect Spanish pronunciation.

© Cengage Learning 2013

7 **¿Cómo respondes?** Choose the best response to each statement.

1. Me llamo Rubén.
   a. Adiós.   b. Un placer.   c. Hasta mañana.

2. Quiero presentarte a Cristina.
   a. Igualmente.   b. Bueno, tengo que irme.   c. Mucho gusto.

3. Mucho gusto en conocerte.
   a. Chau.   b. Igualmente.   c. Mi nombre es Santiago.

4. Bueno, tengo que irme.
   a. Hasta luego.   b. Encantado(a).   c. El gusto es mío.

8 **Quiero presentarte a…** Introductions are a normal part of everyday life. Study the drawing and, with a partner, create four short conversations in which one person introduces another person to a third party. In each conversation, pick one of the characters in the group and play that role. The labels show the four groups.

Grupo 1

Grupo 2

Grupo 3

Grupo 4

© Cengage Learning 2013

9 Fiesta You're at a party and you meet someone you really like who speaks only Spanish. Write out the conversation you might have with that person. Include the following:

> greeting
> response
> introduction
> exchange of phone numbers and e-mail addresses
> exchange of addresses
> goodbyes

10 Un e-mail Write an e-mail to your Spanish instructor introducing yourself. In it, give your name, address, e-mail address, phone number, and any other information you think your Spanish instructor should know about you. Send it!

¡Hola, profesora!

Me llamo Gretchen Murray. Soy estudiante en su clase de español. Mi dirección electrónica es gmurray@xyzmail.com. Vivo en el campus. Mi número de teléfono es el 5-12-49-47. ¡Nos vemos pronto!

Saludos,
Gretchen

© Cengage Learning 2013

11 ¡Mucho gusto en conocerte!
You are at a party with a group of four or five classmates. Greet each other, introduce yourselves, present at least one other member of the group to the others, and then carry on as lively a conversation as you can, exchanging as much personal information as you normally would. Find a natural way to end the conversation and then say goodbye to each other.

Juan Silva/Getty Images

A ver

ESTRATEGIA

Viewing a segment several times

When you first hear authentic Spanish, it may sound very fast. Stay calm! Remember that you don't have to understand everything and that, with video, you have the opportunity to replay. The first time you view the segment, listen for the general idea. The second time, listen for details.

Antes de ver 1 How many of the characters in this video segment do you already know? Go back to pages 8, 10, and 13 and identify the people you see in the photos there.

Antes de ver 2 Review some of the key words and phrases used in the video.

Ha sido un placer.	*It's been a pleasure.*
Marqué…	*I dialed . . .*
¡Tengo prisa!	*I'm in a hurry!*
Voy a marcar…	*I'm going to dial . . .*

Antes de ver 3 Before you watch the video, read items 1–3. Then, as you watch, listen for this information.

1. Las personas que hablan por celular: ¿Cómo se llaman?
2. Las personas al final: ¿Cómo se llaman?
3. _____ tiene *(has)* el celular de _____.

▶ **Ver** Now watch the video segment as many times as necessary to answer the questions in **Antes de ver 3**.

Después de ver Are the following statements about the video segment true **(cierto)** or false **(falso)**? Correct the false statements.

1. Javier tiene el celular de Anilú.
2. Anilú es una amiga de Javier.
3. Beto es un amigo de Anilú.
4. El número del teléfono celular que tiene Javier es el 3-39-71-94.
5. El número de teléfono de Beto es el 3-39-71-94.
6. Anilú le presenta Javier a Beto.

© Cengage Learning 2013

Voces de la comunidad

▶ >> Voces del mundo hispano

In this video segment, people from around the Spanish-speaking world introduce themselves. First read the statements below. Then watch the video as many times as needed to say whether the statements are true (**cierto**) or false (**falso**).

1. Ela y Sandra son de Puerto Rico.
2. Aura y Dayramir son de Honduras.
3. Claudio tiene 42 años (*is 42 years old*).
4. David tiene 19 años.

5. Ricardo es estudiante universitario.
6. Patricia y Constanza son profesoras de español.

◀)) >> Voces de Estados Unidos

Track 2

Spanish speakers in North America

In 1787, Thomas Jefferson had this advice for his nephew, Peter Carr: ❝Apply yourself to the study of the Spanish language with all of the assiduity you can. It and the English covering nearly the whole of America, they should be well known to every inhabitant who means to look beyond the limits of his farm.❞

Today, the U.S. is the fourth-largest Spanish-speaking country in the world. The 44 million Hispanics (or Latinos) who make their home in this country represent the fastest-growing segment of the U.S. population, comprising nearly 16.66% of the total population. For its part, Canada is also home to a thriving community of over 300,000 Hispanics.

U.S. Hispanics are enjoying a period of unprecedented prosperity. Their estimated buying power of $800 billion a year more than doubles the combined buying power of all other Spanish-speaking countries in the world. Through Spanish-language websites, publications, and advertising aimed at the lucrative Hispanic market, U.S. companies are continually striving to better understand, entice, and serve Latino consumers.

The **Voces de la comunidad** section of Chapters 2–20 of *Cuadros* features an outstanding North American Hispanic from these and other areas, people whose contributions have direct relevance to the theme of the chapter.

¿Y tú? What are your reasons for studying Spanish? Do you want to use it for personal or professional reasons?

¡Prepárate!

>> ## Gramática útil 1

Identifying people and objects: Nouns and articles

Cómo usarlo

Nouns identify people, places, and things: **señora Velasco, calle,** and **teléfono** are all nouns. *Articles* supply additional information about the noun.

1. *Definite* articles refer to a specific person, place, or thing.

   La Avenida Central es **la** calle más importante de **la** universidad. *(You already know which avenue and university you are talking about.)*

   *Central Avenue is **the** most important street in **the** university.*

2. *Indefinite* articles refer to a noun without identifying a specific person, place, or thing.

   Un amigo es **una** persona que te gusta. *(You are making a generalization, true of any friend.)*

   *A friend is **a** person you like.*

Cómo formarlo

LO BÁSICO

- *Number* indicates whether a word is singular or plural: **la calle** *(sing.),* **las calles** *(pl.),* **un escritorio** *(sing.),* **unos escritorios** *(pl.)*
- *Gender* indicates whether a word is masculine or feminine: **una avenida** *(fem.),* **el teléfono** *(masc.)*

The idea of gender for non-person nouns and for articles does not exist in English, although it is a feature of Spanish and other languages. When learning new Spanish words, memorize the article with the noun to help remember gender.

3. Noun gender and number

   - **Gender:** Often you can tell the gender of a Spanish noun by looking at its ending. Here are some general guidelines.

Masculine	Feminine
1. Nouns ending in **-o: el amigo, el muchacho**	Exception to rule #1: **la mano** *(hand)*
Exceptions to rule #2: words ending in **-ma: el sistema, el problema, el tema, el programa;** also **el día, el mapa**	2. Nouns ending in **-a: la compañera de cuarto, una chica**
Exceptions to rule #3: **el avión, el camión**	3. Nouns ending in **-ión, -dad, -tad,** and **-umbre** are usually feminine: **la información, una universidad, una costumbre** *(custom)*

When nouns ending in **-ión** become plural, they lose the accent on the **o: la corporación,** but **las corporaciones.**

Nouns referring to people often reflect gender by changing a final **o** to an **a** (**chico / chica, amigo / amiga**) or adding an **a** to a final consonant (**profesor / profesora**). For nouns ending in -**e**, -**ista**, or -**a** that refer to people, the article or context indicates gender (**el estudiante / la estudiante, el guitarrista / la guitarrista, Juan / Juanita es atleta**).

- **Number:** Spanish nouns form their plurals in several ways.

Singular	Plural
Ends in vowel: **calle**	Add **s: calles**
Ends in consonant: **universidad**	Add **es: universidades**
Ends in -**z: lápiz**	Change **z** to **c** and add **es: lápices**

Décima Feria
de las Mascotas

sábado, 11 de mayo, 10:00 a 14:00, Plaza Central

¡Ven a ver y a llevarte algunos de los perros, gatos, pájaros, lagartos y serpientes más raros del mundo!

How many plural nouns can you identify in this poster for a pet fair? Can you find the two definite articles?

4. Definite and indefinite articles

- Here are the Spanish definite articles, which correspond to the English article *the*.

	Singular	Plural
Masculine	**el amigo** *the friend (male)*	**los amigos** *the friends (male or mixed group)*
Feminine	**la amiga** *the friend (female)*	**las amigas** *the friends (female)*

In the past, **los** and **unos**, rather than **las** and **unas**, were used to refer to groups containing one or more males. The **Real Academia de la Lengua Española** recently ruled that the feminine forms should be used for groups with more females than males, but usage is changing slowly.

- Here are the Spanish indefinite articles, which correspond to the English articles *a*, *an*, and *some*.

	Singular	Plural
Masculine	**un amigo** a friend *(male)*	**unos amigos** some friends *(male or mixed group)*
Feminine	**una amiga** a friend *(female)*	**unas amigas** some friends *(female)*

- Remember that you use masculine articles with masculine nouns and feminine articles with feminine nouns. When a noun is in the plural, the corresponding plural article (masculine or feminine) is used: **el hombre, los hombres.**

- When referring to a person's *profession*, the article is omitted: **Liana es profesora y Ricardo es dentista.**

- However, when you use a *title* to refer to someone, the article is used: **Es el profesor Gómez.** When you address that person directly, using their title, the article is not used: **Buenos días, profesor Gómez.**

> When the noun is modified, the article is used: **Liana es una profesora excelente.**

The following titles are typically used with the article when referring to a person, and without the article when addressing that person directly.

señor (Sr.)	*Mr.*	**señorita (Srta.)**	*Miss / Ms.*
señora (Sra.)	*Mrs. / Ms.*	**profesor / profesora**	*professor*

ACTIVIDADES

1 **¿Femenino o masculino?** Listen to the speaker name a series of items and people. First, write whether the noun mentioned is masculine **(M)** or feminine **(F)**, or both **(M/F)**. Next, write the singular form of the noun with its correct definite article. Lastly, write the plural noun with its correct definite article.

MODELO *M*
el libro
los libros

2 **¿Definido o indefinido?** Work with a partner. Try to guess from the context whether it makes more sense to use the definite article, the indefinite article, or no article in each of the following pairs of sentences. Then say which article to use if one is required. If no article is required, mark X.

1. Es _____ calle en mi colonia.
   Es _____ calle central de mi colonia.

2. Es _____ profesor en mi universidad.
   Es _____ profesor de español.

3. Es _____ estudiante *(fem.)* más *(most)* inteligente de mi clase.
   Es _____ estudiante.

4. Es _____ avenida más importante de mi colonia.

   Es _____ avenida en mi colonia.

5. Es _____ universidad en mi estado *(state)*.

   Es _____ universidad más importante de mi estado.

3 Presentaciones With a partner, complete the following introductions with the correct definite or indefinite articles where needed. If no article is needed, mark with an X.

1. —Sra. Oliveros, quiero presentarle a _____ Srta. Martínez.

   —Un placer. ¿Dónde vive usted?

   —Vivo en _____ calle Colón, en _____ colonia Robles.

2. —Oye, Ricardo, quiero presentarte a mi amiga Rebeca. Ella es _____ dentista.

   —¡Mucho gusto, Rebeca! Yo soy _____ profesor de matemáticas.

   —¿De veras? Yo tengo *(I have)* _____ amigo que es profesor también.

3. —Buenas tardes. Yo soy _____ Sr. Bustelo.

   —Sr. Bustelo, ¿cuál es su número de teléfono?

   —Es _____ 8-21-98-32.

4. —¡Hola!

   —Buenos días. ¿Puedo hablar con _____ Sr. Lezama?

   —Lo siento. No está.

   —Por favor, dígale que llamó _____ Sra. Barlovento. Tenemos *(We have)* clase de administración mañana y necesito darle *(I need to give him)* _____ apuntes.

4 Más presentaciones Introduce yourself to another classmate. Exchange information about where you live, phone numbers, and e-mail addresses. Then prepare to introduce your classmate to the entire class.

© Cengage Learning 2013

Gramática útil 2

Identifying and describing: Subject pronouns and the present indicative of the verb ser

Estar, which you have already used in the expression **¿Cómo estás?,** also means *to be.* You will learn other ways to use **estar** in **Chapter 4.**

Cómo usarlo

The Spanish verb **ser** can be used to identify people and objects, to describe them, to make introductions, and to say when something will take place. It is one of two Spanish verbs that are the equivalents of the English verb *to be.*

Mi teléfono **es** el 2-39-71-49.	*My telephone number **is** 2-39-71-49.*
Yo **soy** Mariela y ella **es** Elena.	*I **am** Mariela and this **is** Elena.*
La fiesta **es** el miércoles.	*The party **is** on Wednesday.*

Cómo formarlo

LO BÁSICO

- *Pronouns* are words used to replace nouns. (Some English pronouns are *it, she, you, him,* etc.)
- Verbs change form to reflect *number* and *person. Number* refers to singular versus plural. *Person* refers to different subjects.
- A verb's *tense* indicates the time frame in which an event takes place (for example, *talk, talked, will talk*). The *present indicative tense* refers to present-time events or conditions (*I talk, I am talking*).

1. Subject pronouns

- Subject pronouns are pronouns that are used as the subject of a sentence. Here are the subject pronouns in Spanish.

© Cengage Learning 2013

¿**Tú** eres Javier?

Singular		Plural	
yo	*I*	**nosotros / nosotras**	*we*
tú	*you (fam.)*	**vosotros / vosotras**	*you (fam.)*
usted (Ud.)	*you (form.)*	**ustedes (Uds.)**	*you (fam., form.)*
él, ella	*he, she*	**ellos, ellas**	*they*

- The **vosotros / vosotras** forms are primarily used in Spain. They allow speakers to address more than one person informally. In most other places, Spanish speakers use **ustedes** to address several people, regardless of the formality of the relationship. The **vosotros** forms of verbs are provided in *Cuadros* so that you can recognize them, but they are not included for practice in activities.

2. Formal vs. familiar

English has a single word—*you*—to address people directly, regardless of how well you know them. As you have already seen, Spanish has two basic forms of address: the **tú** form and the **usted** form.

- **Tú** is used to address a family member, a close friend, a child, or a pet.
- **Usted** (often abbreviated **Ud.**) is a more formal means of address used with older people, strangers, acquaintances, and sometimes with colleagues.
- Remember that the **ustedes** form is normally used to address more than one person in both *informal* and *formal* contexts (except in Spain, where **vosotros**(as) is used in informal contexts).

Levels of formality vary throughout the Spanish-speaking world, so it's important when traveling to listen to how **tú** and **usted** are used and to follow the local practice.

In some countries, you will hear **vos** forms (Argentina and parts of Uruguay, Chile, and Central America). This is a variation of **tú** that is used only in these regions.

To show respect, you sometimes hear the titles **don** and **doña** used with people you address as **usted**. **Don** and **doña** are used with the person's first name: **don Roberto, doña Carmen**.

3. The present tense of the verb **ser**

The present indicative forms of the verb **ser** are as follows. Note the subject pronouns associated with each form.

ser *(to be)*	
Singular	
yo soy	*I am*
tú eres	*you (s. fam.) are*
usted es	*you (s. form.) are*
él es	*he is*
ella es	*she is*
Plural	
nosotros / nosotras somos	*we are*
vosotros / vosotras sois	*you (pl. fam.) are*
ustedes son	*you (pl. form. or pl. fam.) are*
ellos son	*they (masc. or mixed) are*
ellas son	*they (fem.) are*

In Spanish, it is not always necessary to use the subject pronoun with the verb, as long as the subject is understood. For example, it's less common to say **Yo soy Rafael**, because **Soy Rafael** is clear enough on its own.

5 **Descripciones** With a partner, match each of the following descriptions with the correct group of individuals.

_____ 1. two teens   a. Son compañeras de cuarto.

_____ 2. one professor   b. Es profesor de periodismo (*journalism*).

_____ 3. two roommates   c. Somos profesores en la universidad.

_____ 4. two professors   d. Son estudiantes.

6 **Manuel** Manuel writes an e-mail to a new Facebook friend describing himself and his two best friends. Complete his e-mail with the correct forms of **ser**.

¡Hola! Yo (1) _____ Manuel Ybarra. (2) _____ estudiante en la Universidad Nacional Autónoma de México, que (3) _____ una de las universidades más importantes de las Américas. ¡La población estudiantil (4) _____ de más de 270.000 estudiantes!

Tengo dos amigos íntimos. Mi amiga Susana (5) _____ una persona muy sincera. Ella y yo (6) _____ inseparables. Mi amigo Hernán (7) _____ muy cómico. Hernán y yo (8) _____ compañeros de cuarto. Susana y Hernán (9) _____ buenos amigos también. Y tú, ¿cómo (10) _____?

7 **¿Quiénes son?** Use **ser** to say who the following people are.

1. [Nombre] _____ mi compañero(a) de clase.
2. [Nombre] _____ el profesor (la profesora) de español.
3. [Nombre] _____ el instructor (la instructora) en la clase de español.
4. Nosotros _____ estudiantes de español.
5. Tú…
6. Usted…
7. Ustedes…
8. Ellos…

8 **Le presento a…** In groups of three or four, act out an introduction in front of the class. Decide beforehand the ages and the social standing of the people you are role-playing, as well as how informal or formal the situation is. The class must guess whether the introduction is formal or informal. Follow the model.

MODELO (formal)
    —*Buenos días, profesora García.*
    —*Buenos días, Susana.*
    —*Profesora García, le presento a mi amigo Paul.*
    —*Encantada, Paul.*

>> Gramática útil 3

Expressing quantity: **Hay** + nouns

Cómo usarlo

Aquí **hay** un problema.

1. **Hay** is the Spanish equivalent of *there is* or *there are* in English.

   Hay una reunión en la cafetería.   ***There is*** *a meeting in the cafeteria.*
   Hay tres estudiantes en la clase.   ***There are*** *three students in the class.*
   Hay unos libros en la mesa.   ***There are*** *some books on the table.*
   Hay una fiesta el viernes.   ***There is*** *a party on Friday.*

2. **Hay** is used with both singular and plural nouns, and in both affirmative and negative contexts.

   Hay un bolígrafo, pero no **hay** lápices en la mesa.

3. **Hay** can be used with numbers or with indefinite articles (**un, una, unos, unas**), but it is never used with definite articles (**el, la, los, las**).

   ¡**Hay** tres profesores en la clase,   ***There are*** *three professors in the class,*
   pero sólo **hay** una estudiante!   *but **there is** only one student!*

4. With a plural noun or negative, typically no article is used with **hay** unless you are providing extra information.

   Hay papeles en la mesa.   ***There are papers*** *on the table.*
   No hay libros en el escritorio.   ***There aren't (any) books*** *on the desk.*
   Hay quince personas en la clase.   ***There are fifteen people*** *in the class.*

   BUT:

   Hay unas personas interesantes   ***There are some interesting people***
   en la clase.   *in the class.*

Cómo formarlo

Hay is an *invariable verb form* because it never changes to reflect number or person. That is why **hay** can be used with both singular and plural nouns.

ACTIVIDADES

9 **¿Sí o no?** Look at the form and then answer the questions using **hay** or **no hay.** Follow the model.

> **Nombre:** Alicia Monteverde Salinas
> **Dirección:** 1742 NE Cleary Street, Portland, OR 97208
> **Número de teléfono:**
>   casa: _____ celular: 971-555-2951 oficina: 503-555-8820
> **Contacto personal:** _____
> **Dirección electrónica:** Alims@netista.org
> **Referencia:** _____

MODELOS ¿Hay... *un nombre?*
Sí, hay.
¿Hay... *un número de teléfono de la casa?*
No, no hay.

¿Hay...

1. ...una dirección?
2. ...un número de teléfono de la oficina?
3. ...un número del celular?

4. ...un contacto personal?
5. ...una dirección electrónica?
6. ...una referencia?

10 **Hay…** Say how many of the following things are in the places mentioned.

MODELO ventana (5): salón de clase
Hay cinco ventanas en el salón de clase.

1. computadora (15): laboratorio
2. policía (2): calle
3. libro (5): escritorio
4. profesor (3): reunión

5. estudiante (40): cafetería
6. persona (20): fiesta
7. verbo (35): pizarra
8. celular (1): mochila

11 **¿Cuántos (How many) hay?** In groups of four or five, find out how many of the following objects there are in your group.

MODELO *Hay tres teléfonos celulares en el grupo.*

1. teléfonos celulares
2. cuadernos
3. diccionarios

4. computadoras portátiles
5. MP3 portátiles
6. ¿…?

12 **¿Hay o no hay…?** With a classmate, take turns asking and answering whether the items indicated are in the classroom.

Objetos posibles: una computadora, un escritorio, un libro, un mapa, una mesa, una mochila, una pizarra digital interactivo, una ventana, ¿...?

Sonrisas

Comprensión Answer the following questions about the cartoon.

1. Según *(According to)* Dieguito, ¿qué hay en su cuarto?
2. En realidad, ¿qué hay en el cuarto de Dieguito?
3. Según el papá de Dieguito, ¿qué hay en el jardín *(garden)*?
4. En realidad, ¿hay un elefante en el jardín?

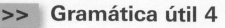

>> Gramática útil 4

Expressing possession, obligation, and age: **Tener, tener que, tener + años**

© Cengage Learning 2013

Tienes el cellular de mi amigo Beto.

Cómo usarlo

1. The verb **tener** means *to have*. It is used in Spanish to express possession and to give someone's age. You can also use it with **que** and another verb to say what you have to do: **Tengo que irme.** *(I have to go.)*

Tengo dos teléfonos en casa.	*I **have** two telephones in my house.*
Elena **tiene** veinte años. ¿Cuántos años **tienen** Sergio y Dulce?	*Elena **is** twenty years old. How old **are** Sergio and Dulce?*
Tengo que irme porque **tengo** clase.	*I **have to** go because I **have** class.*

2. When **tener** is used to express possession, the article is usually omitted, unless number is emphasized or you are referring to a specific object.

3. Note that where Spanish uses **tener… años** to express age, the English equivalent is *to be . . . years old.*

Cómo formarlo

> Remember, it's better to use the verb without a subject pronoun unless the subject is unclear or you want to emphasize it.

1. Here are the forms of the verb **tener** in the present indicative tense.

tener *(to have)*			
yo	**tengo**	nosotros / nosotras	**tenemos**
tú	**tienes**	vosotros / vosotras	**tenéis**
Ud., él, ella	**tiene**	Uds., ellos, ellas	**tienen**

2. When talking about age, it's helpful to know the months of the year so that you can say when people's birthdays are celebrated.

¿Cuándo es tu cumpleaños? *When is your birthday?*

> In Spanish the word for birthday is **cumpleaños**, which literally means "completes **(cumple)** years **(años)**." Many Spanish speakers celebrate their saint's day **(el día de su santo)**, which is the birthday of the saint whose name is the same as or similar to their own. For example: **El 19 de marzo es el día de San José.**

enero	julio
febrero	agosto
marzo	septiembre
abril	octubre
mayo	noviembre
junio	diciembre

3. When giving dates in Spanish, the day of the month comes first: **el quince de abril** = *April 15th.* When writing the date with numbers, the day always comes before the month: 15/4/10 = **el quince de abril de 2010.**

13 **¿Qué tienen?** Say what each person has or has to do.

MODELO Yo _tengo_ un cuaderno en el escritorio.

1. Yo _____ un celular en la mochila.
2. Nosotros _____ que leer el libro.
3. Ellos _____ unos apuntes en el cuaderno.
4. Tú _____ dos libros en la mochila.
5. El profesor _____ cinco lápices en el escritorio.
6. Ustedes _____ que escuchar el audio.

14 **¿Cuántos años tienen?** Tell a friend the birthdays and ages of the following people.

> The number **veintiuno** shortens to **veintiún** when it's used with a noun: **veintiún años**.

MODELO Arturo (28/3; 25 años)
> _El cumpleaños de Arturo es el veintiocho de marzo._
> _Tiene veinticinco años._

1. Martín (12/4; 21 años)
2. Sandra y Susana (14/7; 24 años)
3. mamá (16/6; 45 años)
4. papá (22/2; 47 años)
5. Gustavo (7/9; 17 años)
6. Irma y Daniel (19/1; 19 años)

15 **La fiesta** Listen to the conversation between Marta and Juan. They are talking about the birthdays and ages of various friends. Write down the age and the birthday of each person.

Track 4

	Edad	Cumpleaños
1. Miguel		
2. Arturo		
3. Enrique		
4. Isabel		

16 **Yo tengo...** With a classmate, take turns asking and telling which of the following objects you have and don't have with you today. Follow the model.

MODELO Tú: _¿Tienes un libro?_
> Compañero(a): _Sí. Tengo tres libros._

Objetos posibles: bolígrafo, celular, computadora portátil, cuaderno, diccionario, lápiz, marcador, mochila, ¿...?

¡Explora y exprésate!

El español: ¡una lengua global!

Información general ▶

- Spanish is the official language of 21 countries.
- With almost 500 million native and second-language speakers internationally, Spanish is one of the most widely spoken languages in the world.
- Spanish ranks second worldwide for number of native speakers, with 329 million. (Chinese is first, with 1.2 billion native speakers, and English is a close third, with 328 million speakers.)
- Spanish is spoken by 34.5 million people in the United States and by approximately 480,000 people in Canada. It is one of the most widely studied and fastest-growing languages in both countries.

Top 5 languages on the Internet	Internet users by language	Internet users as percentage of total
English	536,564,837	27.3%
Chinese	444,948,013	22.6%
Spanish	153,308,074	7.8%
Japanese	99,143,700	5.0%
Portuguese	82,548,200	4.2%

Adapted from Top Ten Languages Used in the Web chart at http://www.internetworldstats.com/stats7.htm, Copyright © 2010, Miniwatts Marketing Group. All rights reserved worldwide.

Ryan McVay/Getty Images

Vale saber...

- Spanish originated on the Iberian Peninsula as a descendant of Latin.
- King Alfonso X tried to standardize the language for official use in the 13th century in the Castile region of Spain.
- By 1492, when Christopher Columbus headed for the Western Hemisphere, Spanish had already become the spoken and written language that we would recognize today.
- Spanish was brought to the New World by explorers who colonized the new territories under the Spanish flag for the Spanish Empire. At its peak, *el Imperio español* was one of the largest empires in world history.
- Today, there are far more Spanish speakers in Latin America than there are in Spain.

Prisma Archivo/ Alamy

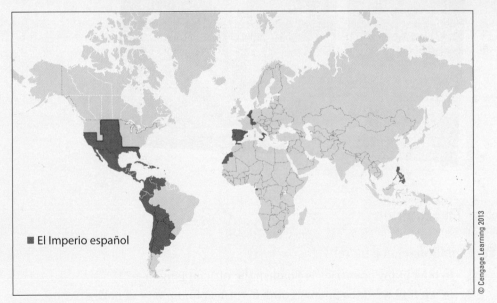

■ El Imperio español

© Cengage Learning 2013

Idioma

- Spanish is referred to as either **español** or **castellano**.
- Like all languages, Spanish exhibits some regional variations, limited mainly to vocabulary and pronunciation. In spite of these variations, Spanish speakers from all over the world communicate without difficulty.
- Spanish and English share many cognates, due to the fact that many of their words have the same linguistic roots in Latin and Arabic.

| family | *familia* | computer | *computadora* |

Profesiones

■ Here are just a few of the professions where Spanish is in high demand in the United States:

law	investment banking
medicine	sales and marketing
tourism	government
social sciences	human resources
education	interactive media

Marty Lederhandler/AP Images

>> En resumen

La información general

1. In how many countries is Spanish the official language?
2. In what place does Spanish rank in terms of numbers of native speakers?
3. Where did Spanish originate?
4. Who tried to standardize Spanish in the 13th century?
5. What do English and Spanish have in common?

†† Los países de habla hispana Did you place the countries in the correct areas? With a partner, check your list from **¿Qué sabes?** on page 7 against the list below to see how many you got right.

África	Guinea Ecuatorial
El Caribe	Cuba, Puerto Rico*, República Dominicana
Centroamérica	Costa Rica, El Salvador, Guatemala, Honduras, Nicaragua, Panamá
Europa	España
Norteamérica	Canadá, Estados Unidos**, México
Sudamérica	Argentina, Bolivia, Chile, Colombia, Ecuador, Paraguay, Perú, Uruguay, Venezuela

*Es un Estado Libre Asociado (Commonwealth), no un país independiente.
**Se habla español, pero el español no es la lengua oficial.

†† Los beneficios de hablar el español With a partner, discuss your reasons for studying Spanish. What professional or personal benefits do you expect to get out of your study of this language? Do a search for key words such as "medical careers in Spanish" to find out why knowing Spanish will be useful to you in your career.

⊕ ¿QUIERES SABER MÁS?

Return to the chart that you started at the beginning of the chapter. Add all the information that you already know in the column **Lo que aprendí**. Then look at the column labeled **Lo que quiero aprender**. Are there some things that you still don't know? Pick one or two of these, or choose from the topics listed below, to investigate further online. You can also find more key words for different topics at **www.cengagebrain .com.** Be prepared to share this information with the class.

Palabras clave: (Historia) la Península Ibérica, la influencia árabe, el Nuevo Mundo, Cristóbal Colón **(Profesiones)** derecho, medicina, finanzas, tecnología, turismo, traducción **(Hispanos históricos célebres)** Alfonso X de Castilla y León, los Reyes Católicos.

⊕ Tú en el mundo hispano To explore opportunities to use your Spanish to study, volunteer, or hold internships in any part of the Spanish-speaking world, follow the links at **www.cengagebrain.com.**

✎ Ritmos del mundo hispano Follow the links at **www.cengagebrain.com** to hear music from across the Spanish-speaking world.

A leer

ESTRATEGIA

Identifying cognates to aid comprehension

You have already learned a number of *cognates*—words that look similar in both Spanish and English but are pronounced differently. Some cognates you have already learned are **regular, terrible,** and **teléfono.** Cognates help you get a general idea of content, even if you don't know a lot of words and grammar.

¡OJO! *False cognates* are words that look similar in English and Spanish but mean different things. For example, **dirección** usually means *address,* not *direction,* in English. If a word that looks like a cognate doesn't make sense, you may need to look it up in a dictionary to discover its true meaning.

¡OJO! (literally, "Eye!") is used in Spanish to direct a person's attention to something. It is similar to saying "Watch out!" or "Be careful!" in English.

1 Look at the headline and the four sections of the following article. See if you can get the main idea of the article by relying on cognates and words you already know.

1. Put a check mark by the words that you already know in the title and the four bulleted sections.
2. Underline the cognates that appear in these sections. Can you guess their general meaning, based on context and where they appear in the sentence?

2 Now read the article, concentrating on the cognates and words you already know. Then answer the following questions, based on what you have read.

1. Según (*According to*) el artículo, las personas que tienen una dirección electrónica con su nombre son…
   - a. misteriosas
   - c. emocionales
   - b. honestas
   - d. introvertidas

2. Las personas que son lógicas y poco emocionales tienen una dirección electrónica…
   - a. con números
   - c. de fantasía
   - b. con su nombre
   - d. descriptiva

3. Las personas que se describen (*describe themselves*) con su dirección electrónica son…
   - a. un poco inocentes
   - c. agresivas
   - b. aventureras
   - d. introvertidas

4. ¿Cuál es el nombre de fantasía que usan en el artículo?

5. En tu opinión, ¿es correcta o falsa la información sobre tu personalidad?

LECTURA

¡Tu dirección electrónica revela tu personalidad!

¿Es simbólica la dirección electrónica que usas? Muchas personas creen[1] que no, pero en realidad, los "nombres de computadora" que usamos revelan información importante sobre nuestras características más secretas. ¿Revela todo[2] tu dirección electrónica? ¡Vamos a ver!

Escoge[3] el tipo de dirección electrónica más similar a la tuya[4]...

Nombre

ejemplo: lucidíaz@woohoo.net

En este caso, la dirección electrónica puede[5] representar a una persona directa y honesta. Prefiere la realidad y es práctica y realista. No le interesa el misterio o la fantasía. Estas personas son muy aptas para los negocios[6] a causa de su estilo directo.

Números

ejemplo: 1078892@compluservicio.com

Las personas con los números en las direcciones electrónicas no tienen mucho interés en las cortesías diarias o las interacciones sociales. ¡Prefieren el mundo[7] súper racional de los números y las matemáticas puras! Otra explicación es que prefieren ser anónimos —quieren[8] mantener su misterio con un nombre que revela muy poco[9]!

Autodescripción

ejemplo: románticoloco29@universidad.edu

Las personas que se describen con la dirección electrónica necesitan comprensión y cariño[10]. Pueden ser amables, afectuosas y un poco ingenuas o inocentes. Pero, ¡cuidado[11]! ¡Estos nombres pueden ser totalmente falsos! Los nombres que indican que una persona es honesta o responsable pueden distorsionar la realidad completamente...

Fantasía

ejemplo: frodo4ever@ciberífico.net

Por lo general, estas personas consideran el ciberespacio como una oportunidad para la reinvención personal. Prefieren identificarse como un personaje imaginario para participar en lo que es, para ellos, ¡un drama cibernético! Pueden ser aventureras, emocionales y extrovertidas. Estos nombres también pueden atraer a las personas introvertidas que tienen la fantasía de presentarse completamente diferente de su realidad diaria.

[1]think [2]everything [3]Choose [4]yours [5]can [6]business [7]world [8]they want to [9]very little [10]affection [11]careful

>> Después de leer

3 With a partner, try to invent as many names in each of the last two categories (**autodescripción** and **fantasía**) as you can. Use cognates from the reading when possible and be as creative as you can!

4 Now take the list of e-mail names you created in **Activity 3** and add your own e-mail name to the list. (Or, if your e-mail name is simply your name or number, create a name that you would like to use.) Then, with your partner from **Activity 3,** form a group with two other pairs. Share your lists and see if you can guess each other's e-mail addresses.

> All of the reading passages in *Cuadros* include translations of key (but not all) unknown words. Try to get the gist of the passage before you look for the definitions. Saving them as a last resort allows you to read the passage more quickly and to concentrate on getting the main idea.

A escribir

As you use *Cuadros,* you will learn to write by using a *process* that moves from prewriting (identifying ideas and organizing them) through writing (creating a rough draft) and ends with revising (editing and commenting on writing). In each **A escribir** section, you will learn strategies that help you improve your techniques in each of the three phases of the writing process.

ESTRATEGIA

Prewriting—Identifying your target audience

Before you write, consider who will read your work. Your intended reader's identity is the crucial element that helps you establish the format, tone, and content of your written piece. Imagine you are writing two descriptions of the same event. How would your description vary if you were writing it for a close friend or for someone you have never met? Remembering your audience is the first step toward creating an effective written piece.

1 You are going to write an e-mail to your new Spanish-speaking roommate whom you have not yet met. With a partner, create a list of the information you should include in your message and identify its tone.

2 Taking your list of information from **Activity 1**, study the following partial model and see if you have included everything you need.

Para:		Enviar
Sujeto:		Adjuntar

B	I	U	T		≣	≢	≣	■

<nombre>,

Me llamo… . Soy tu nuevo(a) compañero(a) de cuarto. Vivo en… . (*Ask about him/her.*)

Aquí tienes mi dirección…, mi teléfono… y mi dirección electrónica…. (*Ask for his/her personal information.*)

Tengo un estéreo, un refrigerador y un televisor para el cuarto. ¿Qué tienes tú?

Bueno, es todo por ahora.

Tu nuevo(a) compañero(a) de cuarto,
<tu nombre>

© Cengage Learning 2013

Composición

3 Using the previous model, write a rough draft of your e-mail. Try to write freely without worrying too much about mistakes or misspellings. You will have an opportunity to revise your work later. Here are some additional words and phrases.

una cafetera	*coffee maker*
Es todo por ahora.	*That's all for now.*
un estéreo	*stereo*
una impresora	*printer*
una lámpara	*lamp*
un microondas	*microwave oven*
para el cuarto	*for the room*
un refrigerador	*refrigerator*
un televisor	*television set*

Yellow Dog Productions/Getty Images

Después de escribir

4 Exchange your rough draft with a partner. Read each other's work and comment on its content and structure. For example, put a check mark next to places where you would like more information. Put a star by the sentence you like best. Put a question mark where the meaning is not clear. Underline any places where you are not certain the spelling and grammar are correct.

5 Now go back over your letter and revise it. Incorporate your partner's comments. Use the following checklist to check your final copy. Did you . . .

- make sure you included all the necessary information?
- match the tone of your writing to your audience?
- follow the model provided in **Activity 2**?
- check to make sure you used the correct forms of **ser** and **tener**?
- watch to make sure articles and nouns agree?
- look for misspellings?

Vocabulario

Para saludar *How to greet*

Hola. *Hello.*
¿Qué tal? *How are things going?*
¿Cómo estás (tú)? *How are you? (s. fam.)*
¿Cómo está (usted)? *How are you? (s. form.)*
¿Cómo están (ustedes)? *How are you? (pl.)*
¿Cómo te va? *How's it going with you? (s. fam.)*

¿Cómo le va? *How's it going with you? (s. form.)*
¿Cómo les va? *How's it going with you? (pl.)*
¿Qué hay de nuevo? *What's new?*
Buenos días. *Good morning.*
Buenas tardes. *Good afternoon.*
Buenas noches. *Good night. Good evening.*

Para responder *How to respond*

Bien, gracias. *Fine, thank you.*
Bastante bien. *Quite well.*
(No) Muy bien. *(Not) Very well.*
Regular. *So-so.*
¡Terrible! / ¡Fatal! *Terrible! / Awful!*

No mucho. *Not much.*
Nada. *Nothing.*
¿Y tú? *And you? (s. fam.)*
¿Y usted? *And you? (s. form.)*

Para pedir y dar información personal *Exchanging personal information*

¿Cómo te llamas? *What's your name? (s. fam.)*
¿Cómo se llama? *What's your name? (s. form.)*
Me llamo… *My name is . . .*
(Yo) soy… *I am . . .*
¿Cuál es tu número de teléfono? *What's your phone number? (s. fam.)*
¿Cuál es su número de teléfono? *What's your phone number? (s. form.)*
Mi número de teléfono es el 3-71-28-12. *My phone number is 371-2812.*
Es el 3-71-28-12. *It's 371-2812.*
¿Dónde vives? *Where do you live? (s. fam.)*
¿Dónde vive? *Where do you live? (s. form.)*
Vivo en… *I live at . . .*
  la avenida… *avenue . . .*
  la calle… *street . . .*
  el barrio… / la colonia… *neighborhood . . .*

¿Cuál es tu dirección? *What's your address? (s. fam.)*
¿Cuál es su dirección? *What's your address? (s. form.)*
Mi dirección es… *My address is . . .*
¿Cuál es tu dirección electrónica? *What's your e-mail address? (s. fam.)*
¿Cuál es su dirección electrónica? *What's your e-mail address? (s. form.)*
Aquí tienes mi dirección electrónica. *Here's my e-mail address. (s. form.)*
Aquí tiene mi dirección electrónica. *Here's my e-mail address. (pl.) (s. form.)*
arroba *@*
punto com *.com*

Para presentar a alguien *Introducing someone*

Soy… *I am . . .*
Me llamo… / Mi nombre es… *My name is . . .*
Quiero presentarte a… *I'd like to introduce you (s. fam.) to . . .*

Quiero presentarle a… *I'd like to introduce you (s. form.) to . . .*
Quiero presentarles a… *I'd like to introduce you (pl.) to . . .*

Para responder *How to respond*

Mucho gusto. *My pleasure.*
Mucho gusto en conocerte. *A pleasure to meet you.*
Encantado(a). *Delighted to meet you.*

Igualmente. *Likewise.*
El gusto es mío. *The pleasure is mine.*
Un placer. *My pleasure.*

Para despedirse *Saying goodbye*

Adiós. *Goodbye.*
Hasta luego. *See you later.*
Hasta mañana. *See you tomorrow.*
Hasta pronto. *See you soon.*

Nos vemos. *See you later.*
Chau. *Bye.*
Bueno, tengo que irme. *Well / OK, I have to go.*

Para hablar por teléfono *Talking on the telephone*

Familiar

—**¡Hola!** *Hello?*
—**Hola. ¿Qué estás haciendo?** *Hi. What are you doing?*
—**Nada, ¿y tú?** *Nothing, and you?*
—**¿Quieres hacer algo?** *Do you want to do something?*
—**Claro. ¿Nos vemos donde siempre?** *Sure. See you at the usual place?*
—**Está bien. Hasta luego.** *OK. See you later.*
—**Chau.** *Bye.*

Formal

—**¡Hola! / ¿Aló?** *Hello?*
—**Hola. ¿Puedo hablar con…?** *Hi, may I speak with . . . ?*
—**Sí. Aquí está.** *Yes. Here he/she is..*
—**Lo siento. No está.** *Sorry. He's/she's not here.*
—**Por favor, dígale que llamó (nombre).** *Please tell him/her that (name) called.*
  Mi número es el… *My number is . . .*
—**Muy bien.** *OK.*
—**Muchas gracias.** *Thank you very much.*
—**De nada. Adiós.** *You're welcome. Goodbye.*
—**Adiós.** *Goodbye.*

¿Cuándo es tu cumpleaños? *When is your birthday?*

enero *January*
febrero *February*
marzo *March*
abril *April*
mayo *May*
junio *June*

julio *July*
agosto *August*
septiembre *September*
octubre *October*
noviembre *November*
diciembre *December*

Palabras útiles *Useful words*

Títulos
don *title of respect used with male first name*
doña *title of respect used with female first name*
señor / Sr. *Mr.*
señora / Sra. *Mrs., Ms.*
señorita / Srta. *Miss, Ms.*

Los artículos definidos
el, la, los, las *the*

Los artículos indefinidos
un, una *a*
unos, unas *some*

Los pronombres personales
yo *I*
tú *you (fam.)*
usted (Ud.) *you (form.)*

él *he*
ella *she*
nosotros / nosotras *we*
vosotros / vosotras *you (fam. pl.)*
ustedes (Uds.) *you (fam. or form. pl.)*
ellos / ellas *they*

Los verbos
estar *to be*
hay *there is, there are*
ser *to be*
tener *to have*
tener… años *to be . . . years old*
tener que *to have to (+ verb)*

Expresiones
Tengo prisa. *I'm in a hurry.*

Repaso y preparación

Complete these activities to check your understanding of the new grammar points in **Chapter 1** before you move on to **Chapter 2**.

The answers to the activities in this section can be found in **Appendix B**.

Nouns and articles (p. 18)

1 For each blank, decide whether an article is needed. If it is, write the correct definite or indefinite article. If no article is needed, write X.

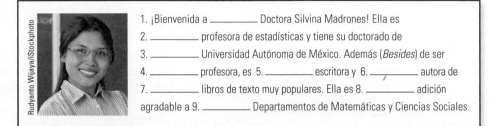

1. ¡Bienvenida a _____ Doctora Silvina Madrones! Ella es
2. _____ profesora de estadísticas y tiene su doctorado de
3. _____ Universidad Autónoma de México. Además (*Besides*) de ser
4. _____ profesora, es 5. _____ escritora y 6. _____ autora de
7. _____ libros de texto muy populares. Ella es 8. _____ adición agradable a 9. _____ Departamentos de Matemáticas y Ciencias Sociales.

Subject pronouns and the present indicative of the verb ser (p. 22)

2 For sentences 1–3, write in the missing subject pronouns. For sentences 4–6, write in the missing forms of the verb **ser** in the present indicative.

1. _____ eres dentista.
2. _____ somos profesores.
3. _____ soy veterinario.
4. Ella _____ taxista.
5. Uds. _____ arquitectos.
6. Nosotras _____ actrices.

Hay + nouns (p. 25)

Remember to leave out the indefinite article with **no hay: Hay una silla, pero no hay escritorio.**

3 Say whether the drawing shows the following items. If you see more than one of an item, say how many there are.

1. ¿una chica?
2. ¿un hombre?
3. ¿una mujer?
4. ¿un niño?
5. ¿una computadora?
6. ¿una mochila?
7. ¿una serpiente?
8. ¿un elefante?

Tener, tener que, tener + años (p. 28)

4 Complete each sentence with the correct present indicative form of **tener**.

1. Marcos, ¿———— un bolígrafo?
2. Profesor Martín, ¿———— la tarea?
3. Yo ———— tu dirección.
4. Nosotras ———— muchos amigos.
5. Ellos no ———— el libro.
6. Tú ———— las fotos.

5 Write forms of **tener que** to tell what the following people have to do.

1. Yo ———— presentarte a mis amigos.
2. ¡Ellos ———— conocerte!
3. Nosotros ———— entregar la tarea.
4. Él ———— contestar la pregunta.
5. Tú ———— escuchar el audio.
6. Ustedes ———— leer el capítulo.

6 Say how old each person is, based on the year he or she was born.

1. tú (1957)
2. ellos (2005)
3. usted (1962)
4. ella (1975)
5. yo (1992)
6. nosotros (1990)
7. ustedes (1983)
8. tú y yo (1995)

LWA/Dann Tardif/Getty Images

¿Cuántos años tiene?

>> Preparación para el Capítulo 2

Starting in **Chapter 2,** the **Preparación** section provides review and practice of grammar topics presented in *previous* chapters. The objective of this section is to help you remember previously learned structures that will be useful when you learn new grammar topics in the next chapter. Because this is the first chapter, however, there is no previous grammar to review.

To prepare for **Chapter 2,** reread **Chapter 1: Gramática útil 1.**

¿Qué te gusta hacer?

GUSTOS Y PREFERENCIAS

We express aspects of our personalities through our likes and dislikes. In this chapter, we explore the relationship between personalities and preferences.

How do you think that the activities you like and dislike define who you are?

Communication

By the end of this chapter you will be able to
- express likes and dislikes
- compare yourself to other people and describe personality traits
- ask and answer questions
- talk about leisure-time activities
- indicate nationality

Felix Sánchez/Getty Images

Un viaje por las áreas hispanohablantes de Estados Unidos

Estos diez estados *(states)* tienen las poblaciones más grandes *(biggest)* de hispanohablantes de Estados Unidos. ¿Puedes *(Can you)* identificar los cinco estados con las poblaciones más grandes?

Orden	Estado
	Arizona
	California
	Colorado
	Florida
	Georgia
	Illinois
	Nueva Jersey
	Nuevo México
	Nueva York
	Texas

Some U.S. states have Spanish equivalents that are fairly common in speech, while others do not. *Cuadros* provides the Spanish state name only if it is frequently used by native speakers, e.g., Nueva York, Nuevo México. Otherwise, the English name is provided, e.g., Rhode Island, Massachusetts.

¿Qué sabes? Di si las siguientes oraciones son **C (ciertas)** o **F (falsas)**.

1. No hay ningún *(none)* estado del Medio Oeste *(Midwest)* en la tabla.
2. La mayoría *(Most)* de los estados con muchos hispanohablantes están en el Sur *(South)*, el Suroeste *(Southwest)* o el Oeste.
3. Los nombres de algunos *(some)* de los estados son de origen español.

Lo que sé y lo que quiero aprender Completa la tabla del **Apéndice A**. Escribe algunos datos que **ya sabes** sobre los hispanohablantes de Estados Unidos en la columna **Lo que sé** *(What I already know)*. Después, añade *(add)* algunos temas que **quieres aprender** a la columna **Lo que quiero aprender** *(What I want to learn)*. Guarda *(Save)* la tabla para usarla otra vez en la sección **¡Explora y exprésate!** en la página 71.

Cultures

By the end of this chapter you will have explored

- world nationalities
- bilingual culture in the U.S. and Canada
- some statistics about Hispanics in the U.S.
- Hispanic groups in the U.S.: brief overview of their history and culture
- some famous U.S. Hispanics talking about themselves and their heritage

Globe Art: Adapted from Shutterstock//rtguest

¡Imagínate!

BETO: Autora14, **¿qué te gusta hacer** los domingos?

DULCE: Los domingos generalmente **estudio** en la biblioteca.

ANILÚ: ¡Qué aburrida!

BETO: **¡Estudias!**

ANILÚ: Dile que **bailas** y **cantas** y **escuchas** música.

BETO: ¿No te gusta hacer otras cosas?

DULCE: Pues sí. A veces mis amigos y yo **tomamos un refresco** en el Jazz Café o **alquilamos un video**.

>> **Las actividades** *Activities*

A ti, ¿qué te gusta hacer los fines de semana (los viernes, los sábados y los domingos)?

What do you like to do on the weekends (Fridays, Saturdays, and Sundays)?

1 Los verbos What Spanish verbs do you associate with the following? Choose from the list. (Some items can have more than one answer.)

1. _____ los murales
2. _____ la música
3. _____ los deportes
4. _____ una presentación oral
5. _____ un instrumento musical
6. _____ la familia

a. preparar
b. pintar
c. tocar
d. visitar
e. escuchar
f. practicar
g. conversar
h. estudiar
i. mirar

2 Le gusta… Your friends like to participate in certain activities. Say what they like to do, based on the information provided.

MODELOS Ernestina: murales
Le gusta pintar.
Leo: orquesta de música clásica
Le gusta tocar un instrumento musical.

1. Neti: ballet
2. Antonio: himnos y ópera
3. Javier: paella y enchiladas
4. Clara: cámara

5. Ernesto: estéreo
6. Beti: programas de comedia, noticias
7. Susana: celular
8. Luis: páginas web

3 Mis actividades favoritas

1. Make a list of five activities you like to do.

MODELO *Me gusta patinar en el parque.*

2. Now ask three other students what their favorite activities are and record their responses.

MODELO —*¿Qué te gusta hacer?*
—*Me gusta caminar.*
You write: *A Heather le gusta caminar.*

3. Compare responses to see who, if anyone, has similar favorite activities, and share this list with the class.

MODELO *A Marta y a Juan les gusta sacar fotos.*

4. Make a list of the most frequent activities mentioned by your classmates. Write a short paragraph about what students like to do and what activities they don't like to do.

¡Fíjate! "Spanglish": la mezcla de dos idiomas

With permission of Ferseus Books

When two cultures are in close proximity, eventually their languages will influence each other. Because native speakers of Spanish and native speakers of English have lived side by side for hundreds of years in the United States, a new hybrid form of the two languages has begun to spring up in conversation on the street, in poetry and fiction, and even in the articles of academic linguistic journals.

Strict language purists, including parents who want their children to be fluent and literate in both languages, and intellectuals who view the mixing of languages as a degradation of the original languages, do not approve of the casual use of Spanglish among the newer generations of Latino Americans. Ilan Stavans, a Mexican native, award-winning essayist, and the Lewis-Sebring professor in Latin American and Latino Culture at Amherst College, illustrates this point in his book *Spanglish: The Making of a New American Language:*

> Asked by a reporter in 1985 for his opinion on el espanglés, . . . Octavio Paz, the Mexican author of *The Labyrinth of Solitude* (1950) and a recipient of the Nobel Prize for Literature, is said to have responded with a paradox: "ni es bueno ni es malo, sino abominable"—it is neither good nor bad but abominable. This wasn't an exceptional view: Paz was one of scores of intellectuals with a distaste for the bastard jargon, which, in his eyes, didn't have gravitas.

"Cover of Ballantine edition", copyright © 1993 by Ballantine, from DREAM IN CUBAN by Cristina Garcia. Used by permission of Ballantine, a division of Random House, Inc.

> Spanglish is not easy to master. It takes a profound understanding of the nuances of both English and Spanish in order to syncopate the linguistic components of each and produce a comprehensible and communicative statement. Bilingual puns, bilingual wordplay, and bilingual sentence fusion can be found in the works of many Latino American writers such as Francisco Alarcón, Julia Álvarez, Sandra Cisneros, Cristina García, Tato Laviera, and Junot Díaz.

Even Stavans admits, "Over the years my admiration for Spanglish has grown exponentially. . . ," and he continues:

> And, atención, Spanglish isn't only a phenomenon that takes place en los Unaited Esteits: in some shape or form, with English as a merciless global force, it is spoken—and broken: no es solamente hablado sino quebrado—all across the Hispanic world, from Buenos Aires to Bogotá, from Barcelona to Santo Domingo.
> Beware: Se habla el espanglés everywhere these days!

Práctica

1. How do you feel about the mixing of two languages? Can you find any other instances in the history of the world where this has occurred?
2. Do you know any bilingual speakers? Do you know of any books that use the fusion of Spanish and English in some form? Do some research in your community or on the web and try to find two or three examples of a bilingual statement that amuses you.

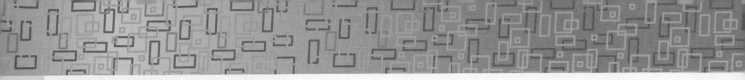

>> Vocabulario útil 2

SERGIO: ¿Con quién hablas?

BETO: No sé. Es una estudiante de la Universidad. Su nombre electrónico es Autora14.

SERGIO: Dile que tienes un amigo muy **guapo.**

>> **Características físicas** *Physical traits*

Notice that you say **Tiene el pelo negro / rubio / castaño**, etc., but when someone is a redhead, you say **Es pelirrojo(a)**. You can also say **Es rubio(a)** to indicate that someone is a blond. **Es moreno(a)** may indicate that someone is either a brunette or has dark skin.

ACTIVIDADES

4 **Sergio, Beto, Anilú y Dulce** Complete the following descriptions of the video characters.

1. Sergio…
   a. es rubio.
   b. es muy, muy pequeño.
   c. es guapo.

2. Anilú…
   a. es pelirroja.
   b. tiene el pelo castaño.
   c. es gorda.

3. Beto…
   a. es viejo.
   b. es gordo.
   c. es delgado.

4. Dulce…
   a. tiene el pelo negro.
   b. tiene el pelo rubio.
   c. es baja.

5 **Descripciones** Describe the people in the illustrations below. Use as many physical descriptions as you can.

1. Eduardo
2. el señor Bernal
3. Sofía
4. Roque

© Cengage Learning 2013

6 **¿Cómo soy yo?** Describe yourself in a paragraph for your Internet blog. You can also include activities that you like to do. Read your description to your partner. Then have him or her read their description to you.

MODELO *Soy alta y tengo el pelo negro. Me gusta tomar el sol y escuchar música.*

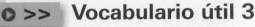

Vocabulario útil 3

ANILÚ: Y tú, Experto10, ¿qué te gusta hacer los domingos?

SERGIO: Autora14, soy un hombre **activo.** Bailo, canto, toco la guitarra, cocino…

BETO: ¡Sergio! **¡Mentiroso!** ¡No me gusta bailar, no me gusta cantar, no toco la guitarra y no cocino!

SERGIO: ¡Qué **aburrido** eres, hombre!

>> **Características de la personalidad** *Personality traits*

aburrido(a)	divertido(a); interesante	*boring / fun; interesting*
activo(a)	perezoso(a)	*active / lazy*
antipático(a)	simpático(a)	*unpleasant / pleasant*
extrovertido(a)	introvertido(a); tímido(a)	*extroverted / introverted; timid, shy*
generoso(a)	egoísta	*generous / selfish, egotistic*
impaciente	paciente	*impatient / patient*
impulsivo(a)	cuidadoso(a)	*impulsive / cautious*
inteligente	tonto(a)	*intelligent / silly, stupid*
mentiroso(a)	sincero(a)	*liar / sincere*
responsable	irresponsable	*responsible / irresponsible*
serio(a)	cómico(a)	*serious / funny*
trabajador(a)	perezoso(a)	*hard-working / lazy*

ACTIVIDADES

7 **Diferentes** You and a partner have differing opinions of the same person. Your partner will say that this imaginary person is a certain way, and you will counter by saying they are just the opposite. Take turns describing several imaginary people this way. Follow the model.

MODELO Tú: *Arturo es activo.*

Compañero(a): *¡No! Arturo es perezoso.*

Compañero(a): *Carmela es impulsiva.*

Tú: *¡No! Carmela es cuidadosa.*

8 **¿Cómo son?** Benjamín describes himself and several of his friends and relatives. Which adjective best describes each person?

1. No me gusta mirar televisión. Prefiero practicar deportes o levantar pesas.
   a. serio b. activo c. impulsivo

2. A mi amiga Marta le gusta ayudar *(to help)* a sus amigos.
   a. antipática b. mentirosa c. generosa

3. Mi profesora es una maestra muy buena. Explica la lección y repite todas las instrucciones.
   a. paciente b. impaciente c. interesante

4. Mi amigo Joaquín tiene una imaginación muy buena. Le gusta inventar historias falsas.
   a. tímido b. tonto c. mentiroso

5. Mi amigo Alberto habla y habla y habla... ¡pero no es muy interesante!
   a. aburrido b. serio c. divertido

6. Mi amiga Linda tiene muchas ideas buenas sobre qué hacer los fines de semana. Además es una persona muy cómica.
   a. inteligente b. tonta c. divertida

9 **La clase de psicología** What personality traits does it take to succeed in various professions? Choose characteristics on the right that you think best fit the professions on the left. Follow the model.

MODELO *Los políticos tienen que ser honestos,...*

Profesiones	Características	
los políticos	sistemáticos	serios
los artistas	deshonestos	estudiosos
los criminales	honestos	sinceros
los actores	inteligentes	pacientes
los científicos	creativos	talentosos
los doctores	simpáticos	impulsivos
los policías	extrovertidos	egoístas
los estudiantes	trabajadores	mentirosos
	curiosos	cuidadosos
	temperamentales	¿...?
	responsables	

10 **Mis amigos** Describe two people from your family to your partner. Provide both physical and personality traits in your descriptions. Then have your partner describe two people from his or her family.

MODELO —*Es una persona alta y delgada. Tiene el pelo castaño. También (Also) es una persona cómica y divertida...*

> Notice that you use the **-a** form of all the adjectives in this activity because the adjectives modify the feminine noun **persona**. You will learn more about adjective endings later in this chapter.

A ver

Antes de ver Review these key words and phrases used in the video.

apagar	*to turn off*
Dile que...	*Tell him/her that . . .*
No sé.	*I don't know.*

ESTRATEGIA

Using questions as an advance organizer

One way to prepare yourself to watch a video segment is to familiarize yourself with the questions you will answer after viewing. Look at the questions in **Después de ver 1**. Before you watch the video, use these questions to create a short list of the information you need to find. Example: **la dirección electrónica de Beto, la dirección electrónica de Dulce, el nombre del amigo de Beto**, etc.

Ver Now watch the video segment as many times as needed to find the information in your list.

Después de ver 1 Answer (in Spanish) the following questions about the video.

1. ¿Cuál es la dirección electrónica de Beto? ¿Y la de Dulce?
2. ¿Cómo se llama el amigo de Beto? ¿Y la amiga de Dulce?
3. ¿Cuáles son las actividades preferidas de Dulce?
4. Según *(According to)* Sergio, ¿cuáles son las actividades preferidas de Experto10?

Después de ver 2 Now say whether the following statements about the video segment are true (**cierto**) or false (**falso**).

1. Según Anilú, Dulce es una persona muy aburrida.
2. Sergio es una persona muy sincera.
3. Dulce generalmente estudia en casa los domingos.
4. A Beto le gusta bailar, cantar y tocar la guitarra.
5. Según Anilú, un hombre que cocina y canta y baila es el hombre ideal.
6. Sergio apaga la computadora porque Anilú quiere *(wants)* su número de teléfono.

© Cengage Learning 2013

Voces de la comunidad

▶ >> Voces del mundo hispano

In this video segment, the speakers say where their families are from and talk about their personalities and pastimes. First read the statements below. Then watch the video as many times as needed to say whether the statements are true (**cierto**) or false (**falso**).

1. La mamá de Nicole es de Guatemala.
2. El papá de Liana es de la República Dominicana.
3. Según Inés, ella es activa, extrovertida y feliz (*happy*).
4. Según los amigos y familiares de Inés, ella es alegre, cuidadosa y tímida.
5. A Constanza le gusta caminar.
6. A Jessica y Ana María les gusta leer.

🔊 >> Voces de Estados Unidos

Track 5

Isabel Valdés, ejecutiva y autora

❝Hispanics are becoming more and more entrenched in American society. Their participation is reflected in the growing number of Hispanic associations, libraries, research centers, and businesses throughout the United States. Furthermore, Hispanics are increasingly active in government at the federal, state, county, and city levels. They have also made significant contributions to American art, theater, literature, film, music, and sports. ❞

Isabel Valdés es responsable de muchas campañas publicitarias en español en Estados Unidos y Latinoamérica. Sus clientes incluyen firmas tales como PepsiCO y Frito-Lay. Esta chilena-estadounidense es autora de cuatro libros sobre el mercado (*market*) hispano en Estados Unidos. Es además la directora de IVC, una empresa (*business*) consultora que ofrece servicios estratégicos a compañías para alcanzar (*to reach*) a consumidores multiculturales en EEUU y los mercados globales. Valdés dedica mucho tiempo al trabajo voluntario para ayudar a (*help*) varias organizaciones, entre ellas *The Nacional Council of La Raza* y *The Latino Community Foundation*.

¿Y tú? What are your interests? Do you identify yourself as part of a market segment? If so, which one(s)?

¡Prepárate!

Gramática útil 1

Describing what you do or are doing:
The present indicative of regular -ar verbs

Bailo, canto, toco la guitarra, **cocino...**

The use of the present tense to talk about future plans is used more in some regions of the Spanish-speaking world than others.

Cómo usarlo

In English we use a variety of structures to express different present-tense concepts. In Spanish many of these are communicated with the same grammatical form. The present indicative tense in Spanish can be used. . .

- to describe routine actions:

  ¡Estudias mucho!   *You study a lot!*

- to say what you are doing now:

  Estudias matemáticas hoy.   *You are studying mathematics today.*

- to ask questions about present events:

  ¿**Estudias** con Enrique todas las semanas?   *Do you study with Enrique every week?*

- to indicate plans in the immediate future:

  Estudias con Enrique el viernes, ¿no?   *You're going to study with Enrique on Friday, right?*

Notice how the same form in Spanish, **estudias**, can be translated four different ways in English.

Cómo formarlo

LO BÁSICO

- An *infinitive* is a verb before it has been conjugated to reflect person and tense. **Bailar** *(To dance)* is an infinitive.
- A *verb stem* is what is left after you remove the **-ar, -er,** or **-ir** ending from the infinitive. **Bail-** is the verb stem of **bailar.**
- A conjugated verb is a verb whose endings reflect person *(I, you, he/she, we, you, they)* and tense *(present, past, future, etc.).* **Bailas** *(You dance)* is a conjugated verb (person: *you familiar singular;* tense: *present*).

1. Spanish infinitives end in **-ar**, **-er**, or **-ir**. For now, you will learn to form the present indicative tense of verbs ending in **-ar**. To form the present indicative tense of a regular **-ar** verb, simply remove the **-ar** and add the following endings.

bailar *(to dance)*			
yo	bail**o**	nosotros / nosotras	bail**amos**
tú	bail**as**	vosotros / vosotras	bail**áis**
Ud., él, ella	bail**a**	Uds., ellos, ellas	bail**an**

2. Remember, as you learned in **Chapter 1**, you do not need to use the subject pronouns (**yo, tú, él, ella**, etc.) unless the meaning is not clear from the context of the sentence, or you wish to clarify, add emphasis, or make a contrast.

Camino en el parque todos los días.	*I walk in the park every day.*

But:

Yo camino en el parque, pero Lidia camina en el gimnasio.	*I walk in the park, but Lidia walks in the gymnasium.*

3. You may use certain conjugated present-tense verbs with infinitives. However, do not use two conjugated verbs together unless they are separated by a comma or the words **y** *(and)*, **pero** *(but)*, or **o** *(or)*.

Necesitamos trabajar el viernes.	*We have to work on Friday.*
Los sábados, **trabajo, practico** deportes y **visito** a amigos.	*On Saturdays I work, play sports, and visit friends.*
Los domingos, **dejo de trabajar.**	*On Sundays I stop working.*
¡**Bailo, canto** o **escucho** música!	*I dance, sing, or listen to music!*

> Notice that in this usage, Spanish infinitives are often translated into English as *-ing* forms: *I stop working.*

4. To say what you don't do or aren't planning to do, use **no** before the conjugated verb.

¡**No estudio** los fines de semana!	*I don't study on the weekends!*

5. Add question marks to turn a present-tense sentence into a *yes/no* question.

¿**No estudias** los fines de semana?	*Don't you study on the weekends?*
¿**Tienes que estudiar** este fin de semana?	*Do you have to study this weekend?*

6. Other regular **-ar** verbs:

apagar	*to turn off*	**llegar**	*to arrive*
acabar de (+ infinitive)	*to have just done something*	**necesitar** (+ infinitive)	*to need (to do something)*
buscar	*to look for*	**pasar**	*to pass (by); to happen*
cenar	*to eat dinner*	**preparar**	*to prepare*
comprar	*to buy*	**regresar**	*to return*
dejar de (+ infinitive)	*to leave; to stop (doing something)*	**usar**	*to use*
descansar	*to rest*	**viajar**	*to travel*
llamar	*to call*		

> The expression **acabar de** can be used with any infinitive to say what activity you and others have just completed: **Acabo de llegar.** *(I just arrived.)* **Acabamos de cenar.** *(We just ate dinner.)*

1 **Beto** Beto describes his day in an e-mail to a friend. Complete his description with the correct form of the verb in parentheses.

A las siete de la mañana, (1. caminar) a la universidad. (2. Llegar) a las siete y media. Si tengo tiempo, (3. estudiar) un poco antes de las clases.

A veces (4. necesitar) comprar unos libros. (5. Comprar) los libros en la librería. Generalmente (6. cenar) en la cafetería. Después (7. pasar) por un café y (8. tomar) un café o un té. (9. Regresar) al dormitorio a las siete de la noche. (10. Hablar) con mis amigos por teléfono o (11. navegar) por Internet.

2 **Anilú y Sergio** Anilú and Sergio do different things. Say what each of them does. Use **pero** *(but)* to contrast what they do. Follow the model.

MODELO   Anilú: cenar en un restaurante; Sergio: cocinar en casa
         Anilú cena en un restaurante, pero Sergio cocina en casa.

1. Anilú: bailar; Sergio: levantar pesas
2. Anilú: trabajar; Sergio: descansar
3. Anilú: tomar un refresco; Sergio: tomar café
4. Anilú: estudiar; Sergio: navegar por Internet
5. Anilú: alquilar un video; Sergio: mirar televisión
6. Anilú: escuchar música rap; Sergio: tocar la guitarra

3 **Tú** Interview a partner about his or her activities.

MODELO   estudiar en la biblioteca
         Tú: *¿Estudias en la biblioteca?*
         Compañero(a): *Estudio en la biblioteca.*

1. caminar a la universidad
2. tocar la guitarra
3. visitar mucho a la familia
4. trabajar los fines de semana
5. cenar en la cafetería
6. necesitar una computadora

4 **Ellos y nosotros** Work in pairs to compare the activities of you and your friends (**nosotros**) and someone else's friends (**ellos**).

MODELO   estudiar
         Nosotros estudiamos en la biblioteca. Ellos estudian en casa.

1. estudiar
2. cenar
3. trabajar
4. visitar a la familia
5. necesitar
6. llegar a la universidad
7. navegar por Internet
8. ¿…?

5 **Los fines de semana** What do you generally do on the weekends? First, make a chart like the one below and fill in the **Yo** column. Compare your list with those of two classmates. Then write a paragraph comparing your typical weekend to theirs. (**¡OJO!: por la mañana / tarde / noche** = *in the morning / afternoon / night*)

¿Cuándo?	Yo	Amigo(a) #1	Amigo(a) #2
viernes por la noche:	*Descanso en casa.*		
sábado por la mañana:			
sábado por la tarde:			
sábado por la noche:			
domingo por la mañana:			
domingo por la tarde:			
domingo por la noche:			

MODELO *Los viernes por la noche generalmente descanso en casa.*
　　　　　Mi amigo Eduardo generalmente…

6 **¿Quién?** You work at a dating service and you have to decide who to introduce to whom. You have some descriptions in writing and some on audio. First read the following profiles. Then listen to the audio descriptions. For each description you hear, write the person's name next to the profile below that is most compatible with that person.

Track 6

Perfiles: Andrés, Marta, Jorge, Ángela, Rudy, Sara

Rosa: Me gusta escuchar música de todo tipo. ¡Soy muy divertida!
Sugerencia para Rosa: _____

Isidro: Levanto pesas tres veces por semana. Soy muy atlético.
Sugerencia para Isidro: _____

Roberta: Me gusta mirar películas. No practico deportes.
Sugerencia para Roberta: _____

Carmen: Uso Internet mucho en mis estudios. Soy introvertida.
Sugerencia para Carmen: _____

José Luis: Estudio mucho. Soy un poco serio.
Sugerencia para José Luis: _____

Antonio: Todos los días hablo por teléfono con mis amigos. Mis amigos son muy divertidos.
Sugerencia para Antonio: _____

Now use the information above to find the best match for you and your classmates, based on the information you provided in **Activity 5.**

MODELO *Antonio es la persona más compatible con (with) Katie.*

>> Gramática útil 2

Saying what you and others like to do: **Gustar** + infinitive

Un hombre que cocina...
y también ¡**le gusta bailar**
y **cantar!**

Cómo usarlo

The Spanish verb **gustar** can be used with an infinitive to say what you and your friends like to do. Note that **gustar**, although often translated as *to like*, is really more similar to the English *to please*. **Gustar** is always used with pronouns that indicate *who is pleased* by the activity mentioned.

—**Me gusta bailar** salsa.	***I like to dance** salsa. (**Dancing** salsa **pleases me**.)*
—¿**Te gusta bailar** también?	***Do you like to dance**, too? (**Does dancing please you**, too?)*
—No, pero a **Luis le gusta** mucho.	*No, but **Luis likes it** a lot. (No, but it pleases Luis a lot.)*

Cómo formarlo

LO BÁSICO

The pronouns used with **gustar** are indirect object pronouns. They show the person who is being pleased or who likes something. You will learn more about them in **Chapter 8**.

1. When **gustar** is used with one or more infinitives, it is always used in its third-person singular form **gusta**. Sentences with **gusta** + *infinitive* can take the form of statements or questions without a change in word order.

—**Nos gusta cocinar** y **cenar** en restaurantes.	***We like to cook** and **to eat** dinner in restaurants.*
—¿**Te gusta cocinar** también?	***Do you like to cook** also?*

¡OJO! Do not confuse **me, te, le, nos, os,** and **les** with the subject pronouns **yo, tú, él, ella, Ud., nosotros, vosotros, ellos, ellas,** and **Uds.** that you have already learned.

2. **Gusta** + *infinitive* is used with the following pronouns.

gusta + *infinitive*	
Me gusta cantar. *I like to sing.*	**Nos** gusta cantar. *We like to sing.*
Te gusta cantar. *You like to sing.*	**Os** gusta cantar. *You (fam. pl.) like to sing.*
Le gusta cantar. *You (form.) / He / She like (s) to sing.*	**Les** gusta cantar. *You (pl.) / They like to sing.*

3. When you use **gusta**, you can also use **a** + *person* to emphasize or clarify *who* it is who likes the activity mentioned. Clarification is particularly important with **le** and **les,** because they can refer to several people.

Le gusta navegar por Internet.	***He/She likes*** *to browse the Internet. (Who does?)*
A Beto / A él le gusta navegar por Internet.	***Beto / He likes*** *to browse the Internet.*
A ellos les gusta cantar.	***They like*** *to sing.*
A nosotros nos gusta conversar.	***We like*** *to talk.*
A Sergio y a Anilú les gusta bailar.	***Sergio and Anilú like*** *to dance.*

4. If you want to emphasize or clarify what you or a close friend like, use **a mí** (with **me gusta**) and **a ti** (with **te gusta**).

A mí me gusta alquilar películas, pero **a ti te gusta** mirar televisión.	*I **like** to rent movies, but **you like** to watch television.*

> Notice that **mí** has an accent, but **ti** does not.

5. To create negative sentences with **gusta** + *infinitive*, place **no** before the *pronoun* + **gusta**.

No nos gusta trabajar.	***We don't like to work.***
A Roberto **no le gusta cocinar.**	*Roberto **doesn't like to cook**.*

6. To express agreement with someone's opinion, use **también**. If you want to disagree, use **no** or **tampoco**. If you want to ask a friend if they like an activity you've already mentioned, ask **¿Y a ti?**

—¿Te gusta cocinar?	*Do you like to cook?*
—**A mí, no.** No me gusta. Me gusta comer en restaurantes. **¿Y a ti?**	***No, not me.*** *I don't like it. I like to eat in restaurants. **And you?***
—**A mí también.** Pero no me gusta comer en restaurantes elegantes.	***Me too.*** *But I don't like to eat in fancy restaurants.*
—**¡A mí tampoco!**	***Me neither!***

A mí me gusta sacar fotos.

Konstantin Sutyagin/Shutterstock

ACTIVIDADES

7 **Atleta 23** Can you tell what the following people like to do, based on their online names? Pick their preferred activities from the column to the right.

MODELO Cantante29

A Cantante29 le gusta cantar.

1. Pianista18
2. Atleta23
3. Artista12
4. Estudiante31
5. Fotógrafo11
6. Cocinero13
7. Bailarina39

estudiar
cocinar
cantar
tocar el piano
sacar fotos
bailar
practicar deportes
pintar

8 **En el parque** With a partner, describe what everyone in the illustration likes to do.

© Cengage Learning 2013

9 **Les gusta** Susana and Alberto like to participate in certain activities together, but prefer to do other things alone. First listen to what they say and decide who likes to do the activity mentioned. After you listen, use the verbs indicated to create a sentence saying who likes to do what. Follow the models.

MODELOS *(A Susana y a Alberto) Les gusta bailar.*

	Susana	Alberto	Susana y Alberto
bailar			x

(A Susana) Le gusta caminar en el parque.

	Susana	Alberto	Susana y Alberto
caminar en el parque	x		

	Susana	Alberto	Susana y Alberto
1. hablar por teléfono			
2. cocinar comida mexicana			
3. sacar fotos			
4. navegar por Internet			
5. tocar la guitarra			

10 **El estudiante hispanohablante** A new Spanish-speaking student is arriving at your dorm today. You want to let him know what activities you and your friends like to do so he can think about which activities he'd like to do with you. Write a note to post on your door that tells him what you and your friends typically like to do and where, so that when he arrives, he can decide what he wants to do with you.

1. First fill out the following chart to help you organize the information. Here are some possible locations: **el parque, el gimnasio, el restaurante, la cafetería, la residencia estudiantil, la biblioteca, la discoteca, el café, la oficina**.

Me gusta...	Nos gusta...	¿Dónde?

2. Once you complete the chart, use the information to write a note to welcome the new student, telling what you and your friends like to do and where, so that he can make plans to join you or not.

Gramática útil 3

Describing yourself and others: Adjective agreement

Cómo usarlo

Creative Study Gat®, "Se busca" advertisement for www.bitsandcream.com.
Used with permission from Gat Publicidad.

> Find at least three adjectives in this advertisement from a Spanish magazine. What nouns do they modify?

As you learned in **Chapter 1,** Spanish nouns must agree with definite and indefinite articles in both gender and number. This agreement is also necessary when using Spanish adjectives. Their endings change to reflect the number and gender of the nouns they modify.

Anilú es **delgada**.	*Anilú is **thin***.
Sergio y Beto son **inteligentes**.	*Sergio and Beto are **intelligent***.
Sergio es un hombre **alto**.	*Sergio is a **tall** man*.
Dulce y Anilú son mujeres **jóvenes**.	*Dulce and Anilú are **young** women*.

Notice that in these cases the adjectives go *after* the noun, rather than before, as in English.

Cómo formarlo

LO BÁSICO

A *descriptive adjective* is a word that describes a noun. It answers the question *What is . . . like?*

To modify is to limit or qualify the meaning of another word. A descriptive adjective *modifies* a noun by specifying characteristics that apply to that noun: **un estudiante** vs. **un estudiante inteligente**.

1. **Gender**: If an adjective is used to modify a masculine noun, the adjective must have a masculine ending. If it is used to modify a feminine noun, it must have a feminine ending.

   ■ The masculine ending for adjectives ending in **-o** is the **o** form.
   ■ The feminine ending for adjectives ending in **-o** is the **a** form.
   ■ Adjectives ending in **-e** or most consonants don't change to reflect gender.
   ■ Adjectives ending in **-or** add **a** to the ending for the feminine form.

Un profesor	Una profesora
simpátic**o**	simpátic**a**
interesant**e**	interesant**e**
trabajad**or**	trabajad**ora**

2. **Number**: If an adjective is used to modify a plural noun or more than one noun, it must be used in its plural form.

   ■ To create the plural of an adjective ending in a vowel, add **s**.
   ■ To create the plural of an adjective ending in a consonant, add **es**.
   ■ To create the plural of an adjective ending in **-or**, add **es** to the masculine form and **as** to the feminine form.
   ■ To create the plural of an adjective ending in **-z**, change the **z** to **c** and add **es**.

El profesor	Los profesores	Las profesoras
simpátic**o**	simpático**s**	simpática**s**
interesant**e**	interesante**s**	interesante**s**
trabajad**or**	trabajador**es**	trabajador**as**
feli**z**	feli**ces**	feli**ces**

3. As with articles and subject pronouns, adjectives that apply to mixed groups of males and females typically use the masculine form.

4. Most descriptive adjectives are used *after* the noun, rather than before.

5. If you want to use more than one adjective, you can use **y** *(and)* or **o** *(or)*.
   El estudiante es simpático **y** trabajador.
   ¿Es el profesor alto **o** bajo?
   Mis amigos son activos, generosos **y** cómicos.
   ¿Son ellas extrovertidas **o** introvertidas?

   ■ If **y** appears before a word that begins with an **i**, it changes to **e**.
   La instructora es divertida **e** interesante.

   ■ If **o** appears before a word that begins with an **o**, it changes to **u**.
   Hay siete **u** ocho estudiantes buenos en la clase.

Numbers do not change to match the number or gender of the nouns they describe. They go *before* the noun, rather than after.

Note that Spanish does not use a serial comma, as English does optionally. In the following English sentence, the comma after *generous* can be kept or omitted: *My friends are active, generous, and funny.* In Spanish, you do not use a comma after **generosos: Mis amigos son activos, generosos y cómicos.**

Remember that Puerto Ricans are U.S. citizens.

6. Adjectives of nationality follow slightly different rules. These adjectives add **a / as** feminine endings for nationalities whose names end in **-l, -s,** and **-n**. See the nationalities in the following group for examples. Adjectives of nationality are always used after the noun.

Nacionalidades		
África		
ecuatoguineano(a) Guinea Ecuatorial		
Asia		
chino(a) China	**indio(a)** India	
coreano(a) Corea	**japonés, japonesa** Japón	
Australia		
australiano(a) Australia		
Centroamérica y el Caribe		
costarricense Costa Rica	**guatemalteco(a)** Guatemala	**panameño(a)** Panamá
cubano(a) Cuba	**hondureño(a)** Honduras	**puertorriqueño(a)** Puerto Rico
dominicano(a) República Dominicana	**nicaragüense** Nicaragua	**salvadoreño(a)** El Salvador
Europa		
alemán, alemana Alemania	**francés, francesa** Francia	**italiano(a)** Italia
español, española España	**inglés, inglesa** Inglaterra	**portugués, portuguesa** Portugal
Norteamérica		
canadiense Canadá	**estadounidense** Estados Unidos	**mexicano(a)** México
Sudamérica		
argentino(a) Argentina	**colombiano(a)** Colombia	**peruano(a)** Perú
boliviano(a) Bolivia	**ecuatoriano(a)** Ecuador	**uruguayo(a)** Uruguay
chileno(a) Chile	**paraguayo(a)** Paraguay	**venezolano(a)** Venezuela

Estados Unidos is often abbreviated as **EEUU** or **EE.UU.** in Spanish. Some native speakers do not use the article **los** with **EEUU: en Estados Unidos** or **en EEUU**.

Notice the umlaut on the **ü** in **nicaragüense**. It is called a **diéresis** in Spanish. The **diéresis** is placed on the **u** in the syllables **gue** and **gui** to indicate that the **u** needs to be pronounced. Compare: **bilingüe, pingüino** and **guerra, Guillermo**.

7. Several adjectives in Spanish may be used *before* or *after* the noun they modify. Three common adjectives of this type are **bueno** *(good)*, **malo** *(bad)*, and **grande** *(big, large)*. When **bueno** and **malo** are used before a singular masculine noun, they have a special shortened form. Whenever **grande** is used before any singular masculine or feminine noun, its shortened form **gran** is used. Note that **grande** has different meanings when used *before* the noun *(great, famous)* and *after* the noun *(big, large)*.

un estudiante bueno	BUT:	un **buen** estudiante
una estudiante buena		una buena estudiante
un día malo	BUT:	un **mal** día
una semana mala		una mala semana
un hotel grande	BUT:	un **gran** hotel
una universidad grande	BUT:	una **gran** universidad

11 **El profesor y la profesora** Say whether the description refers to **la profesora, el profesor**, or if it could refer to both of them.

MODELO Es trabajadora.
la profesora

1. Es serio.
2. Es activo.
3. Es extrovertida.
4. Es responsable.
5. Es inteligente.

6. Es cuidadosa.
7. Es paciente.
8. Es interesante.
9. Es sincera.
10. Es generoso.

12 **Marcos y María** Marcos and María are two of your best friends. They are not at all similar. Describe what they are like. Follow the model.

MODELO Marcos es divertido.
María no es divertida. Es aburrida.

1. Marcos es paciente.
2. María es responsable.
3. Marcos es extrovertido.
4. María es perezosa.

5. Marcos es sincero.
6. María es antipática.
7. Marcos es rubio.
8. María es delgada.

13 **También** Your partner tells you that a person you both know has a certain personality or physical trait. Say that two of your friends are just like that person.

MODELO Compañero(a): *Rocío es alta.*
Tú: *Tomás y Marcelo también son altos.*

Rocío

1. Gerardo

2. Ángela

3. Miguel

4. Carmela

5. Pablo

6. Jimena

© Cengage Learning 2013

†† 14 Las nacionalidades With your partner, take turns asking the nationalities of the following people. Then mention another person of the same nationality.

MODELO   Orlando Bloom (Inglaterra)
          Tú: *¿De qué nacionalidad es Orlando Bloom?*
          Compañero(a): *Es inglés.*
          Tú: *¿De veras? Robert Pattinson es inglés también.*

1. Penélope Cruz y Rafael Nadal (España)
2. Manny Ramírez (República Dominicana)
3. Sonia Sotomayor (Puerto Rico)
4. Audrey Tautou (Francia)
5. Diego Luna y Gael García Bernal (México)
6. Gabriel García Márquez (Colombia)
7. Rigoberta Menchú (Guatemala)
8. Venus y Serena Williams (Estados Unidos)
9. Celia Cruz y Fidel Castro (Cuba)

††† 15 Personas famosas In groups of four or five, each person takes a turn describing a famous person. The rest of the group tries to guess who is being described.

Palabras útiles: actor (actriz), atleta, cantante, músico(a), político(a)

MODELO   Tú: *Es actriz. Es estadounidense. Es alta, delgada y rubia. Es muy*
          inteligente y simpática. Habla inglés, francés y español. ¿Quién es?
          Grupo: *Es Gwyneth Paltrow.*

†† 16 Tus cualidades You are appearing in a play and the director wants you to write a short bio for the theatre program. First, make a list of the personal and physical qualities you want to include. Then make a list of all of your favorite and least favorite activities. (If you want to use adjectives and activities you haven't learned yet, look for them in a Spanish-English dictionary.) Exchange your lists with a classmate and suggest changes you think would be helpful.

††† 17 Tu descripción Now, using the information you listed in **Activity 16,** write your description. Make sure you write at least five complete sentences, using the third person, since that is how these descriptions normally appear in theatre programs. Then, in groups of three or four, exchange your descriptions and see if you can guess whose ad is whose. If possible, as a follow-up, post your description on the class website under a false name and see if others can guess who it is.

MODELOS   *Shannon Silvestre es una actriz buena... También es... Le gusta...*
          Shaun Perales es un actor cómico... No le gusta..., pero sí le gusta...

Sonrisas

Comprensión Answer the following questions about the cartoon.

1. Según el gato *(cat)*, ¿cómo es?
2. Según el perro, ¿cómo es?
3. En realidad, ¿cómo es el gato? ¿Y el perro?
4. ¿Tienen consecuencias serias las mentiras del gato? En tu opinión, ¿son sinceras o mentirosas las personas cuando se comunican por Internet?

¡Explora y exprésate!

Doble identidad: Los latinos en EEUU y Canadá ▶

Andresr/Shutterstock

Los cinco grupos de latinos de mayor número en Estados Unidos son los méxicoamericanos (o los chicanos), los puertorriqueños, los cubanoamericanos, los dominicanos y los salvadoreños. Cada grupo tiene una historia larga y distinta. Sin embargo, tienen en común la doble identidad del bilingüe. El censo de 2010 indica que hay más de 50 millones de latinos en Estados Unidos.

En Canadá, viven 480.000 hispanos de varios países. La población va creciendo (*is increasing*), aumentando un 6% cada año.

When expressing numbers with numerals, Spanish uses a period where English uses a comma (480.000 rather than 480,000). It also uses a comma instead of a period to express decimals (6,5 rather than 6.5).

Latinos en Estados Unidos*	
mexicanos	31.673.700
puertorriqueños	4.411.604
salvadoreños	1.736.221
cubanos	1.677.158
dominicanos	1.360.476
guatemaltecos	1.077.412
colombianos	916.616
hondureños	624.533
españoles	613.585
ecuatorianos	611.457
peruanos	557.107

*Pewhispanic.org, 2009

Los cinco estados con las poblaciones hispanas más concentradas*	
California	14.014.000
Texas	9.461.000
Florida	4.224.000
Nueva York	3.417.000
Illinois	2.028.000

*http://pewhispanic.org/files/reports/140.pdf

Los méxicoamericanos o chicanos

Vale saber...

- After the Mexican-American War in 1848, Mexico ceded California, Texas, and parts of New Mexico, Arizona, Utah, Nevada, Colorado, Kansas, and Wyoming to the U.S. The majority of Mexicans in these areas elected to stay and were granted citizenship.
- The Chicano movement was born in the 1960s as Mexican-Americans attempted to regain a sense of pride in their Mexican heritage and culture.
- The integration of Mexican culture can be seen in vibrant areas such as the Riverwalk in San Antonio, Texas, the Pilsen and La Villita communities in Chicago, and the Mission District in San Francisco.

The term "Chicano" was adopted by Americans of Mexican descent during the American civil rights movement to distinguish themselves from Mexicans native to Mexico. There are many theories about its origin, none of which can be proven. The term was used by Mexican American activists who wanted to claim a unique ethnic and political identity.

Los grandes muralistas chicanos

Diego Rivera, José Orozco y David Siquieros eran *(were)* grandes muralistas mexicanos que usaban sus murales para expresar su visión política y reclamar sus orígenes indígenas. El arte del mural como expresión cultural ha sido adoptado *(has been adopted)* por los chicanos en EEUU.

Justin Sullivan/AP Images

Los puertorriqueños

Vale saber...

- In 1898, after the Spanish American War, Spain ceded Puerto Rico to the U.S. Nine years later, President Woodrow Wilson signed the Jones Act, which granted American citizenship to all Puerto Ricans.
- Many Puerto Ricans settled in New York City or in other parts of New York State, but younger Puerto Ricans have moved to Texas, Florida, Pennsylvania, New Jersey, Massachusetts and other states.
- El Museo del Barrio, La Marqueta, and el Desfile Puertorriqueño de Nueva York are all testimony to the bicultural life of the "Nuyoricans", also known as "nuyorquinos" or "nuevarriqueños."

Los poetry slams

Miguel Algarín, profesor de Rutgers, empezó *(began)* The Nuyorican Poets Café en su apartamento del East Village en 1973. Hoy día el Café es una organización sin fines de lucro *(non-profit agency)* que se ha transformado en un foro para poesía, música, hip hop, video, artes visuales, comedia y teatro. Los Poetry Slams son eventos muy populares en el Café.

Philip Scalia/Alamy

Los cubanoamericanos

Vale saber…

- All of Florida and Louisiana were provinces of Cuba prior to the Louisiana Purchase and the Adams-Onís Treaty of 1819.
- The largest community of Cuban Americans in the United States is in Miami-Dade County in Florida.
- La Pequeña Habana in Miami is the cultural center of Cuban American life.

Jeff Greenberg/PhotoEdit

La música

El Buena Vista Social Club era un club en La Habana donde se juntaban los músicos en los años 40. La ilustre historia musical de Cuba sigue en los Estados Unidos con los cantantes Jon Secada, Albita, Celia Cruz, Gloria Estefan y el saxofonista Paquito D'Rivera—todos ganadores del premio Grammy.

Los dominicanos y los centroamericanos

Vale saber…

- New York City has had a Dominican population since the 1930s. They largely settled in Quisqueya Heights, an area of Washington Heights in Manhattan. Nowadays, Dominicans also reside in New Jersey, Massachusetts, and Miami.
- In the 1980s and 90s, Dominican immigration to the United States was at its height.
- In the 1980s, political conflicts in Guatemala, El Salvador, and Nicaragua led to a big wave of immigration to the U.S. Many Central Americans made their homes in cities like Los Angeles, Houston, Washington, D.C., New York, and Miami.

LatinContent/Getty Images

La literatura revolucionaria

El conflicto produce la literatura. La tarea del escritor es captar la verdad (*truth*) de la vida diaria. En países que pasan por una revolución, es urgente describir las condiciones del ser humano por escrito (*in writing*). Testimonio de la necesidad de escribir en tiempos de conflicto es la importante literatura centroamericana de escritores como Gioconda Belli, Rigoberta Menchú Tum, Claribel Alegría, Ernesto Cardenal y Roque Dalton.

La información general Say which Hispanic group each statement describes.

1. Los **nuyoricans** son personas de este grupo que viven *(live)* en Nueva York.
2. Este grupo en Estados Unidos adopta esta forma de arte como expresión cultural.
3. Los conflictos en los países de origen de este grupo produce una literatura revolucionaria.
4. **Chicano** es otro nombre para una persona de este grupo.
5. Esta sección de Miami es el centro cultural de este grupo.
6. La inmigración de este grupo a Estados Unidos ocurre principalmente en las décadas de los 80 y los 90.

🌐 **¿QUIERES SABER MÁS?**

Return to the chart that you started at the beginning of the chapter. Add all the information that you already know in the column **Lo que aprendí.** Then, look at the column labeled **Lo que quiero aprender.** Are there some things that you still don't know? Pick one or two of these, or from the topics listed below, to further investigate online. You can also find more key words on different topics at **www.cengagebrain.com.** Be prepared to share this information with the class.

Palabras clave: (méxicoamericanos): the Mexican-American War, Treaty of Guadalupe Hidalgo, 5 de mayo**; (puertorriqueños):** Treaty of Paris, Jones Act, Luis Muñoz Rivera**; (cubanoamericanos):** calle Ocho, Ybor City, Louisiana Purchase, Adams-Onís Treaty**; (dominicanos y centroamericanos):** *El Norte*, Rafael Trujillo, Anastasio Somoza, Sandinistas, Civil War in El Salvador

🌐 **Tú en el mundo hispano** To explore opportunities to use your Spanish to study, volunteer, or do internships in the U. S. and Canada, follow the links at **www.cengagebrain.com.**

🎞 **Ritmos del mundo hispano** Follow the links at **www.cengagebrain.com** to hear music in Spanish from the U.S. and Canada.

A leer

ESTRATEGIA

Looking up Spanish words in a bilingual dictionary

When reading in Spanish, try to understand the general meaning of what you read and don't spend time looking up every unknown word. But if there are key words you can't understand, using a dictionary can save you time.

Try to look up only one or two words from each page of text. Focus on words that you cannot guess from context and that you must understand to get the reading's general meaning. When you do look up the word, don't settle on the first definition! Look at the different English translations provided. Which one seems to best fit with the overall content of the reading?

When looking up verbs, remember that you must look up the infinitive form (**-ar**, **-er**, or **-ir**) and not the conjugated form. (**Ser** instead of **soy**, **hablar** instead of **hablas**, etc.) When you look up adjectives, look up the masculine form (**bueno** instead of **buena**, etc.).

> For more on using a bilingual dictionary, see the **A escribir** section on page 76.

 1 When celebrities are interviewed, they often describe themselves and talk about their backgrounds. The point of the interview is to share personal information with the viewer and reader.

1. Look at the quotes of the seven U.S. Hispanics featured on pages 73–74. Read the translated words at the bottom of each page, then skim the quotes themselves. What words don't you know that you might need in order to get the main idea? Make a list of 5 to 10 words.

2. Can you guess from context any of the words you identified? For example, Albert Pujols is listed as a **pelotero** and in his photo he is wearing a uniform. Based on that information, can you guess what a **pelotero** is?

3. Of the remaining words, how many do you really need to know in order to understand the basic idea of what the person is saying? With a partner, create a list that contains only the words you think are necessary to get the main idea.

2 Now that you have narrowed down your list of unknown but key words, work with a partner to look them up in the dictionary. Be sure to read all the English definitions. Which one(s) fit(s) best in the context of the article?

¿Cómo soy yo?

Roberto Pfeil/dapd/AP Images

Carlos Santana
músico de ascendencia mexicana
"Soy un músico serio, como Paco de Lucía. Serio, pero divertido. Nunca invertí[1] energía en ser rico o famoso".

Charles Sykes/AP Images

Zoe Saldana
actriz de ascendencia puertorriqueña y dominicana
"Como latina, pienso que[2] tenemos que sentirnos[3] muy orgullosos de nuestra herencia. Tendemos[4] a buscar raíces[5] europeas y a rechazar las indígenas y las africanas, y eso es un asco, una vergüenza[6]. El latino es una composición de todos".

Isabel Toledo
diseñadora de ropa de ascendencia cubana
"Ser latina es ser quien soy, no cómo me defino... Es una cultura enamorada de la moda".

Kathy Willens/AP Images

Albert Pujols
pelotero de ascendencia dominicana
"Yo quiero que la gente me recuerde[7], no sólo como Albert Pujols el buen pelotero, sino por la persona que yo soy, bien humilde[8] y que trata de ayudar[9] a los que lo necesitan".

MLB Photos via Getty Images

[1]*I never invested* [2]*I think that* [3]*to feel* [4]*We tend to* [5]*roots* [6]**un...:** *it's disgusting and a shame* [7]**Yo...:** *I want people to remember me* [8]*humble* [9]**trata...:** *that tries to help*

Eva Longoria
actriz de ascendencia mexicana

"Somos mexicanos de quinta[10] generación en Texas y estoy[11] orgullosa de ser latina y de representar a los latinos en todas partes... Ser mexicana es muy importante en quién soy yo".

Wilmer Valderrama
actor de ascendencia venezolana

"Yo soy muy agradecido por mis raíces latinas... A mí me da mucha dicha[12] y un orgullo muy grande cuando la gente latina admira cualquier[13] trabajo que he hecho[14]".

César Millán
entrenador de perros ("El Encantador de Perros"), de ascendencia mexicana

"Sólo soy un tipo instintivo que vive en el momento".

[10]*fifth* [11]*I am* [12]**me...**: *it gives me a lot of happiness* [13]*whatever* [14]**he...**: *I have done*

3 Now work with a partner to match the descriptions on the right with each person on the left.

_____ 1. Carlos Santana

_____ 2. Zoe Saldana

_____ 3. Albert Pujols

_____ 4. Isabel Toledo

_____ 5. César Millán

_____ 6. Eva Longoria

_____ 7. Wilmer Valderrama

a. Es muy agradecido por su herencia latina.

b. Vive en el presente, no en el futuro.

c. Es mexicana y muy orgullosa de su herencia.

d. Habla de ser una composición de culturas.

e. Es una persona muy humilde.

f. Es serio, pero divertido.

g. Es de una cultura enamorada de la moda.

4 With a classmate, take turns interviewing each other and writing down your responses. Answer the following questions based on your own personality or that of a famous celebrity.

1. ¿Cuál es tu herencia? (Soy de ascendencia...)
2. ¿Cómo eres? (Soy...)
3. ¿Qué te gusta hacer? (Me gusta...)

5 Now, choose a famous Spanish speaker and do a search for him or her online. Find enough information to answer the three questions in **Actividad 4** about that person—**¡en español, por favor!** Be prepared to share your information with the class.

Rafael Nadal, España

Paulina Rubio, México

A escribir

ESTRATEGIA

Prewriting—Looking up English words in a bilingual dictionary

Since no textbook can provide you with all the words you may want to use when you write, you will want to use a bilingual dictionary to supplement the words you already know. Here's how to use the dictionary most effectively.

1. Decide on the English word you want to translate: for example, *lively*.

2. Think of several English synonyms for that word: *vivacious, energetic*.

3. Look up the original English word in the English-Spanish part of the dictionary and write down all the Spanish equivalents given. Note that semicolons are used to separate groups of words that are similar in meaning. Example: *lively:* **vivo, vivaz, vivaracho; rápido, apresurado; gallardo, galán, airoso; vigoroso, brioso, enérgico; animado, bullicioso; eficaz, intensivo.**

4. Take a Spanish equivalent from each group and look it up in the Spanish part of the dictionary. What is given as its English equivalent? As you look up each word, you'll see that often the different Spanish words express very different ideas in English.

   Example: **Rápido** and **apresurado** are words that apply more to actions, since they are translated as *rapid, quick, swift* and *brief, hasty*.

5. Now look up the English synonyms you listed in step #2 and see what Spanish equivalents are given. Are any of them the same as those that turned up for the first word? Example: *vivacious:* **vivaz, animado, vivaracho;** *energetic:* **enérgico, activo, vigoroso.**

6. Focus on the words that came up more than once: **vivaz, vivaracho, animado, enérgico.** If you need to, look these words up a final time. Which best expresses the shade of meaning you want to use?

1 You are going to write a short description of a sculpture by Fernando Botero, the well-known Colombian painter and sculptor.

Look at the photo of the sculpture on page 77. What words might you need to describe it? Here are some to get you started, but look up any new words you might require in a bilingual dictionary. **¡OJO!** Remember to cross-check the words you choose in order to get the one that best fits what you are trying to say.

Palabras útiles: escultura *(sculpture)*, **estatua** *(statue)*, **montado a caballo** *(on horseback)*, **sombrero** *(hat)*.

La escultura *Hombre montado a caballo* de Fernando Botero

Composición

2 Write three to five sentences that describe the sculpture, using the list of words you generated in **Actividad 1.** Try to write freely without worrying too much about mistakes and misspellings.

Después de escribir

3 Now go back over your review and revise it. Use the following checklist to guide you. Did you . . .

- include all the necessary information?
- check to make sure that the adjectives and nouns agree in gender and number?
- make sure that the verbs agree with their subjects?
- look for misspellings?

Vocabulario

Para expresar preferencias *Expressing preferences*

¿Qué te gusta hacer? *What do you like to do?*
A mí me gusta... *I like . . .*
A ti te gusta... *You like . . .*
A... le gusta... *You/He/She like(s) . . .*
A... les gusta... *You (pl.)/They like . . .*
¿Y a ti? *And you?*

alquilar videos / películas *to rent videos/movies*
bailar *to dance*
caminar *to walk*
cantar *to sing*
cocinar *to cook*
escuchar música *to listen to music*
estudiar en la biblioteca / en casa *to study at the library/at home*
hablar por teléfono *to talk on the phone*
levantar pesas *to lift weights*

mirar televisión *to watch television*
navegar por Internet *to browse the Internet*
patinar *to skate*
pintar *to paint*
practicar deportes *to play sports*
sacar fotos *to take photos*
tocar un instrumento musical *to play a musical instrument*
    la guitarra *the guitar*
    el piano *the piano*
    la trompeta *the trumpet*
    el violín *the violin*
tomar un refresco *to have a soft drink*
tomar el sol *to sunbathe*
trabajar *to work*
visitar a amigos *to visit friends*

Para describir *Describing*

¿Cómo es? *What is he/she/it like?*

muy *very*

Características de la personalidad *Personality traits*

aburrido(a) *boring*
activo(a) *active*
antipático(a) *unpleasant*
bueno(a) *good*
cómico(a) *funny*
cuidadoso(a) *cautious*
divertido(a) *fun, entertaining*
egoísta *selfish, egotistic*
extrovertido(a) *extroverted*
generoso(a) *generous*
impaciente *impatient*
impulsivo(a) *impulsive*
inteligente *intelligent*
interesante *interesting*

introvertido(a) *introverted*
irresponsable *irresponsible*
malo(a) *bad*
mentiroso(a) *dishonest, lying*
paciente *patient*
perezoso(a) *lazy*
responsable *responsible*
serio(a) *serious*
simpático(a) *nice*
sincero(a) *sincere*
tímido(a) *shy*
tonto(a) *silly, stupid*
trabajador(a) *hard-working*

Características físicas *Physical traits*

alto(a) *tall*
bajo(a) *short*
delgado(a) *thin*
feo(a) *ugly*
gordo(a) *fat*
grande *big, great*
guapo(a) *handsome, attractive*
joven *young*

lindo(a) *pretty*
pequeño(a) *small*
viejo(a) *old*

Es pelirrojo(a) / rubio(a). *He/She is redheaded/ blond(e).*
Tiene el pelo negro / castaño / rubio. *He/She has black/brown/blond hair.*

Nacionalidades *Nationalities*

alemán (alemana) *German*
argentino(a) *Argentinian*
australiano(a) *Australian*
boliviano(a) *Bolivian*
canadiense *Canadian*
chileno(a) *Chilean*
chino(a) *Chinese*
colombiano(a) *Colombian*
coreano(a) *Korean*
costarricense *Costa Rican*
cubano(a) *Cuban*
dominicano(a) *Dominican*
ecuatoguineano(a) *Equatorial Guinean*
ecuatoriano(a) *Ecuadoran*
español(a) *Spanish*
estadounidense *U. S. citizen*
francés (francesa) *French*

guatemalteco(a) *Guatemalan*
hondureño(a) *Honduran*
indio(a) *Indian*
inglés (inglesa) *English*
italiano(a) *Italian*
japonés (japonesa) *Japanese*
mexicano(a) *Mexican*
nicaragüense *Nicaraguan*
panameño(a) *Panamanian*
paraguayo(a) *Paraguayan*
peruano(a) *Peruvian*
portugués (portuguesa) *Portuguese*
puertorriqueño(a) *Puerto Rican*
salvadoreño(a) *Salvadoran*
uruguayo(a) *Uruguayan*
venezolano(a) *Venezuelan*

Los verbos

acabar de (+ inf.) *to have just done something*
apagar *to turn off*
buscar *to look for*
cenar *to eat dinner*
comprar *to buy*
dejar *to leave*
dejar de (+ inf.) *to stop (doing something)*
descansar *to rest*

llamar *to call*
llegar *to arrive*
necesitar *to need*
pasar *to pass (by)*
preparar *to prepare*
regresar *to return*
usar *to use*

Otras palabras

los fines de semana *weekends*
los viernes *Fridays*
los sábados *Saturdays*
los domingos *Sundays*
el gato *cat*

el perro *dog*
pero *but*
también *also*
tampoco *neither*

>> Repaso del Capítulo 2

The present indicative of regular **-ar** verbs (p. 54)

1 Look at the illustrations and say what the people indicated are doing.

1.
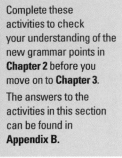
Esteban y Carolina

2.

usted

3.
Loreta

4.

yo

5.

nosotros

6.
tú

7.
ustedes

8.
tú y yo

© Cengage Learning 2013

Gustar + infinitive (p. 58)

2 Read the description of each person. Then say what activity he or she likes to do, choosing from the list. Follow the model.

Actividades: estudiar, mirar televisión, pintar, practicar deportes, visitar a amigos, trabajar.

MODELO   Ellos son muy trabajadores.
A ellos les gusta trabajar.

1. Yo soy muy serio.
2. Tú eres muy perezosa.
3. Usted es muy extrovertido.

4. Nosotras somos muy artísticas.
5. Ustedes son muy activos.

Adjective agreement (p. 62)

3 Use forms of **ser** to describe each person using the cues provided.

1. Gretchen y Rolf / Alemania / sincero
2. Brigitte / Francia / divertido
3. nosotras / España / simpático

4. yo (feminino) / Estados Unidos / generoso
5. usted (feminino) / Japón / interesante
6. tú (masculino) / Italia / activo

Preparación para el Capítulo 3

Nouns and articles (Chapter 1)

4 Complete the description with the definite and indefinite articles that are missing. Make sure the articles agree with the nouns they modify.

A mí me gustan 1. _____ clases que tengo hoy. 2. _____ profesor de historia es muy inteligente y 3. _____ profesora de español es muy interesante. Tengo 4. _____ amigos en 5. _____ clase de ingeniería y por eso es muy divertida. Solamente tengo 6. _____ clase por la tarde. Pero no es 7. _____ día normal. Normalmente tengo clases por 8. _____ mañana y también por 9. _____ tarde. ¡Pero por lo menos, no tengo clases por 10. _____ noches!

Complete these activities to review some previously learned grammatical structures that will be helpful when you learn the new grammar in **Chapter 3**.

Be sure to reread **Chapter 2: Gramática útil 1** and **2** before moving on to the **Chapter 3** grammar sections.

Subject pronouns and the present indicative of the verb ser (Chapter 1)

5 Match the illustrations on the left with the sentences on the right. Then write in the missing forms of the verb **ser**.

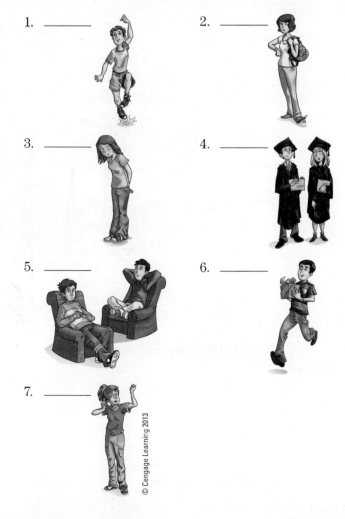

1. _____

2. _____

3. _____

4. _____

5. _____

6. _____

7. _____

a. Ella _____ muy tímida.

b. Nosotros _____ muy perezosos.

c. Yo _____ muy extrovertida.

d. Usted _____ muy impaciente.

e. Tú _____ generoso.

f. Él _____ activo.

g. Ustedes _____ inteligentes.

© Cengage Learning 2013

¿Qué clases vas a tomar?

¡VIVIR ES APRENDER!

Los estudiantes asisten a clases formales y estudian muchas materias. Pero en un sentido *(sense)* menos formal, todos somos estudiantes. Aprendemos algo nuevo todos los días—de nuestros *(our)* amigos, familiares y experiencias.

Para ti, ¿cuál es la mejor manera *(the best way)* de aprender?

Communication

By the end of this chapter you will be able to

- talk about courses and schedules and tell time
- talk about present activities and future plans
- talk about possessions
- ask and answer questions

Glowimages RF

Un viaje por Cuba, Puerto Rico y la República Dominicana

Estos tres países están situados en el mar Caribe y tienen un clima tropical. Todos también tienen montañas. La República Dominicana comparte *(shares)* una isla con Haití.

Pais / Área	Tamaño y fronteras *(Size and Borders)*	Sitios *(Places)* de interés
Cuba 110.860 km²	un poco más pequeño que Pensilvania	las cavernas de Bellamar, la Vieja Habana, la península de Guanahacabibes
Puerto Rico 8.950 km²	casi tres veces *(almost three times)* el área de Rhode Island	Vieques, El Morro, Viejo San Juan
República Dominicana 48.380 km²	más de dos veces el área de Nuevo Hampshire; frontera con Haití	Pico Duarte, la sierra *(mountains)* de Samaná, La Universidad Autónoma de Santo Domingo

¿Qué sabes? Di si las siguientes oraciones son ciertas (**C**) o falsas (**F**).

1. Estos tres países están en el mar Caribe.
2. La República Dominicana es casi dos veces el tamaño de Puerto Rico.
3. No hay una zona vieja en Cuba.

Lo que sé y lo que quiero aprender Completa la tabla del **Apéndice A**. Escribe algunos datos que **ya sabes** sobre estos países caribeños en la columna **Lo que sé**. Después, añade algunos temas que **quieres aprender** a la columna **Lo que quiero aprender**. Guarda la tabla para usarla otra vez en la sección **¡Explora y exprésate!** en la página 111.

Cultures

By the end of this chapter you will have explored

- facts about Puerto Rico, Cuba, and the Dominican Republic
- Cuba: the campaign for literacy
- Puerto Rico: the bilingual education of the **boricuas**
- República Dominicana: the oldest university in the New World
- the 24-hour clock
- three unusual schools in the Caribbean

¡Imagínate!

>> Vocabulario útil 1

CHELA: Para empezar, dime, ¿cuántas clases tienes?

ANILÚ: Ay, ¡qué aburrido!, ¿no crees? Si voy a salir por Internet, quiero hacer más que recitar mis clases: **computación, diseño gráfico, psicología**, bla, bla, bla…

CHELA: Comprendo que no son las preguntas más interesantes del mundo, pero…

ANILÚ: Prefiero hablar de mi tiempo libre, los **sábados**, por ejemplo.

Notice that many of the courses of study are cognates of their English equivalents. Be sure to notice the difference in spelling, accentuation, and pronunciation, for example: **geografía**: *geography*.

>> Campos de estudio

Los cursos básicos
la arquitectura
las ciencias políticas
la economía
la educación
la geografía
la historia
la ingeniería
la psicología

Las humanidades
la filosofía
las lenguas / los idiomas
la literatura

**Las lenguas /
Los idiomas**
el alemán
el chino
el español
el francés
el inglés
el japonés

Las matemáticas
el cálculo
la computación /
la informática
la estadística

Las ciencias
la biología
la física
la medicina
la química (*chemistry*)
la salud (*health*)

Los negocios
la administración de
empresas
la contabilidad
(*accounting*)
el mercadeo (*marketing*)

**La comunicación
pública**
el periodismo
(*journalism*)
la publicidad

Las artes
el arte
el baile
el diseño gráfico
la música
la pintura

Lugares en la universidad

¿Dónde tienes la clase de...?	*Where does your . . . class meet?*
En el centro de computación.	*In the computer center.*
...el centro de comunicaciones.	*. . . the media center.*
...el gimnasio.	*. . . the gymnasium.*
la cafetería	*the cafeteria*
la librería	*the bookstore*
la residencia estudiantil	*the dorm*

>> **Los días de la semana**

lunes	martes	miércoles	jueves	viernes	sábado	domingo
8	9	10	11	12	13	14

Notice that the week begins on Monday in most Spanish-speaking countries. Also notice that the days of the week are not capitalized in Spanish as they are in English.

To say that something happens *on* a certain day, use the singular article with the day of the week: **La fiesta va a ser** *el* sábado.

To say that something happens on the same day every week, use the plural article with the day of the week: ***Los* sábados visito a mi madre.** Notice that there is no preposition **en** *(on)* in these cases.

ACTIVIDADES

1 **Las carreras** Say what course you would take if you were interested in a certain career.

MODELO journalist
el periodismo

1. psychologist
2. accountant
3. software programmer
4. architect
5. graphic designer
6. teacher

2 **Las clases de Mariana** With a partner, say on which days Mariana has each of her classes, based on her class schedule.

MODELO economía
Mariana tiene economía los lunes, los miércoles y los viernes.

1. psicología
2. literatura
3. francés
4. contabilidad
5. pintura
6. música

	lunes	martes	miércoles	jueves	viernes
8:00	economía		economía		economía
10:00	psicología	literatura	psicología	literatura	
11:30	francés	francés	francés	francés	francés
3:00		contabilidad		contabilidad	
4:00	pintura		música	pintura	música

3 **Mis clases** Create a chart with your class schedule. Include days, times, and locations. Then, with a partner, ask each other questions about each day of the week. Be sure to save your schedule for later activities.

MODELO   Tú: *¿Qué clases tienes los lunes?*
Compañero(a): *Los lunes tengo psicología, arte y computación.*

4 **¿Dónde?** Ask your partner where he/she does certain activities.

MODELO   levantar pesas
Tú: *¿Dónde levantas pesas?*
Compañero(a): *En el gimnasio.*

1. visitar a tus amigos
2. navegar por Internet
3. escuchar los CDs de la clase de español
4. practicar deportes
5. comprar libros
6. vivir
7. tener clase de baile
8. estudiar

5 **Entrevista** Imagine that you are like Chela in the video and you must approach someone in your class for an interview about their daily schedule. Use as much language as you can from previous chapters. Make a list of questions beforehand. Then record the interview and upload for the class to view or summarize the interview in class. You can use the following questions or make up your own.

Preguntas:
Buenos días, ¿qué tal?
¿Cómo te llamas?
¿De dónde eres?
¿Cuántos años tienes?
¿Qué te gusta hacer los domingos?
¿Qué estudias?
¿Cuántas clases tienes?
¿Dónde tienes la clase de…?
¿Cuál es tu clase preferida?
¿Qué día de la semana te gusta más?

6 **Mi blog** Write a blog post about the interview you did in Activity 5. What were some of the interesting things you learned about your partner?

MODELO   *Mi compañero estudia psicología, pero su clase preferida es la clase de baile.*

¡Fíjate! El reloj de veinticuatro horas

The 24-hour clock is used globally, and in all Spanish-speaking countries, for schedules and official times. The system is based on counting the hours of the day from zero through twenty-four. The first twelve hours of the day (from midnight until noon) are represented by the numbers 0–12. Any time after noon is represented by that time +12. The **h** after the time stands for **horas**.

For example:
1:00 P.M. = 1:00 + 12 = 13:00h
2:30 P.M. = 2:30 + 12 = 14:30h
5:45 P.M. = 5:45 + 12 = 17:45h

To go from a 24-hour clock time to a 12-hour clock time, you must subtract 12 hours from the 24-hour clock time.

For example:
13:00h − 12 = 1:00 P.M.
14:30h − 12 = 2:30 P.M.
17:45h − 12 = 5:45 P.M.

Próximas Salidas
Cercanías   Regionales y L. Rec

The 24-hour clock is almost always used in written form. In conversation, Spanish speakers use the 12-hour format, adding **de la mañana** (morning, A.M.), **de la tarde** (afternoon, P.M.), and **de la noche** (evening, P.M.) for clarification.

Práctica 1 With a partner, look at the schedules below. Convert the times on the 24-hour clock to the 12-hour clock. Follow the model.

MODELO 21:20h = *9:20 P.M.*

1. 23:20h =   3. 18:30h =   5. 15:10h =
2. 14:45h =   4. 16:25h =   6. 19:15h =

Práctica 2 With a partner, look at the schedules that you used in **Activity 3**. Convert the times on your schedules to hours on the 24-hour clock. Follow the model.

MODELO Tú: *Mi (My) clase de matemáticas es a las 3:00 de la tarde.*
Compañero(a): *Tu (Your) clase de matemáticas es a las 15:00 horas.*

Vocabulario útil 2

© Cengage Learning 2013

CHELA:	¿Qué haces los sábados?
ANILÚ:	**Por la mañana**, corro por el parque. **A las dos de la tarde**, tengo clase de danza afrocaribeña.
CHELA:	¿Y **por la noche**?
ANILÚ:	Por la noche escucho música con mis amigos o vamos al cine o a un restaurante.
CAMARÓGRAFO:	Uy, **¿qué hora es?** ¡Tengo que irme!
CHELA:	Pero, ¿adónde vas? ¡Necesito otra entrevista!
CAMARÓGRAFO:	¡Tengo clase **a las once**!
CHELA:	**Son las once menos cuarto.** Espera un minuto, por favor.

Compare the following two questions and responses.

¿Qué hora es? *(What time is it?)*

Es la una. *(It's one o'clock.)*

¿A qué hora es la clase de español? *([At] What time is Spanish class?)*

Es a la una. *(It's at one o'clock.)*

>> **Para pedir y dar la hora** *Asking for and giving the time*

¿Qué hora es? *What time is it?*

Es la una.

Son las dos.

Son las cinco y cuarto.
Son las cinco y quince.

Son las cinco y media.

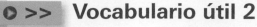

Son las cinco y diez.

Son las cinco menos cuarto.
Faltan quince par las cinco.

© Cengage Learning 2013

—**¿Tienes tiempo** para tomar un café?

—**Sí, es temprano.** / —¡Ay, no, **ya es muy tarde**!

Mañana, tarde o noche
Mira **el reloj** para **decir la hora**.

Morning, afternoon, or night
Look at the clock to tell the time.

Son las ocho de la mañana.

Son las tres de la tarde.

Son las nueve de la noche.

Es mediodía.	*It's noon.*
Es medianoche.	*It's midnight.*
Es tarde.	*It's late.*
Es temprano.	*It's early.*

De la mañana is used for the morning hours between midnight and noon. **De la tarde** is used for daylight hours after noon. **De la noche** is used only for nighttime hours. These hours vary from country to country, given that in some countries it gets dark earlier or stays light later.

Compare the use of **de** and **por** in the following sentences.

> La clase es a las diez **de la mañana**.

> En general estudio **por la mañana**.

Note that you use **de la mañana / tarde / noche** to give a specific time of day. You use **por la mañana / tarde / noche** to give a more general time frame.

ACTIVIDADES

7 ¿Qué hora es? Ask your partner what time it is. He/She will tell you what time it is. Take turns asking the time.

MODELO 1:00 P.M.
> Tú: *¿Qué hora es?*
> Compañero(a): *Es la una de la tarde.*

1. 3:15 P.M.	3. 10:30 A.M.	5. 6:55 A.M.
2. 2:45 P.M.	4. 12:00 noon	6. 9:25 P.M.

8 Mi horario Get out the agenda page that you completed for **Activity 3.** Ask your partner about his/her class schedule. You name a day and a time, and your partner tells you what class he/she has at that time. Talk about all five days of the week.

MODELO Tú: *Es lunes y son las diez de la mañana.*
> Compañero(a): *Tengo clase de cálculo.*

9 Tu horario Exchange your agenda page with your partner. Your partner names a day and a time, and you tell him/her where he/she is at that time. Take turns with each other's schedules.

MODELO Compañero(a): *Es viernes y son las dos de la tarde. ¿Dónde estoy?*
> Tú: *Estás en la clase de danza afrocaribeña.*

CHELA: ¿Así que te gustan más los fines de semana que los días de **entresemana**?

ANILÚ: Pues sí, por supuesto. Los fines de semana son mucho más divertidos. Ay, **es tarde**. Yo también tengo clase a las once.

CHELA: Gracias por la entrevista. …

ANILÚ: Oye, ¿cuándo sale la entrevista en la red?

CHELA: **Mañana.**

>> **Para hablar de la fecha** *Talking about the date*

¿Qué día es hoy? *What day is today?*
Hoy es martes treinta. *Today is Tuesday the 30th.*

¿A qué fecha estamos? *What is today's date?*
Es el treinta de octubre. *It's the 30th of October.*
Es el primero de noviembre. *It's the first of November.*

¿Cuándo es el Día de las Madres? *When is Mother's Day?*
Es el doce de mayo. *It's May 12th.*

el día *day*
la semana *week*
el fin de semana *weekend*
el mes *month*
el año *year*
todos los días *every day*
entresemana *during the week/on weekdays*

ayer *yesterday*
hoy *today*
mañana *tomorrow*

10 **¿Qué es?** Say what each of the following time periods are.

MODELO febrero
el mes

1. enero
2. sábado y domingo
3. 2012
4. el 7 de septiembre
5. 7 de noviembre a 14 de noviembre
6. hoy

11 **Las fechas** Form pairs and look at a current yearly calendar. Your professor will give each team five minutes to answer the following questions. Write out your answers in Spanish. There are some words that you might not know. Try to guess at their meaning, but don't let it hold you up!

1. ¿Qué día de la semana es Navidad (25 de diciembre) este año?
2. ¿Qué día de la semana es el Día de la Independencia (4 de julio) este año?
3. ¿Qué día de la semana es el Día de los Enamorados (14 de febrero) este año?
4. ¿A qué fecha estamos? ¿Cuándo es el próximo *(next)* examen de español?
5. ¿Cuándo son las próximas vacaciones? ¿Qué día regresan los estudiantes de las próximas vacaciones?

12 **Fechas importantes** Write out in Spanish ten to fifteen dates that are important for you. Then copy them into your calendar. The following are some examples of the dates you might include.

los cumpleaños de los miembros de mi familia
los cumpleaños de mis amigos
el Día de las Madres
el Día del Padre
las fechas de las vacaciones
el aniversario de…
las fechas de mis exámenes finales

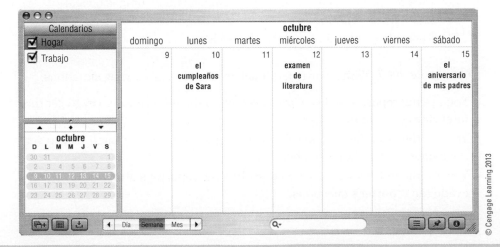

© Cengage Learning 2013

A ver

ESTRATEGIA

Using body language to aid in comprehension

When you observe the body language of the person speaking, you can get clues to a person's meaning by watching facial expressions, gestures, hand movements, and so on. For example, if you ask someone a question and the person shrugs and walks away, the meaning is clear, even if no words were uttered!

As a previewing strategy to help guide your comprehension of the video segment, read the items in **Después de ver 1** *before* you view the video.

Antes de ver Review these key words used in the video.

la entrevista	*the interview*
transmitir	*to transmit*
la red	*the Internet*

© Cengage Learning 2013

Ver Now watch the video segment for **Chapter 3** without sound. Pay special attention to the characters' body language.

Después de ver 1 Say whether statements 1-4 are true (**cierto**) or false (**falso**), based on your observation of the characters' body language. Then watch again with sound and complete statements 5–9.

1. Muchos estudiantes prefieren no participar en la entrevista con Chela.
2. Chela indica algo *(something)* al estudiante con la cámara.
3. El estudiante con la cámara no tiene prisa *(is not in a hurry)*.
4. Anilú observa a Javier (el estudiante que aparece al final del segmento) con mucho interés.
5. En la opinión del estudiante con la cámara y de Anilú, el tema del programa de Chela es _____.
6. Anilú tiene clases de computación, diseño gráfico y _____.
7. Los _____, Anilú corre en el parque.
8. Los sábados por la noche, Anilú escucha música con amigos o va al _____ o a un restaurante.
9. El estudiante con la cámara tiene clase a las _____.

Después de ver 2 With a partner, dramatize one of the following situations.

- You are the reporter and you are attracted to the interviewee. Try to get the interviewee's phone number.
- You are the interviewee and you are attracted to the cameraman. Try to get the cameraman's phone number.
- You are the interviewee and you don't like the reporter's attitude. Try to evade the reporter's questions.

Voces de la comunidad

▶ >> Voces del mundo hispano

In this video segment, the speakers talk about their studies and pastimes. First read the statements below. Then watch the video as many times as needed to say whether the statements are true (**cierto**) or false (**falso**).

1. Sandra estudia administración de empresas.
2. Jessica estudia química.
3. A Javier le gusta ver *(to see)* películas.
4. A Dayramir le gusta bailar salsa con sus amigos.
5. Durante los fines de semana, Ela va *(goes)* al parque.
6. Durante los fines de semana, Inés visita a su familia.

© Cengage Learning 2013

◀)) >> Voces de Estados Unidos

Track 8

Sonia Sotomayor, jueza, Corte Suprema de Estados Unidos

❝ **Creo que si las caras de los jueces** *(judges' faces)* **no reflejan la población a la que sirven, la gente va a tener menos confianza en el sistema de justicia. Es importante que todos los grupos de Estados Unidos estén representados en la función más importante de la sociedad.** ❞

Pablo Martínez Monsivais/AP Images

Sonia Sotomayor, la primera persona de ascendencia hispana en la Corte Suprema de los Estados Unidos, es la personificación del sueño *(dream)* americano. Nacida *(Born)* en un proyecto público en El Bronx a padres puertorriqueños, la jueza es conocida por su inteligencia, capacidad de trabajo y respeto por sus raíces. Dos tragedias en su niñez forman su carácter: la muerte *(death)* de su padre a los nueve años y la diabetes juvenil. Con la ayuda *(help)* de su madre, Sotomayor triunfa sobre estas adversidades. Asiste a Princeton, y después a la escuela de derecho de Yale. Sin embargo, la jueza nunca olvida sus raíces *(never forgets her roots)*. Sus experiencias como empleada en una dulcería *(candy store)* y una tienda de ropa *(clothing store)* y como camarera *(waitress)* le dan una especial sensibilidad hacia las necesidades de las personas comunes.

¿Y tú? ¿ Are you interested in working in the public sector? Why or why not?

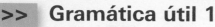

¡Prepárate!

>> Gramática útil 1

Asking questions: Interrogative words

© Cengage Learning 2013

¿**Cuántas** entrevistas tenemos que hacer?

Cómo usarlo

You have already seen, learned, and used a number of interrogative words to ask questions. ¿**Cómo te llamas?**, ¿**Cuál es tu dirección electrónica?**, ¿**Dónde vives?**, and ¿**Qué tal?** are all questions that begin with interrogatives: **cómo, cuál, dónde, qué.**

As in English, we use interrogatives in Spanish to ask for specific information. Here are the Spanish interrogatives.

¿**Cuál(es)?**	*What? Which one(s)?*	¿**Dónde?**	*Where?*
¿**Qué?**	*What? Which?*	¿**Adónde?**	*To where?*
¿**A qué hora?**	*(At) What time?*	¿**De dónde?**	*From where?*
¿**De qué?**	*About what? Of what?*	¿**Quién(es)?**	*Who?*
¿**Cuándo?**	*When?*	¿**De quién(es)?**	*Whose?*
¿**Cuánto(a)?**	*How much?*	¿**Cómo?**	*How?*
¿**Cuántos(as)?**	*How many?*	¿**Por qué?**	*Why?*

1. ¿**Qué?** and ¿**cuál?** may appear interchangeable at first sight, but they are used in very specific ways.

   ¿**Qué?** is . . .

   ■ used to ask for a definition: ¿**Qué es el reloj de veinticuatro horas?**

   ■ used to ask for an explanation or further information: ¿**Qué vas a estudiar este semestre?**

   ■ generally used when the next word is a noun: ¿**Qué libros te gustan más?** ¿**Qué clase tienes a las ocho?**

   ¿**Cuál?** is . . .

   ■ used to express a choice between specified items: ¿**Cuál de los libros prefieres?**

   ■ used when the next word is a form of **ser** but the question is *not* asking for a definition: ¿**Cuál es tu número de teléfono?** ¿**Cuáles son tus clases favoritas?**

2. ¿**Dónde?** is used to ask where something is.

   ¿**Dónde** está la biblioteca?   *Where is the library?*

3. **¿Adónde?** is used to ask where someone is going.

¿**Adónde** vas ahora?   *Where are you going now?*

4. **¿De quién es?** and **¿De quiénes son?** are used to ask about possession. You answer using **de**.

—**¿De quién** es la computadora?   *Whose computer is this?*
—**Es de** Miguel.   *It's Miguel's.*

—**¿De quiénes** son los libros?   *Whose books are those?*
—**Son de** Anita y Manuel.   *They're Anita's and Manuel's.*

5. Questions using **¿por qué?** can be answered using **porque** *(because).*

—**¿Por qué** tienes que trabajar?   *Why do you have to work?*
—**¡Porque** necesito el dinero!   *Because I need the money!*

> Notice that **dónde** and **adónde** are both translated the same way into English.

> Note that the interrogative is two separate words with an accent on **qué**. **Porque** is one single word with no accent.

Cómo formarlo

1. Interrogatives are always preceded by an inverted question mark (**¿**). The question requires a regular question mark (**?**) at the end.

2. Notice that in a typical question the subject *follows* the verb.

¿Dónde **estudia Marcos**?   *Where does **Marcos study**?*
¿Qué instrumento **tocan** ustedes?   *What instrument do **you play**?*

3. **¿Quién?** and **¿cuál?** change to reflect number.

¿**Quién** es el hombre alto? / ¿**Quiénes** son los hombres altos?
¿**Cuál** de los libros tienes? / ¿**Cuáles** son tus idiomas favoritos?

4. **¿Cuánto?** changes to reflect both number and gender.

¿**Cuánto** dinero tienes?   ***How much** money do you have?*
¿**Cuánta** comida compramos?   ***How much** food should we buy?*
¿**Cuántos** años tienes?   ***How many** years old are you? /*
                                      ***How old** are you?*

¿**Cuántas** personas hay?   ***How many** people are there?*

5. When you want to ask *how much* in a general way, use **¿cuánto?**

¿Cuánto es?   **¿Cuánto necesitamos?**

6. Note that interrogatives always require an accent.

7. You have already learned how to form simple *yes/no* questions by adding **no** to a sentence.

¿**No escribes** e-mails   ***Aren't you writing** any*
   hoy?   *e-mails today?*

8. You can also form simple *yes/no* questions by adding a tag question, such as **¿verdad?** *(Isn't that right?)* and **¿no?** to the end of a statement.

Cantas en el coro con   *You sing in the chorus with*
   Ana, **¿no?**   *Ana, **right**?*
Enrique baila salsa muy   *Enrique dances salsa very*
   bien, **¿verdad?**   *well, **right**?*

> When a Spanish speaker adds **¿verdad?** or **¿no?** to a question, he or she is expecting an affirmative answer.

🔊
Track 9

1 **Las preguntas** What question would you have to ask to produce the response shown? You will hear three questions. Choose the correct one.

_____ 1. La clase de informática es a las once de la mañana.

_____ 2. Tengo que ir al centro de computación para la clase de informática.

_____ 3. La computadora portátil es de mi compañero de cuarto.

_____ 4. Hay que comprar tres libros para la clase de informática.

_____ 5. Porque me gustan mucho las computadoras y quiero aprender a programarlas.

_____ 6. La señora Delgado es la profesora de informática.

2 **En la cafetería** You overhear a conversation between two students in the cafeteria. Fill in the correct form of the question words to complete their conversation.

—¿(1) _____ clases tienes este semestre?
—Tengo arte, literatura, cálculo, química y economía.

—¿(2) _____ son tus clases favoritas?
—El arte y la literatura.

—¿(3) _____ son tus autores favoritos?
—Gabriel García Márquez, Mario Vargas Llosa, Julia Álvarez e Isabel Allende.

—¿(4) _____ es tu profesor de literatura?
—El señor Banderas.

—¿(5) _____ libros necesitas para la clase de literatura?
—Diez, más o menos, pero son libros que puedo sacar de la biblioteca.

—¿A (6) _____ hora tienes la clase de literatura?
—A las diez de la mañana.

—¿(7) _____ vas ahora?
—Al centro de computación.

—¿(8) _____ vas allí?
—Porque necesito usar las computadoras para hacer mi tarea.

—Pero tienes computadora portátil. ¿(9) _____ es la computadora portátil?
—Es de mi compañero de cuarto. ¡Haces demasiadas *(You ask too many)* preguntas!

3 **Más preguntas** For each activity indicated, take turns asking and answering questions with a partner.

MODELO   bailar (cuándo)
              Estudiante #1: *¿Cuándo bailas?*
              Estudiante #2: *Bailo los viernes.*

1. estudiar (qué)
2. visitar a amigos (cuándo)
3. hablar con la profesora (por qué)
4. caminar (adónde)
5. tener años (cuánto)
6. imprimir los informes (dónde)

4 **¡Qué curiosidad!** In groups of three or four, take turns coming up with as many questions as you can for each activity listed. (Take turns writing down the questions or keep your own list.) Then compare your group's questions with another group to see who has the most questions for each activity.

1. correr
2. comer
3. tener muchos amigos
4. escuchar música
5. comprar muchos libros
6. tomar clases

5 **Encuesta #1** In the chapter activities labeled **"Encuesta"** you will gather information from your fellow students in order to write a description of life at your college or university in the **A escribir** section at the end of the chapter.

1. First prepare a questionnaire by creating two questions for each category, using the cues provided or coming up with your own.

   El horario: clases por día / semana, lugar preferido para estudiar

   El trabajo: lugar de trabajo, horas de trabajo

   La computadora: tiempo que pasas en la computadora, sitios interesantes en Internet

   La universidad: clases difíciles y fáciles, las horas por semana que estudias, profesores buenos y malos

2. Now work with another group and ask the members to answer your questionnaire. Be sure to answer their questions as well. Keep track of your results. You will need them later in the chapter.

Gramática útil 2

Talking about daily activities: The present indicative of regular -er and -ir verbs

Por la mañana, **corro** en el parque.

Cómo usarlo

In **Chapter 2,** you learned how to use the present indicative of regular **-ar** verbs to talk about daily activities. The present indicative of **-er** and **-ir** verbs are used in the same contexts.

Remember:

1. The present indicative, depending on how it is used, can correspond to the following English usages: *I read* (in general), *I am reading, I am going to read, I do read,* and, if used as a question, *Do you read?*

2. You can often omit the subject pronoun when the subject is clear from the verb ending used or from the context of the sentence.

   Leo en la biblioteca todos los días.   *I read in the library every day.*
   Lees en la residencia estudiantil, ¿no?   *You read in the dorm, right?*

3. You may use an infinitive after certain conjugated verbs.

   ¿Tienes que imprimir esto?   *Do you have to print this?*
   ¿Necesitas leer este libro?   *Do you need to read this book?*
   ¡Dejo de leer después de medianoche!   *I stop reading after midnight!*

4. However, do not use two verbs conjugated in the present tense together unless they are separated by a comma or the words **y** *(and)* or **o** *(or).*

   Leo, estudio y **escribo** composiciones en la biblioteca.   *I read, study, and write compositions in the library.*

5. Remember that you can negate sentences in the present indicative tense to say what you don't do or aren't planning to do.

   No comemos en la cafetería hoy.   *We're not eating in the cafeteria today.*
   No leo todos los días.   *I don't read every day.*

Cómo formarlo

To form the present indicative tense of **-er** and **-ir** verbs, simply remove the **-er** or **-ir** and add the following endings.

comer *(to eat)*			
yo	**como**	nosotros / nosotras	**comemos**
tú	**comes**	vosotros / vosotras	**coméis**
Ud. / él / ella	**come**	Uds. / ellos / ellas	**comen**

vivir (to live)			
yo	**vivo**	nosotros / nosotras	**vivimos**
tú	**vives**	vosotros / vosotras	**vivís**
Ud. / él / ella	**vive**	Uds. / ellos / ellas	**viven**

Notice that the present indicative endings for **-er** and **-ir** verbs are identical except for the **nosotros** and **vosotros** forms.

Here are some commonly used **-er** and **-ir** verbs.

-er verbs			
aprender a (+ infinitive)	to learn to (do something)	**creer (en)**	to believe (in)
beber	to drink	**deber** (+ infinitive)	should, ought (to do something)
comer	to eat	**leer**	to read
comprender	to understand	**vender**	to sell
correr	to run		

-ir verbs			
abrir	to open	**escribir**	to write
asistir a	to attend	**imprimir**	to print
compartir	to share	**recibir**	to receive
describir	to describe	**transmitir**	to broadcast
descubrir	to discover	**vivir**	to live

ACTIVIDADES

6 **¿Qué hacen?** Based on the information provided, what do the people indicated do? Choose verbs from the list. Follow the model.

MODELOS   Carlos ya no necesita esa cámara digital.
   Vende la cámara.

   Tú y yo necesitamos hacer ejercicio.
   Corremos en el parque.

Verbos posibles: aprender / asistir / comer / compartir / correr / vender

1. ¡Olivia tiene la clase de biología a las tres y ya son las tres y cinco! _____ a la universidad.
2. A Susana no le gusta esa bicicleta. _____ la bicicleta.
3. Raúl y Enrique tienen que viajar a Puerto Rico en dos meses. _____ español.
4. Elena y yo no comprendemos las lecturas del libro. _____ a una clase de estudio.
5. No me gustan los restaurantes aquí. _____ en la cafetería todos los días.
6. Susana vive con una compañera de cuarto. _____ el apartamento con ella.

7 **La vida estudiantil** Say what the people indicated are doing today on campus. The numbers indicate how many actions are going on for each person.

1. Juan Carlos e Isabel (1)
2. Marcos (2)
3. Cecilia y Marta (2)
4. Radio WBRU (1)
5. Y tú, ¿qué haces *(what are you doing)*?

8 **¿Y tú?** With a partner, take turns asking and answering the following questions.

1. ¿Cuándo asistes a tu primera clase del día?
2. ¿Vives en un apartamento o en una residencia?
3. ¿A qué hora comes la cena *(dinner)*?
4. ¿Recibes muchos e-mails de tu familia?
5. ¿Escribes muchos informes?
6. ¿Dónde lees los libros para tus clases?

9 **¿Qué hacemos?** Using an element from each of the three columns, create eight sentences describing what you and people you know do in and around campus.

MODELO *Yo asisto a clases los lunes, los miércoles y los jueves.*

A	B	C
yo	aprender a hablar	café por la mañana
tú	español	en el centro de comunicaciones
compañero(s)	asistir a	clases *(número)* días de la semana
de cuarto	beber	correspondencia electrónica todos los
profesor(es)	comprender	días
estudiante(s)	correr	en el estadio
amigo(s)	creer (en)	la importancia de Internet
	escribir	clases los *(día de la semana)*
	leer	novelas latinoamericanas en el parque
	recibir	poemas para la clase de literatura
		las lecturas del libro
		mensajes de texto *(text messages)*
		¿…?

10 **Encuesta #2** Use the cues provided to create a questionnaire. Use the interrogatives you learned earlier in the chapter along with the cues provided. Once your group has completed the questionnaire, ask the questions to members of another group. Remember to save your responses for use later in the chapter.

1. leer libros / por semana
2. compartir cuarto / con compañero(a) de cuarto
3. asistir a clase / todos los días / todas las semanas
4. comer en la cafetería / por semana
5. vender / libros de texto

11 **La vida universitaria** Write a message to a friend describing your university life. Mention the following things or anything else you might want to talk about. Save your work for use later in the chapter.

- cuántas clases tienes y los días que asistes a clase
- dónde y cuándo comes
- dónde vives
- qué libros lees
- qué actividades te gustan (correr, levantar pesas, mirar televisión, navegar por Internet, leer, escribir, etc.)

Gramática útil 3

Talking about possessions: Simple possessive adjectives

> What two possessive adjectives do you see in this ad for a gym?

Tus horas son nuestras horas

Abierto 24 horas al día para acomodar los horarios
más exigentes... y a los atletas más dedicados

GIMNASIO EL NOCTÁMBULO

www.elnoctambulo.com

1590 Condado Ave., Condado 907 PR

Photos: Chris Fisher/iStockphoto (moon); Libby Chapman/iStockphoto (bar); Soubrette/iStockphoto (background); text: © Cengage Learning 2013

Cómo usarlo

1. You already have learned to express possession using **de** + a noun or name.

   Es la computadora portátil **de la profesora**.　　*It's **the professor's** laptop computer.*

2. You can also use possessive adjectives to describe your possessions, other people's possessions, or items that are associated with you. You are already familiar with some possessive adjectives from the phrases **¿Cuál es tu dirección?** and **Aquí tienes mi número de teléfono**.

   —¿Cuándo es **tu** clase de historia?　　*When is **your** history class?*
   —A las dos. Y **mi** clase de español es a las tres.　　*At two. And **my** Spanish class is at three.*

3. When you use **su** (which can mean *your*, *his*, *her*, *its*, or *theirs*), the context will usually clarify who is meant. If not, you can follow up with **de** + name.

   Es **su** libro. Es **de la profesora**.　　*It's **her** book. It's **the professor's**.*

LO BÁSICO

Possessive adjectives modify nouns in order to express possession. In other words, they tell who owns the item.

1. Here are the simple possessive adjectives in Spanish.

mi mis	*my*	**nuestro / nuestra** **nuestros / nuestras**	*our*
tu tus	*your (fam.)*	**vuestro / vuestra** **vuestros / vuestras**	*your (fam. pl.)*
su sus	*your (form.), his, her, its*	**su** **sus**	*your (pl.), their*

The subject pronoun **tú** *(you)* has an accent on it to differentiate it from the possessive adjective **tu** *(your)*.

Tú trabajas los lunes, ¿verdad?

Tu libro está en mi casa.

2. Notice that . . .

- all possessive adjectives change to reflect number: **mi clase, mis clases; nuestro compañero de cuarto, nuestros compañeros de cuarto.**
- **mi, tu**, and **su** do not change to reflect gender, but **nuestro** and **vuestro** do: **nuestro libro, nuestros amigos, vuestras clases,** but **mi libro, mi clase.**
- unlike other adjectives, which often go after the noun they modify, simple possessive adjectives always go before the noun: **su profesora, nuestras amigas.**

ACTIVIDADES

12 **¿De quién es?** Say to whom the following things belong.

MODELO computadora portátil (yo)
Es mi computadora portátil.

1. apuntes, tarea, CDs, silla (yo)
2. bolígrafos, lápiz, celular, examen (María)
3. calculadoras, cuadernos, dibujo, mochilas (nosotros)
4. diccionario, notas, escritorio, DVDs (tú)
5. libros, tiza, cuarto, papeles (la profesora Roldán)
6. computadora, fotos, salón de clase, apuntes (ustedes)

13 **¿Es de quién?** Look at the pictures and state what each person has.

MODELO *Marta tiene su guitarra.*

Marta

1.

Martín

2.

Felipe y Eusebio

3.

Sarita y Estela

4.

tú y yo

5.

tú

6.

ustedes

© Cengage Learning 2013

14 **Conversaciones** You just met someone from Cuba. Write a message to him or her asking for more information. Use the following ideas for your message or make up your own questions.

- dirección
- número de teléfono
- cumpleaños
- clases

- amigos / compañeros de cuarto
- actividades favoritas
- ¿...?

15 **Nuestros amigos** Make two semantic maps like the one below—one each for two of your friends. Put your name at the bottom of each map. In groups of four, give one map to each person. The person whose map it is has to start the conversation. Then, each of the others must say something about the friend using a possessive adjective. Notice whom you're addressing!

Mi amigo(a) se llama _____. ¿Cómo es?

¿nacionalidad?	¿características físicas?	¿características de personalidad?	¿nacionalidad de sus papás?
_____	_____	_____	_____

MODELO
Estudiante #1: *Mi amigo es puertorriqueño.*
Estudiante #2: *Tu amigo puertorriqueño es alto.* (talking to Estudiante #1)
Estudiante #3: *Su amigo puertorriqueño es responsable.* (talking to others)
Estudiante #4: *Su amigo se llama Carlos y sus padres son puertorriqueños también.* (talking to others)

Sonrisas

Comprensión In your opinion, how would you describe the characters in the cartoon?

1. En tu opinión, ¿es generoso y romántico o manipulador el hombre? ¿Por qué?
2. En tu opinión, ¿es inocente y romántica o manipuladora la mujer? ¿Por qué?
3. ¿Crees que los contratos prenupciales son una buena idea o una mala idea?

Indicating destination and future plans: The verb **ir**

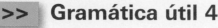

© Cengage Learning 2013

Quiero hacerle una entrevista para un programa que **vamos a transmitir** en la página web de la Universidad.

You have already used similar expressions: **necesitar** + infinitive *(to need to do something)*, **tener que** + infinitive *(to have to do something)*, and **dejar de** + infinitive *(to stop doing something)*.

Cómo usarlo

You can use the Spanish verb **ir** to say where you and others are going. You can also use it to say what you and others are going to do in the near future.

Vamos a la biblioteca mañana.   *We're going to the library tomorrow.*
Vamos a estudiar.   *We're going to study.*

Cómo formarlo

LO BÁSICO

An *irregular verb* is one that does not follow the normal rules, such as **tener**, which you learned in **Chapter 1**.

   A *preposition* links nouns, pronouns, or noun phrases to the rest of the sentence. Prepositions can express location, time sequence, purpose, or direction. *In, to, after, under,* and *for* are all English prepositions.

1. Here is the verb **ir** in the present indicative tense. **Ir**, like the verbs **ser** and **tener** that you have already learned, is an irregular verb.

ir *(to go)*			
yo	**voy**	nosotros / nosotras	**vamos**
tú	**vas**	vosotros / vosotras	**vais**
Ud. / él / ella	**va**	Uds. / ellos / ellas	**van**

2. Use the preposition **a** with the verb **ir** to say where you are going.

Voy a la cafetería.   *I'm going to the cafeteria.*

3. When you want to use the verb **ir** to say what you are going to do, use this formula: **ir** + **a** + *infinitive*.

Vamos a comer a las cinco hoy.   *We're going to eat at 5:00 today.*
Después, **vamos a ir** al   *Afterward, we're going to go to*
concierto.   *the concert.*

4. When you use **a** together with **el**, it contracts to **al**. The same holds true for **de** + **el**: **del**.

$$a + el = al \qquad de + el = del$$

Voy **a la** biblioteca y luego **al** gimnasio. Después, **al** mediodía, voy a estudiar en la biblioteca **del** centro de comunicaciones.

ACTIVIDADES

16 **Vamos a…** Say what the people indicated plan to do and where they are going to do it.

MODELO yo (estudiar: biblioteca)
Voy a estudiar. Voy a la biblioteca.

1. Pedro y Rafael (levantar pesas: gimnasio)
2. mi compañero de cuarto y yo (correr: parque)
3. Fabiola (escuchar los CDs de español: centro de comunicaciones)
4. Tomás, Andrea y yo (tomar un refresco: cafetería)
5. tú (comprar libros: librería)
6. Lourdes (descansar: residencia estudiantil)
7. tú (leer libros: biblioteca)
8. David y Patricia (comer: restaurante caribeño)

17 **¡Pobre Miguel!** Listen as Miguel describes his schedule to his best friend Cristina. As you listen, write down where he goes on each day of the week. Then use **ir** + **a** to create seven complete sentences that describe his schedule.

Track 10

1. los lunes:
2. los martes:
3. los miércoles:
4. los jueves:
5. los viernes:
6. los sábados:
7. los domingos:

18 **Encuesta #3** You need to get more information about student life for the description you will be writing later in this chapter. Find out as much as you can about your partner's leisure activities. Ask questions such as the following and take notes. Then, as a class, tally the information you collected.

El tiempo libre

1. ¿Adónde vas los viernes y los sábados por la noche? ¿Con quién vas?
2. ¿Adónde vas entresemana cuando no estudias? ¿Con quién vas?
3. ¿…?

Vocabulario útil: un club, una discoteca, el cine *(movie theater)*, un restaurante, un centro comercial *(mall)*, un partido *(game)* de fútbol americano / de básquetbol, pasar tiempo en línea, ir a una fiesta, etc.

¡Explora y exprésate!

Cuba

Christian Kober/Getty Images

Información general ▶

Nombre oficial: República de Cuba

Población: 11.477.459

Capital: La Habana (f. 1515) (2.200.000 hab.)

Otras ciudades importantes: Santiago (450.000 hab.), Camagüey (300.000 hab.)

Moneda: peso cubano

Idiomas: español (oficial)

Mapa de Cuba: Apéndice D

Notice that **f.** is the abbreviation for **fundado(a)**, which means *founded*. La Habana, the capital city of Cuba, was founded in 1515.

Notice that **hab.** is the abbreviation for **habitantes**, which means *inhabitants*. This is how population statistics are written in Spanish.

Vale saber...

- La población de la isla es una mezcla *(mixture)* de los nativos originales (taínos), descendientes de esclavos africanos y europeos, mezcla que produce una cultura única. También hay una población china significante, resultado de la inmigración china a Norteamérica y al Caribe durante los años 1800.
- Raúl Castro (hermano de Fidel) es el actual presidente de Cuba.

La educación para todos

Cuba se distingue por tener uno de los mejores sistemas de educación del mundo. Desde la revolución cubana en 1959, el sistema de educación ha sido

Chine Nouvelle/SIPA/Newscom

(has been) prioridad del gobierno cubano, empezando con la Campaña Nacional de Alfabetización en Cuba en 1960. El objetivo de la campaña fue *(was)* eliminar el analfabetismo y llevar maestros *(to bring teachers)* y escuelas *(schools)* a todas las áreas del país. La educación, ¡para todos!

Puerto Rico

Información general

Nombre oficial: Estado Libre Asociado de Puerto Rico (Commonwealth of Puerto Rico)

Población: 3.997.663

Capital: San Juan (f. 1521) (450.000 hab.)

Otras ciudades importantes: Ponce (200.000 hab.), Caguas (150.000 hab.)

Moneda: dólar estadounidense

Idiomas: español, inglés (oficiales)

Mapa de Puerto Rico: Apéndice D

Artifan/Shutterstock

Vale saber...

- A los puertorriqueños también se les conoce como *(are also known as)* "boricuas", ya que antes de la llegada de los europeos en 1493 la isla se llamaba *(was called)* Borinquen.
- Los puertorriqueños son ciudadanos *(citizens)* estadounidenses, pero no votan en elecciones de Estados Unidos.

La educación bilingüe

La educación en Puerto Rico está garantizada constitucionalmente y es gratuita hasta el nivel secundario *(secondary level)*. El español es el idioma de instrucción, pero los estudiantes toman clases de inglés en todos los grados. Los estudios universitarios son iguales al sistema estadounidense: el bachillerato *(bachelor's degree)*, la maestría *(master's degree)* y finalmente el doctorado *(Ph.D)*. Ser boricua es ser bilingüe.

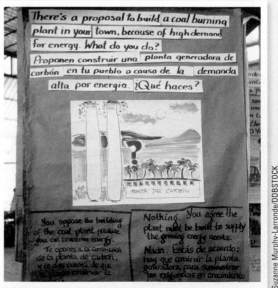

Suzanne Murphy-Larronde/DDBSTOCK

República Dominicana

pashapixel/Shutterstock

Información general ▶

Nombre oficial: República Dominicana

Población: 9.794.487

Capital: Santo Domingo (f. 1492) (2.500.000 hab.)

Otras ciudades importantes: Santiago de los Caballeros (2.000.000 hab.), La Romana (300.000 hab.)

Moneda: peso dominicano

Idiomas: español

Mapa de República Dominicana: Apéndice D

Vale saber…

- La isla que comparten la República Dominicana y Haití se llama La Hispaniola. Estuvo bajo *(It was under)* control español hasta 1697, cuando la parte oeste *(western)* pasó a ser territorio francés.
- Santo Domingo es la primera ciudad del Nuevo Mundo *(New World).* En esta ciudad capital, se construyeron *(were built)* la primera catedral, el primer hospital y la primera universidad del Nuevo Mundo.

Vova Pomortzeff / Alamy

La universidad más antigua del Nuevo Mundo

La Universidad Santo Tomás de Aquino, ahora conocida como la Universidad Autónoma de Santo Domingo, se puede considerar *(can be considered)* la universidad más antigua del Nuevo Mundo. Fundada en 1538—unos cien años antes que Harvard en 1636 y Yale en 1701—empezó *(it began)* con cuatro facultades: medicina, derecho *(law)*, teología y artes. ¡Cómo han cambiado los tiempos! *(How times have changed!)* Hoy día la Universidad ofrece muchos más cursos, entre ellos: ingeniería, arquitectura, economía e informática, por supuesto.

>> En resumen

La información general Answer these questions in English.

1. Look at the maps on page 83. What is the Spanish name of the area in which these three countries are located?
2. Which of the three countries is closest to the United States?
3. Which two countries are islands and which one shares an island with another country?
4. Why are Puerto Ricans called **boricuas**?
5. Which island citizens are also American citizens?
6. Which country boasts the first city in the New World?

El tema de la educación

1. What was the objective of Cuba's "Campaña Nacional de Alfabetización"?
2. Why are "boricuas" bilingual?
3. What were the first four academic departments established in the oldest university of the New World?

🌐 ¿QUIERES SABER MÁS?

On the chart that you started at the beginning of the chapter, add what you already know under **Lo que aprendí**. For the **Lo que quiero aprender** column, pick one or two of the things you would still like to learn, or one or two of the key words below to investigate online. Be prepared to share this information with the class.

Palabras clave: (Cuba) la revolución cubana, José Martí, Celia Cruz; **(Puerto Rico)** Estado Libre Asociado de Puerto Rico, Rosario Ferré, Tito Puente; **(República Dominicana)** Juan Pablo Duarte, las hermanas Mirabal, Sammy Sosa

🌐 **Tú en el mundo hispano** To explore opportunities to use your Spanish to study, volunteer, or do internships in Cuba, Puerto Rico, and the Dominican Republic, follow the links on **www.cengagebrain.com**.

🎬 **Ritmos del mundo hispano** Follow the links at **www.cengagebrain.com** to hear music from Cuba, Puerto Rico, and the Dominican Republic.

A leer

ESTRATEGIA

Using visuals to aid in comprehension

When visuals accompany a text, looking at them first can help you determine the subject. When you approach a reading, look first at the visuals and any captions that accompany them to see if they help you understand the content.

1 Look at the following article about three different schools (**escuelas**) in the Caribbean. Focus on the photos, captions, and headlines, then match the general information on the right with the photos on the left.

1. _____ Foto A
2. _____ Foto B
3. _____ Foto C

a. Aquí los estudiantes estudian técnicas para filmar programas de televisión y cine.

b. Los estudiantes de esta escuela toman clases de música.

c. Esta escuela ofrece cursos de bellas artes, ilustración, diseño gráfico y diseño digital.

2 The following are some unknown words and phrases you will encounter in the reading passages. Although not all the words are cognates, they are somewhat similar to their English counterparts. See if you can match them up.

1. _____ sin pagar nada
2. _____ se han graduado
3. _____ está afiliada con
4. _____ se admiten
5. _____ construyó
6. _____ villa
7. _____ fue inaugurado
8. _____ se ofrecen
9. _____ edición
10. _____ han recibido

a. *was inaugurated*
b. *village*
c. *without paying anything*
d. *editing*
e. *are admitted*
f. *constructed*
g. *have received*
h. *is affiliated with*
i. *have graduated*
j. *are offered*

3 Now, using the information you gained from looking at the visuals, read the article, and focus on getting the main idea. Don't forget to use cognates and active vocabulary to help you understand the content. Try not to worry about unknown words and just focus on getting the main information.

LECTURA

Tres escuelas interesantes del Caribe

La Escuela Libre[1] de Música Ernesto Ramos Antonini

En Puerto Rico muchos estudiantes de música toman cursos sin pagar nada, gracias a cinco escuelas públicas de educación musical. Establecidas a finales de los años 40 por un político local, estas escuelas han graduado a miles[2] de estudiantes. Entre los graduados famosos están el saxofonista de jazz David Sánchez y el cantante salsero Gilberto Santa Rosa.

La escuela más grande es la de San Juan, que está afiliada con el prestigioso Berklee College of Music en Boston. Los cursos de estudio incluyen la música clásica, rock, jazz, contemporánea y tradicional, y el currículum prepara a los estudiantes para estudiar cursos más avanzados en el Conservatorio de Música de Puerto Rico. En San Juan sólo se admiten 100 estudiantes al año, aunque se reciben solicitudes[3] de más de 600 personas, así que los estudiantes de la escuela son unos de los más talentosos de la isla.

La Escuela de Diseño Altos de Chavón

Esta escuela data de los años 70 cuando la República Dominicana construyó un centro cultural en la pequeña villa de Altos de Chavón. La Escuela de Diseño, que forma parte del centro, fue inaugurado por Frank Sinatra en 1982 y está afiliada con el famoso Parsons The New School for Design en la ciudad[4] de Nueva York.

Los 110 estudiantes de La Escuela de Diseño se especializan en campos de estudio como bellas artes e ilustración, diseño gráfico, diseño de modas[5], diseño digital y diseño de interiores.

Más de 1.000 estudiantes dominicanos e internacionales se han graduado de la escuela. Los graduados de la escuela son elegibles para transferirse directamente a Parsons en Nueva York o París.

La Escuela Internacional de Cine y Televisión

En la Escuela Internacional de Cine y Televisión (EICTV) de San Antonio de los Baños, Cuba, se ofrecen cursos de formación audiovisual para estudiantes cubanos e internacionales. La EICTV fue inaugurada en 1986 y es presidida por el famoso escritor colombiano Gabriel García Márquez. Los profesores, además de ser instructores, son cineastas profesionales que dirigen[6] películas y documentales a nivel mundial[7].

Los estudiantes de la EICTV estudian siete especialidades en el curso regular: guión[8], producción, dirección, fotografía, sonido[9], edición y documentales. También se presentan unos veinte talleres[10] especializados cada año. Más de 1.500 estudiantes de unos treinta países se han graduado de la EICTV desde su incepción y los graduados de la escuela han recibido más de 100 premios[11] en varios festivales nacionales e internacionales

A. El saxofonista puertorriqueño David Sánchez, uno de los graduados famosos de "La Libre"

B. Unos estudiantes de arte de La Escuela de Diseño

C. Un estudiante de la Escuela Internacional de Cine y Televisión

[1]*Free* [2]*thousands* [3]**aunque**…: *although they receive applications* [4]*city* [5]*fashion* [6]*they direct* [7]**a**…: *worldwide* [8]*script* [9]*sound* [10]*workshops* [11]*prizes*

4 Answer the following questions about the readings to see how well you understood them.

1. ¿Quiénes son dos graduados famosos de la Escuela Libre de la Música?
2. ¿Con qué institución estadounidense está afiliada la Escuela Libre de la Música?
3. ¿Cuáles son tres tipos de música que los estudiantes estudian en la Escuela Libre?
4. ¿Con qué institución estadounidense está afiliada la Escuela de Diseño Altos de Chavón?
5. ¿Cuáles son cuatro campos de estudio que se ofrecen en la Escuela de Diseño?
6. ¿Cuántos graduados de la Escuela de Diseño hay?
7. ¿Qué autor está afiliado con la EICTV?
8. ¿Cuáles son cuatro campos de estudio que se ofrecen en la EICTV?

5 With a partner, answer the following questions about the reading and about your own interests.

1. ¿Cuál de las tres escuelas les interesa (*interests you*) más?
2. ¿Cuál de los campos de estudio de esa escuela les interesa más?
3. ¿Conocen (*Are you familiar with*) unas escuelas similares en Estados Unidos? ¿Cómo se llaman?

Esta escuela está en Providence, Rhode Island. ¿Sabes (*Do you know*) cómo se llama y cuál es su especialización?

Andre Jenny / Alamy

>> Antes de escribir

ESTRATEGIA

Prewriting—Brainstorming ideas

When you are planning to write and need ideas, try brainstorming. You can do this verbally with a partner, writing down your ideas, or on your own, writing freely and without restriction. The key thing is to write ideas as they occur, without evaluating them. Then take the list of ideas and decide which work best.

It is important to try to brainstorm in Spanish. This will get you to start "thinking" in Spanish, which in turn will lead to increased comfort and ease with the language.

1 Retrieve the information from the three **Encuesta** activities (**Activity 5** on p. 97, **Activity 10** on p. 101, and **Activity 18** on p. 107). With a partner, study the results and brainstorm ideas to describe the life of a typical student at your university.

2 Look at the following partial diary entry, and organize your information into a similar format. Try to use only words you've already learned.

> viernes, 10 de octubre
>
> ¡Tengo muchas actividades hoy! A las ocho, tengo clase de química. Luego, voy a ir al café para estudiar para el examen de historia a las diez...
> Por la tarde, tengo que... Por la noche, voy a...

© Cengage Learning 2013

>> Composición

3 Using the previous model, work with your partner on a rough draft of your diary entry. For now, just write freely without worrying about mistakes. Here are some additional words and phrases that may be useful as you write.

primero	*first*	**finalmente**	*finally*
luego	*later*	**mucho que hacer**	*a lot to do*
entonces	*then*	**un día (muy) ocupado**	*a (very) busy day*
después	*after that*	**con**	*with*

>> Después de escribir

4 Now, with your partner, go back over your diary entry and revise it.

Did you . . .

- make sure you included all the necessary information?
- check to make sure the verbs are conjugated correctly?
- make sure articles, nouns, and adjectives agree?
- use possessive adjectives correctly?
- look for misspellings?

Vocabulario

Campos de estudio   *Fields of study*

Los cursos básicos   *Basic courses*
la arquitectura   *architecture*
las ciencias políticas   *political science*
la economía   *economics*
la educación   *education*
la geografía   *geography*
la historia   *history*
la ingeniería   *engineering*
la psicología   *psychology*

Las humanidades   *Humanities*
la filosofía   *philosophy*
las lenguas / los idiomas   *languages*
la literatura   *literature*

Las lenguas / Los idiomas   *Languages*
el alemán   *German*
el chino   *Chinese*
el español   *Spanish*
el francés   *French*
el inglés   *English*
el japonés   *Japanese*

Las matemáticas   *Mathematics*
el cálculo   *calculus*
la computación   *computer science*

la estadística   *statistics*
la informática   *computer science*

Las ciencias   *Sciences*
la biología   *biology*
la física   *physics*
la medicina   *medicine*
la química   *chemistry*
la salud   *health*

Los negocios   *Business*
la administración de empresas   *business administration*
la contabilidad   *accounting*
el mercadeo   *marketing*

La comunicación pública   *Public communications*
el periodismo   *journalism*
la publicidad   *public relations*

Las artes   *The arts*
el arte   *art*
el baile   *dance*
el diseño gráfico   *graphic design*
la música   *music*
la pintura   *painting*

Lugares en la universidad   *Places in the university*

¿Dónde tienes la clase de...?
   Where does your . . . class meet?
En el centro de computación.
   In the computer center.
...el centro de comunicaciones.
   . . . the media center.
...el gimnasio.   *. . . the gymnasium.*

la cafetería   *the cafeteria*
la librería   *the bookstore*
la residencia estudiantil   *the dorm*

Los días de la semana   *The days of the week*

lunes *Monday*	**miércoles** *Wednesday*	**viernes** *Friday*	**domingo** *Sunday*
martes *Tuesday*	**jueves** *Thursday*	**sábado** *Saturday*	

Para pedir y dar la hora   *Asking for and giving the time*

Mira el reloj para decir la hora... *Look at the clock to tell the time . . .*
¿Qué hora es? *What time is it?*
Es la una. *It's one o'clock.*
Son las dos. *It's two o'clock.*
Son las... y cuarto. *It's . . . fifteen.*
Son las... y media. *It's . . . thirty.*

Son las... menos cuarto. *It's a quarter to . . .*
Faltan quince para las... *It's a quarter to . . .*

tarde *late*
temprano *early*
¿A qué hora es la clase de español? *(At) What time is Spanish class?*
Es a la / a las... *It's at . . .*

Mañana, tarde o noche   *Morning, afternoon, or night*

de la mañana *in the morning* (with precise time)
de la tarde *in the afternoon* (with precise time)
de la noche *in the evening* (with precise time)

Es mediodía. *It's noon.*
Es medianoche. *It's midnight.*

por la mañana *during the morning*
por la tarde *during the afternoon*
por la noche *during the evening*

Para hablar de la fecha   *Talking about the date*

¿Qué día es hoy? *What day is today?*
Hoy es martes treinta. *Today is Tuesday the 30th.*

¿A qué fecha estamos? *What is today's date?*
Es el treinta de octubre. *It's the 30th of October.*
Es el primero de noviembre. *It's the first of November.*

¿Cuándo es el Día de las Madres? *When is Mother's Day?*
Es el doce de mayo. *It's May 12th.*

el día *day*
la semana *week*
el fin de semana *weekend*
el mes *month*
el año *year*
todos los días *every day*
entresemana *during the week/on weekdays*

ayer *yesterday*
hoy *today*
mañana *tomorrow*

Para hacer preguntas   *Asking questions*

¿Cómo? *How?*
¿Cuál(es)? *What? Which one(s)?*
¿Cuándo? *When?*
¿Cuánto(a)? *How much?*
¿Cuántos(as)? *How many?*
¿De quién es? *Whose is this?*

¿De quiénes son? *Whose are these?*
¿Dónde? *Where?*
¿Por qué? *Why?*
¿Qué? *What? Which?*
¿Quién(es)? *Who?*

Verbos

abrir *to open*
aprender *to learn*
asistir a *to attend*
beber *to drink*
comer *to eat*
compartir *to share*
comprender *to understand*
correr *to run*
creer (en) *to believe (in)*
deber *should, ought*
dejar de *to stop (doing something)*

describir *to describe*
descubrir *to discover*
escribir *to write*
imprimir *to print*
ir *to go*
ir a *to be going to (do something)*
leer *to read*
recibir *to receive*
transmitir *to broadcast*
vender *to sell*
vivir *to live*

Adjetivos posesivos

mi(s) *my*
tu(s) *your (fam.)*
su(s) *your (sing. form., pl.) his, her, their*

nuestro(a) / nuestros(as) *our*
vuestro(a) / vuestros(as) *your (pl. fam.)*

Contracciones

al (a + el) *to the*
del (de + el) *from the, of the*

Otras palabras

porque *because*
escuela *school*

Repaso y preparación

>> **Repaso del Capítulo 3**

Complete these activities to check your understanding of the new grammar points in **Chapter 3** before you move on to **Chapter 4**.

The answers to the activities in this section can be found in **Appendix B**.

Interrogative words (p. 94)

1 Complete each sentence in the chat with an interrogative word (**cuál, cuándo, cuántas, por qué, qué, quien**), capitalizing as needed.

> **Finita7:** Marcos, ¿_____ estudias?
>
> **Marcosis:** Historia. ¿_____?
>
> **Finita7:** ¡Necesito tu ayuda! ¡Por favor!
>
> **Marcosis:** ¿_____ es tu problema?
>
> **Finita7:** ¡Tengo que escribir un informe!
>
> **Marcosis:** ¿Para _____ tienes que entregar la tarea?
>
> **Finita7:** ¡Mañana!
>
> **Marcosis:** ¿_____ páginas?
>
> **Finita7:** ¡Cinco!
>
> **Marcosis:** ¿_____ es el profesor?
>
> **Finita7:** ¡Martínez!
>
> **Marcosis** ¡Noooooooooo! Este problema no tiene solución...
>
> **Finita7:** :-O

The present indicative of regular -er and -ir verbs (p. 98)

2 Complete each sentence with the present-tense form of the verb indicated.

1. Marta _____ (escribir) la tarea para la clase de ciencias políticas.
2. Tú y yo _____ (deber) ir a la biblioteca.
3. Yo _____ (comer) pizza mientras estudio.
4. Uds. _____ (vivir) en la Residencia Central, ¿verdad?
5. La profesora de literatura _____ (leer) muchas novelas.

Simple possessive adjectives (p. 102)

3 Complete each sentence with a possessive adjective.

1. No comprendo a _____ padres.
2. ¿Tienes _____ notas?
3. Escribimos _____ tarea.
4. Ella lee _____ papeles.
5. Ellos abren _____ libros.
6. Aquí tienes _____ número.

The verb ir (p. 106)

4 Complete the sentences with the present-indicative forms of **ir**.

1. Si yo _____ a la biblioteca, ¿qué _____ a hacer ustedes?
2. Mi amiga _____ a correr, pero nosotros _____ al gimnasio.
3. Tú _____ a la librería, ¿verdad?

Gustar + infinitive (Chapter 2)

5 Use the cues to create complete sentences. Follow the model.

MODELO (a Marta) / gustar correr
A Marta le gusta correr.

1. (a mí) / gustar leer
2. (a nosotros) / gustar comer
3. (a ustedes) / gustar bailar
4. (a ti) / gustar cocinar
5. (a él) / gustar patinar
6. (a mí) / gustar cantar

Complete these activities to review some previously learned grammatical structures that will be helpful when you learn the new grammar in **Chapter 4**.

Be sure to reread **Chapter 3: Gramática útil 2** before moving on to the new **Chapter 4** grammar sections.

The present indicative of regular -ar verbs (Chapter 2)

6 Complete the description with present indicative forms.

Tengo dos compañeros de cuarto. Roque es muy serio y 1. _____ (estudiar) mucho. También 2. _____ (cocinar) la cena. ¡Es un chef fantástico! El otro, Raul, 3. _____ (tocar) la guitarra y 4. _____ (cantar). A veces, él y Roque 5. _____ (levantar) pesas y 6. _____ (practicar) deportes, como el tenis y el fútbol. Nosotros 7. _____ (mirar) televisión y 8. _____ (alquilar) videos por las noches. ¿Y yo? Pues, yo 9. _____ (trabajar) mucho y a veces 10. _____ (visitar) a amigos. ¡Yo no 11. _____ (pasar) mucho tiempo allí!

Present indicative of **ser** (Chapter 1), Adjective agreement (Chapter 2)

7 Use an adjective from the list to write a sentence with **ser** about each person.

MODELO *Neli es muy trabajadora.*

Adjetivos: activo(a), divertido(a), egoísta, generoso(a), impaciente, perezoso(a), tímido(a) trabajador(a)

Neli

1.

Rogelio y Mauricio

2.

tú

3.

nosotros

4.

yo

5.

Sandra

6.

Néstor y Nicolás

¿Te interesa la tecnología?

CONEXIONES VIRTUALES Y PERSONALES

Las nuevas tecnologías tienen un impacto tremendo en las áreas de las comunicaciones, los negocios y las relaciones personales, entre otras. ¡Nuestro mundo está cambiando *(is changing)* todos los días!

¿Cuáles son tus aparatos electrónicos favoritos y para qué los usas?

Communication

By the end of this chapter you will be able to

- talk about computers and technology
- identify colors
- talk about likes and dislikes
- describe people, emotions, and conditions
- talk about current activities
- say how something is done

British Retail Photography/Alamy

Un viaje por España

España es el único país europeo donde el español es la lengua oficial. España forma la Península Ibérica con Portugal, y por eso tiene costas en el Atlántico, el mar Mediterráneo y el mar Cantábrico. También tiene varias sierras, entre ellas la sierra de Guadarrama en la parte central del país y la sierra Nevada en el sur.

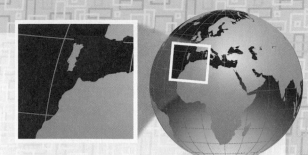

País / Área	Tamaño y fronteras	Sitios de interés
España 499.542 km²	un poco más de dos veces el área de Oregón; fronteras con Portugal, Francia y Andorra y con Marruecos (Ceuta y Melilla)	la Alhambra, el Museo del Prado, el Museo Guggenheim, las Islas Canarias, las Islas Baleares

¿Qué sabes? Di si las siguientes oraciones son ciertas (**C**) o falsas (**F**).

1. España está situada completamente en Europa.
2. Varios grupos de islas también forman parte de España.
3. Hay unos museos importantes en España.
4. España es más pequeña que Oregón.

Lo que sé y lo que quiero aprender Completa la tabla del **Apéndice A.** Escribe algunos datos que **ya sabes** sobre España en la columna **Lo que sé**. Después, añade algunos temas que **quieres aprender** a la columna **Lo que quiero aprender**. Guarda la tabla para usarla otra vez en la sección **¡Explora y exprésate!** en la página 151.

Cultures

By the end of this chapter you will have explored

- the Spanish empire
- the great artists and writers of Spain
- the Arabic influence on Spanish architecture
- Buika, a Spanish singer who blends many musical styles
- a popular Spanish social networking site
- borrowed words on the Internet

⏵ >> Vocabulario útil 1

BETO: ¡Estoy furioso!

CHELA: Pero, ¿por qué?

BETO: Primero llego tarde a la clase de literatura.

CHELA: Llegar tarde no es una tragedia.

BETO: ¡Tenemos examen! Abro mi **computadora portátil**, pero en la **pantalla** dice que no tengo suficiente **memoria** para abrir la **aplicación**.

>> La tecnología
El hardware

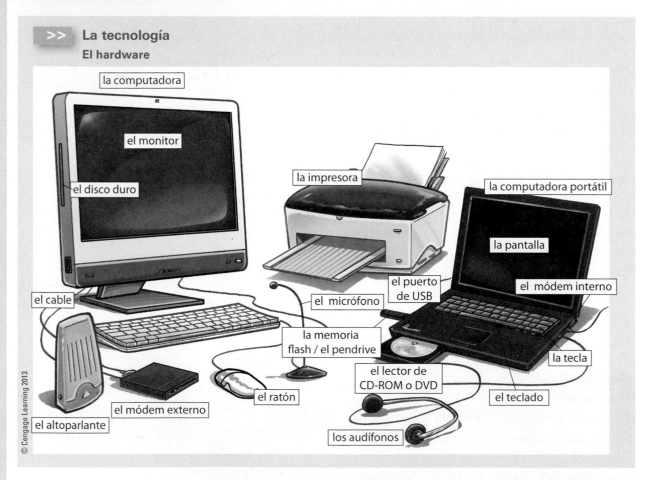

> **Notice:** In Spain, **la computadora** is called **el ordenador**. **El computador** is also used, mostly in Latin America. Another term for **hacer clic** is **pulsar**.

>> La tecnología

El software

la aplicación *application*
los archivos *files*
  el archivo PDF *PDF attachment*
el ícono del programa
  program icon
el juego interactivo
  interactive game
el programa antivirus *antivirus program*
el programa de procesamiento de textos *word processing program*

Funciones de la computadora

archivar *to file*
bajar / descargar *to download*
conectar *to connect*
enviar *to send*
funcionar *to function*
grabar *to record*
guardar *to save*
hacer clic / doble clic *to click / double-click*
instalar *to install*
subir / cargar *to upload*

> **PDF** stands for **el formato de documento portátil** and is pronounced **pe-de-efe**.

> To describe the hard drive of your computer or its processor, use:
> - **un disco duro con capacidad de 500 GB (gigabytes)**
> - **un procesador a 2.4 o 2.53 GHz (gigahercio)**

>> Los colores

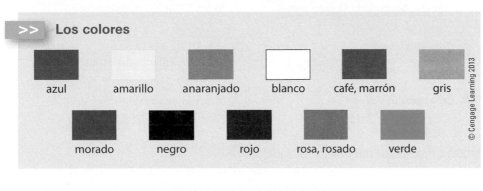

azul   amarillo   anaranjado   blanco   café, marrón   gris

morado   negro   rojo   rosa, rosado   verde

© Cengage Learning 2013

> When a color is used as an adjective, it comes after the noun it modifies.
> - If it ends in **-o**, it changes to match the gender and number of that noun: **la silla negra, los cuadernos rojos**.
> - If the color ends in **-e**, add an **s** to the plural: **las pizarras verdes**.
> - If the color ends in a consonant, add **es** to the plural: **los libros azules**.
> - **Marrón** in the plural changes to **marrones**, with no accent. Can you figure out why, for pronunciation reasons, it loses the accent?
> - Note that **rosa** and **café** change to reflect number, but not gender.
> - If you want to say that a color is dark, use **fuerte** or **oscuro**. For example, **amarillo fuerte** or **amarillo oscuro**. If you want to say that a color is light, use **claro**. For example, **azul claro**.

ACTIVIDADES

1 **La computadora** Un amigo necesita hacer *(needs to do)* ciertas cosas en la computadora. ¿Qué parte de la computadora va a necesitar para hacer lo que quiere? Escoge de la segunda columna.

1. _____ Necesito imprimir el correo electrónico.
2. _____ Necesito ver un video de YouTube.
3. _____ Necesito conectar el teclado al monitor.
4. _____ Necesito escuchar música mientras trabajo.
5. _____ Necesito escribir un documento.
6. _____ Necesito archivar un documento.
7. _____ Necesito grabar un mensaje para enviar a mis amigos.
8. _____ Necesito instalar el programa de procesamiento de textos.

a. los audífonos
b. la pantalla
c. el teclado
d. la memoria flash
e. la impresora
f. el cable
g. el micrófono
h. el lector de DVD-ROM

> Starting in this chapter, many of the activity direction lines will be presented in Spanish. Here are a few words that will help you understand Spanish direction lines: **di** *(say)*, **haz** *(do)*, **escoge** *(choose)*, **luego** *(then, later)*, **siguiente** *(following)*, **oración** *(sentence)*, **párrafo** *(paragraph)*.

2 El sitio web Tu compañero(a) quiere buscar información sobre ciertos temas en el servicio ¡VIVA! Latino. Tú le dices *(You tell him/her)* en qué ícono debe hacer doble clic. Luego, él o ella te dirige a los íconos que corresponden a tus intereses.

In some countries, the Internet is referred to as **la Internet**, in others as **el Internet**, and in others still, it is referred to simply as **Internet**, with no article to indicate gender.

¡VIVA! Latino

Directorio de sitios web

Arte y cultura
Literatura, Teatro, Museos, Guías

Internet y computadoras
WWW, Aplicaciones, Chat, Redes

Educación
Primaria, Secundaria, Universidades

Medios de comunicación
Radio, TV, Revistas, Periódicos

Deportes y ocio
Deportes, Fútbol, Juegos, Turismo

Salud
Medicina, Enfermedades, Ejercicio, Dietas

Espectáculos y diversión
Cine, Actores, Música, Humor

Materias de consulta
Bibliotecas, Diccionarios

MODELO   el Museo del Prado en Madrid
Tú: *Necesito más información sobre el Museo del Prado en Madrid.*
Compañero(a): *Haz doble clic en el ícono rojo.*

1. una dieta vegetariana
2. mi actor (actriz) favorito(a)
3. un diccionario español / inglés
4. la Copa Mundial de Fútbol
5. un programa de procesamiento de textos
6. la Universidad Complutense de Madrid
7. el periódico *El País* de Madrid
8. ¿…?

3 Mi computadora ¿Puedes describir tu computadora? Incluye en tu descripción todos los componentes de tu computadora y menciona el color de cada uno si es apropiado.

If you want to describe the colors of your mousepad, you can say **almohadilla de ratón**, or simply **mousepad**.

MODELO   *El monitor de mi computadora es azul y blanco. Los cables son grises. El ratón es blanco. Los altoparlantes son negros. Las teclas en el teclado son blancas…*

¡Fíjate! El lenguaje de Internet

Pedro Armestra/AFP/Getty Images/Newscom

The Internet is a source of entirely new words in English, a development that has created language issues for translators and Internet users alike. Online word forums in which people from different countries discuss how to translate Internet terms into their own languages are useful in dealing with these issues. In many cases, the universal Internet terms have simply stayed in English. Here are some examples of words that have commonly (or infrequently) used Spanish translations, and others that do not yet (and may never!) have translations.

Blog: This is an abbreviated form of Web-log, and is usually referred to simply as *blog*, losing the *We* of Web. In Spanish, it is common to simply say **blog**, but it can also be defined as: **un diario personal en un sitio web que contiene reflexiones, comentarios, fotos, video o enlaces.**

Forum: Foro is the common Spanish translation. If you are referring to an announcement board, you would say **un tablón de anuncios**. A message board is **un tablón de mensajes**.

Podcast: Un podcast is a radio broadcast that is Portable On Demand. If you want to use only Spanish words, you could say **una emisora radial en Internet. Los podcasts** are downloaded to **un teléfono inteligente** or **un smartphone**, where the user can listen to them at leisure.

Video conferencing: Chat with your friends via Internet using **un sistema de video conferencia**.

Wifi: Most Spanish speakers simply say **wifi**, with a wide variation in pronunciation from country to country. To be technically correct, you could refer to it as **la red inalámbrica. (Alambre** means *wire,* which is why **inalámbrica** means *wireless.)* Although you would be understood with this mouthful of a phrase, you would probably be considered rather geeky. Stick with **wifi** for now.

Text messaging: Everyone texts these days. In Spanish this would be **enviar un mensaje de texto**.

Instant messaging: If you instant message someone, this is referred to as **enviar un mensaje instantáneo**.

Sound files: Music downloads are **archivos de sonido** or **MP3s** that can be transferred directly to **MP3 portátiles** or **los smartphones**.

Las redes sociales: Social networking sites like Facebook and Twitter have become the preferred mode of communication for many people throughout the world.

Without a doubt, the Internet will continue to create new functions and new words as its uses multiply. Don't panic! You can find a site online that will help you find just the Spanish expression you are looking for!

Práctica Escribe una lista de términos de Internet en inglés que no sabes decir en español. Con un(a) compañero(a), busca en Internet un sitio con las traducciones y las pronunciaciones, o simplemente verifica que lo más común es usar el término en inglés.

● >> Vocabulario útil 2

BETO: Empiezo a salir del salón de clases. No sé en dónde, pero entre el salón y la biblioteca, pierdo mi **asistente electrónico**.

CHELA: Ya me voy. Estoy muy **aburrida** con tu cuento trágico.

>> Las emociones

aburrido(a) *bored*
cansado(a) *tired*
contento(a) *happy*
enfermo(a) *sick*
enojado(a) *angry*
furioso(a) *furious*
nervioso(a) *nervous*
ocupado(a) *busy*
preocupado(a) *worried*
seguro(a) *sure*
triste *sad*

>> Aparatos electrónicos

Products like the iPod®, the iPhone®, Android™, the Blackberry®, Bluetooth®, etc., can all be referred to in English when speaking in Spanish. For example, **¿Tienes un iPhone? ¿De qué color es tu iPod?**

el asistente electrónico *electronic notebook*
la cámara digital *digital camera*
la cámara web *webcam*
el MP3 portátil *portable MP3 player*
el reproductor / grabador de discos compactos *CD player / burner*
el reproductor / grabador de DVD *DVD player / burner*
la tableta *tablet computer*
el teléfono inteligente / smartphone *smartphone*
la videocámara *videocamera*

ACTIVIDADES

4 **Las emociones** Las siguientes personas están en ciertas situaciones. ¿Cómo crees que están?

1. A Raúl le gusta navegar por Internet y jugar videojuegos. Hay una tormenta *(thunderstorm)* y por eso no hay electricidad en su casa. No tiene nada *(nothing)* que hacer.
2. Blanca acaba de comprar una computadora portátil pero cuando llega a casa, no funciona.
3. Julio tiene que escribir una composición de diez páginas para su clase de historia mañana y todavía no ha empezado *(hasn't begun)*.
4. Mañana Luis tiene que ir al trabajo por tres horas, estudiar para un examen y hacer una investigación en Internet para la clase de filosofía.
5. Sabrina trabaja diez horas en la biblioteca, va a su clase de aeróbicos y camina a casa del gimnasio.
6. Marcos y Marina toman un refresco, escuchan música y conversan en un café en la Plaza Mayor.

5 **¿Eres un(a) tecnogeek o un(a) tecnófobo(a)?** With a partner, come up with a list of items related to technology. Use a point system of 1–5 to rate how tech-savvy someone is (1 = the least advanced and 5 = the most advanced). Then, in groups of four or five, ask each person in the group about each item. Based on your findings, decide who is the most technologically advanced and who is the most technologically inexperienced in the group. Report your findings to the class.

Sample items

teléfono inteligente	revista *(magazine)* de tecnología
computadora portátil	tomar clases virtuales en línea
tableta	*(take classes online)*
perfil *(profile)* en Facebook	bajar videos de YouTube
más de una dirección de e-mail	

6 **El Corte Inglés** El Corte Inglés es el almacén *(department store)* más grande en España. Con un(a) compañero(a), busca el sitio web del Corte Inglés. Entren en el Departamento de Electrónica y contesten las siguientes preguntas.

1. ¿Cuáles son las subcategorías en el Departamento de Electrónica?
2. Entren en la subcategoría DVD & Blu Ray. Nombren tres productos que hay allí y sus precios en euros (€).
3. Quieren comprarle un regalo *(gift)* a un amigo a quien le gusta la música. Busquen un regalo apropiado. ¿Qué es? ¿Cuánto cuesta?
4. Quieren comprarle un regalo a una amiga a quien le gusta grabar videos, pero no tienen mucho dinero *(money)*. Busquen la videocámara con el precio más bajo *(lowest price)*.
5. ¿Qué producto electrónico quieres comprar? ¿Cuánto cuesta?

BETO: ¿Tú? ¿Tú eres Autora14?

DULCE: Sí, yo soy Autora14. ¿Por qué preguntas?

BETO: No, no, nada. ¿Te gustan los **grupos de conversación**?

DULCE: No, en realidad, no. Prefiero el **correo electrónico**.

You are learning two words for e-mail: **correo electrónico** and **e-mail**. **Correo electrónico** refers more to the whole system of e-mail or a group of e-mails, while **el e-mail** refers to a specific e-mail message.

To say you are going to post something on your Facebook page, you can say:

Voy a publicar un post en mi página de Facebook.

Voy a publicar mi estado (status).

Voy a publicar mis noticias (news).

Voy a publicar algo en el muro (wall) **de mi amigo Javier.**

Voy a subir / bajar fotos / videos a mi página de Facebook.

>> **Funciones de Internet**

acceder to access
el blog blog
el buscador search engine
el buzón electrónico electronic mailbox
chatear to chat online
el ciberespacio cyberspace
la conexión connection
hacer una conexión to get online
cortar la conexión to get offline, disconnect
la contraseña password
el correo electrónico / el e-mail e-mail
en línea online
el enlace link
el foro forum
el grupo de conversación chat room
el grupo de noticias news group
la página web web page
el proveedor de acceso Internet provider
la red mundial World Wide Web
la red social social networking site
el sitio web website
el usuario user
el wifi wifi, wireless connection

7 **¡Gran sorteo!** Completa el cuestionario para el concurso (*contest*) de la revista *DIGITAL en Español*. Compara tus respuestas con las respuestas de diez compañeros de clase. Haz una gráfica como la de la página 130 que muestre (*shows*) los resultados de tu cuestionario. Llena los espacios en blanco (*Fill in the blanks*) con el número de estudiantes que marcaron (*marked*) esa respuesta.

Digital en Español — ¡GRAN SORTEO!

Participe en el sorteo de *Digital en Español* y gánate una impresora multifunción que puede colocarse perfectamente sobre cualquier escritorio. Además, resulta fácil de usar y funciona como impresora, escáner, copiadora y fax. Este modelo puede ser conectado fácilmente a tu computadora con conexiones inalámbricas Bluetooth 2.0 o Wi-Fi.

1. ¿Usas computadora portátil o una de escritorio?
_____ portátil
_____ de escritorio
_____ ninguna de las dos

2. ¿Tienes teléfono inteligente o celular sin capacidades de computadora?
_____ inteligente
_____ celular

3. ¿Tienes tableta?
_____ sí
_____ no

4. ¿Cuál de tus aparatos electrónicos usas con más frecuencia?
_____ teléfono inteligente
_____ teléfono celular
_____ tableta
_____ computadora portátil
_____ otro aparato

5. ¿Cómo usas tu teléfono con más frecuencia?
_____ para hablar por teléfono
_____ para enviar mensajes de texto
_____ para navegar Internet
_____ para publicar en las redes sociales como Facebook y Twitter
_____ otro

6. ¿Para qué usas Internet principalmente? Indica sólo tres usos.
_____ compras
_____ servicios de banco
_____ investigaciones
_____ correo electrónico
_____ redes sociales
_____ para mantener mi sitio web
_____ para publicar un blog
_____ ver videos en YouTube
_____ otro

7. ¿Cuántas veces por día publicas algo en Facebook?
_____ 0
_____ 1-3
_____ 4-6
_____ más de 7

8. ¿Cuál es tu modo preferido de comunicación con tus amigos?
_____ hablar por teléfono
_____ enviar mensajes de texto
_____ enviar e-mails
_____ publicar en Facebook
_____ tuitear
_____ persona a persona
_____ otro

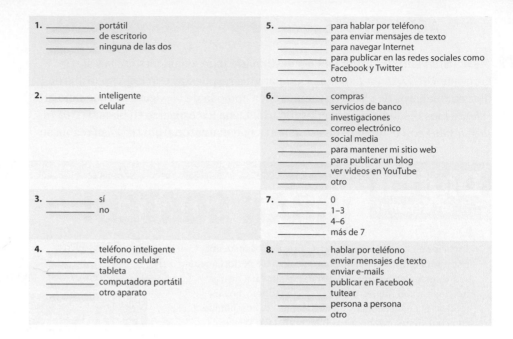

1. _____ portátil
   _____ de escritorio
   _____ ninguna de las dos

2. _____ inteligente
   _____ celular

3. _____ sí
   _____ no

4. _____ teléfono inteligente
   _____ teléfono celular
   _____ tableta
   _____ computadora portátil
   _____ otro aparato

5. _____ para hablar por teléfono
   _____ para enviar mensajes de texto
   _____ para navegar Internet
   _____ para publicar en las redes sociales como
             Facebook y Twitter
   _____ otro

6. _____ compras
   _____ servicios de banco
   _____ investigaciones
   _____ correo electrónico
   _____ social media
   _____ para mantener mi sitio web
   _____ para publicar un blog
   _____ ver videos en YouTube
   _____ otro

7. _____ 0
   _____ 1–3
   _____ 4–6
   _____ más de 7

8. _____ hablar por teléfono
   _____ enviar mensajes de texto
   _____ enviar e-mails
   _____ publicar en Facebook
   _____ tuitear
   _____ persona a persona
   _____ otro

8 **¿Cómo usas Internet?** ¿Qué más quieres saber sobre *(do you want to know about)* los hábitos de tus compañeros acerca de Internet? Escribe cinco preguntas más como las del cuestionario en la **Actividad 7**. Luego, hazle las preguntas a tu compañero(a) de clase y que él o ella te haga *(have him or her ask you)* sus preguntas.

MODELO   *¿Te gustan las redes sociales? ¿Cuántas horas al día pasas en las redes sociales?*
         ¿Tienes un blog? ¿Cuántas veces por semana escribes en tu blog?

9 **Mi blog** Escribe un blog para describir como usas Internet. Ponle todos los detalles que puedas *(that you can)*. Usa las ideas de la **Actividad 8**, de la lista o inventa otras.

Opciones:

- ¿qué te gusta hacer en Internet?
- ¿usas el teléfono inteligente para acceder a Internet?
- ¿cuáles son tus aparatos electrónicos preferidos?
- ¿qué clase de videos te gusta bajar o subir?
- ¿usas la computadora para ver programas de la televisión?
- ¿cuál es tu modo de comunicación preferido?
- ¿…?

10 **La red social** Escribe tu perfil en español para tu página en la red social. Además de la información básica, escribe un párrafo sobre tu personalidad. Explica un poco sobre tu relación con la tecnología. ¿Eres tecnofóbico o tecnomaestro?

11 **¿Qué estás pensando?** Ten una conversación con un(a) compañero(a) sobre un post que piensas publicar en la página de tu red social. El post describe cómo vas a usar la tecnología hoy.

MODELO Tú: *Voy a compartir unas fotos en mi red social.*
Compañero(a): *¡Qué divertido! ¿Estás tú en las fotos?*

12 **Los cursos virtuales** Hoy en día es posible tomar cursos virtuales por Internet. Hay muchas universidades de habla española que ofrecen una gran variedad de cursos a distancia.

En grupos de cuatro, escojan *(choose)* un país de la lista de abajo. Visiten los sitios web que corresponden a ese país, usando la lista de enlaces que está en **www.cengagebrain.com**.

Países: España, México, Argentina

1. ¿Qué cursos virtuales ofrece la universidad o escuela?
2. ¿En el sitio web es posible hacer una visita virtual? ¿Hay información sobre los profesores de los cursos? ¿Sobre los otros estudiantes?
3. Después de obtener toda la información sobre este sitio web, compárenla con la información de los otros grupos.

© Shutterstock/enigmatico

A ver

ESTRATEGIA

Watching without sound

Sometimes it helps to watch a segment first without the sound, especially when it contains a lot of action. As you watch, focus on the characters' actions and interactions. What do you think is happening? Once you have gotten some ideas, watch the segment a second time with the sound turned on.

Antes de ver Lee la lista de eventos que ocurren en este episodio.

_____ Beto descubre que su computadora no tiene suficiente memoria.

_____ Dulce tiene el asistente electrónico de Beto.

_____ Beto está furioso porque tiene que escribir el examen con bolígrafo y papel.

_____ Beto llega tarde a clase.

_____ Beto ve una hoja de papel con el e-mail de Autora14.

_____ Beto deja su asistente electrónico en el salón de clase.

© Cengage Learning 2013

▶ **Ver** Mira el episodio para el **Capítulo 4** sin sonido *(sound)*.

Después de ver 1 Ahora vuelve a *(go back to)* **Antes de ver** y usa números para poner *(to put)* la lista en el órden correcto.

Después de ver 2 Mira el episodio otra vez—ahora con sonido—y completa las oraciones siguientes.

1. Beto llega tarde a la clase de _____.
2. Según Chela, ella está muy _____ con la historia trágica de Beto.
3. La dirección electrónica de _____ es Autora14.
4. Dulce prefiere el correo electrónico a _____.

Después de ver 3 En tu opinión, ¿de qué hablan Dulce y Beto mientras salen juntos al final del episodio? Basándote en lo que ya sabes de sus personalidades, escribe una conversación breve entre ellos mientras se conocen *(they get to know each other)* un poco mejor.

● >> Voces del mundo hispano

© Cengage Learning 2013

En el video para este capítulo Juan Pedro, Patricia y Sergio hablan de los aparatos tecnológicos y sus hábitos con relación a Internet. Lee las siguientes oraciones. Después mira el video una o más veces para decir si las oraciones son ciertas (**C**) o falsas (**F**).

1. Juan Pedro y Patricia tienen una cámara digital.

2. Sergio tiene un reproductor de MP3.

3. A Juan Pedro le gusta mucho su reproductor de discos compactos.

4. A Patricia le gusta usar su ordenador (computadora) para chatear.

5. Patricia sólo usa Internet durante los días de entresemana.

6. A Sergio no le gusta usar e-mail ni *(nor)* Skype.

◀)) >> Voces de Estados Unidos

Track 11

Thaddeus Arroyo, director ejecutivo de información

PRN Images

En la escuela, las matemáticas y la lógica siempre fueron las materias preferidas de Thaddeus Arroyo. Hoy en día, Arroyo, que es Director Ejecutivo de Información *(Chief Information Officer)* en AT&T, es uno de los líderes del campo de la informática y uno de los ejecutivos más importantes del país. Arroyo es conocido mundialmente *(worldwide)* por hacer posible la fusión *(merger)* de Cingular Wireless y AT&T Wireless, creando así la mayor red del país, con unos 60 millones de usuarios. De padre español y madre mexicana, Arroyo explica su éxito *(success)* profesional de esta manera:

❝**Mi mamá y mi papá, los dos, fueron inmigrantes y se concentraron en la educación. Ellos no me permitieron creer que existían barreras insuperables. Creo que más que otra cosa es la fe en el arte de la posibilidad.❞** *("Both my parents were immigrants and focused on education. They would never let me believe there was any barrier I couldn't overcome. I think more than anything else it was believing in the art of the possibility.")*

¿Y tú? En tu opinión, ¿qué tipo de preparación escolar y características personales son necesarias para ser un líder en el campo de la tecnología?

¡Prepárate!

>> Gramática útil 1

Expressing likes and dislikes: **Gustar** with nouns and other verbs like **gustar**

¿**Te gustan** los grupos de conversación?

> Remember that when you use **gustar** + infinitive you only use **gusta: Les gusta comer en la cafetería.**

You will learn more about Spanish indirect object pronouns in **Chapter 8.**

Cómo usarlo

As you learned in **Chapter 2,** you can use **gustar** with an infinitive to say what activities you and other people like to do.

Me gusta estudiar en la biblioteca, pero **a Vicente le gusta estudiar** en la cafetería.

I like to study in the library, but Vicente likes to study in the cafeteria.

You can also use **gustar** with nouns, to say what thing or things you (and others) like or dislike. In this case, you use **gusta** with a single noun and **gustan** with plural nouns or a series of nouns.

—¿**Te gusta** esta **computadora**?
—Sí, ¡pero **me gustan** más estas **portátiles**!

Do you like this computer?
Yes, but I like these laptops more!

When you make negative sentences with **gusta** and **gustan,** you use **no** before the pronoun + **gusta / gustan.**

Nos gustan los programas de diseño gráfico, pero **no nos gustan** los programas de arte.

We like the graphic design programs, but we don't like the art programs.

Cómo formarlo

LO BÁSICO

- In Spanish, an *indirect object pronoun* is used with **gustar** to say who likes something. Because **gustar** literally means to *please*, the indirect object answers the question: *Pleases whom?*
- A *prepositional pronoun* is a pronoun that is used after a preposition, such as **a** or **de.**

1. As you have already learned, you must use forms of **gustar** with the correct indirect object pronoun.

Me gusta	el foro.	**Nos gusta**	el foro.
Me gustan	los foros.	**Nos gustan**	los foros.
Te gusta	el foro.	**Os gusta**	el foro.
Te gustan	los foros.	**Os gustan**	los foros.
Le gusta	el foro.	**Les gusta**	el foro.
Le gustan	los foros.	**Les gustan**	los foros.

2. As you have learned, if you want to *emphasize* or *clarify* who likes what, you can use **a** + name or noun, or **a** + prepositional pronoun. Note that when **a** + prepositional pronoun is used, there is often no direct translation in English. Notice that except for **mí** and **ti**, the prepositional pronouns are the same as the subject pronouns you already know.

Prepositional pronoun	Indirect object pronoun	Form of gustar + noun
A mí	me	gustan los videojuegos.
A ti	te	gustan los videojuegos.
A Ud. / a él / a ella	le	gustan los videojuegos.
A nosotros / a nosotras	nos	gustan los videojuegos.
A vosotros / a vosotras	os	gustan los videojuegos.
A Uds. / a ellos / a ellas	les	gustan los videojuegos.

> Notice that while **mí** takes an accent, **ti** does not.

A mí me gustan los MP3 portátiles pero **a Elena** no le gustan.

*I like MP3 players, but **Elena** doesn't like them.*

A ella le gustan los teléfonos inteligentes que también tocan MP3s.

***She** likes smartphones that also play MP3s.*

3. A number of other Spanish verbs are used like **gustar.** These verbs are usually just used in two forms, as is **gustar.**

—**Me interesan** mucho estos celulares.

***I'm interested** in these cell phones.*

—¿No **te molesta** la recepción mala aquí?

*Doesn't the bad reception here **bother you**?*

Other verbs like gustar	
encantar *to like a lot*	¡Me encanta la tecnología!
fascinar *to fascinate*	A Ana le fascinan esos sitios web.
importar *to be important to someone; to mind*	Nos importa tener acceso a Internet. ¿Te importa si usamos la computadora?
interesar *to interest, to be interesting*	A ellos les interesan las redes sociales.
molestar *to bother*	Nos molestan las computadoras viejas.

> In Spanish-speaking cultures, courtesy is of utmost importance. It is very common to use phrases like **¿Le importa?** or **¿Le molesta?** to ask someone a question. **¿Le importa si uso la computadora?** would be more likely heard than **Voy a usar la computadora** or **¿Puedo usar la computadora?** It's also common to use **por favor** when asking a question and **gracias** upon receiving the answer. Other common expressions of courtesy are:
>
> **¡Perdón! / ¡Disculpe! / ¡Lo siento!** *Pardon me! / Excuse me! / I'm sorry!*
>
> **No hay de qué. / No se preocupe.**
>
> *No problem. / Not to worry.*
>
> **Con permiso.** *Excuse me... / With your permission...*
>
> **Cómo no.** *Of course. / Certainly.*

ACTIVIDADES

1 **¿Te gusta?** Di si te gustan o no las siguientes cosas.

MODELO (Me gustan / No me gustan) las computadoras portátiles.
Me gustan las computadoras portátiles.

1. (Me gustan / No me gustan) los juegos interactivos de tenis.
2. (Me gusta / no me gusta) el sitio web de YouTube.
3. (Me gustan / No me gustan) las clases virtuales.
4. (Me gustan / No me gustan) los aparatos electrónicos.
5. (Me gusta / No me gusta) el nuevo CD de Paulina Rubio.
6. (Me gustan / No me gustan) los sitios web y foros sobre España.

2 **Los gustos** Para cada persona, di si le gustan o no las cosas indicadas.

MODELO los teléfonos inteligentes / Marío (no)
A Mario no le gustan los teléfonos inteligentes.

1. las computadoras portátiles / tú (sí)
2. las cámaras digitales / Sara y Laura (sí)
3. los juegos interactivos / usted (no)
4. las redes sociales / nosotros (sí)
5. los foros sobre los autos / ustedes (no)
6. los podcasts / tú (no)
7. los grupos de noticias / yo (¿…?)
8. las tabletas / yo (¿…?)

3 **¿Qué les gusta o gustan?** Mira los dibujos y di qué les gusta (o gustan) a las personas indicadas. Sigue el modelo y usa **gusta** o **gustan** según la(s) cosa(s) o la actividad indicadas.

MODELOS Martina / navegar en Internet
A Martina le gusta navegar en Internet.

1.

Roque / las computadores portátiles

2.

ustedes / jugar juegos interactivos

3.

nosotros / las tabletas

4.

tú / tu videocámara

5.

yo / mi teléfono inteligente

6.

los niños / ver los videos en la computadora

4 ¿Y ustedes? Pregúntales a varios compañeros de clase sobre sus gustos.

MODELO   Facebook (Twitter, Yelp, Foursquare, ¿...?)
   Tú: *¿Les gusta Facebook?*
   Compañero(a): *Sí, me gusta Facebook, pero no me gusta Twitter.*

1. el grupo de noticias de profesores de español (de artistas chilenos, de actores de teatro, ¿...?)
2. la página web de Yahoo! en español (de *People en español*, de *Newsweek* o *CNN en español*, ¿...?)
3. el foro de estudiantes de español (de profesores de español, de estudiantes de francés, ¿...?)
4. los juegos interactivos (de mesa, de niños, ¿...?)
5. las computadoras portátiles (PC, Mac, ¿...?)
6. el programa de arte (de diseño gráfico, de contabilidad, ¿...?)

5 ¿Te interesa? Pregúntale a un(a) compañero(a) qué opina *(feels)* sobre varios aspectos de la tecnología.

MODELO   interesar: los blogs de personas desconocidas *(strangers)*
   Tú: *¿Te interesan los blogs de personas desconocidas?*
   Compañero(a): *No, no me interesan los blogs de personas desconocidas.*

1. molestar: recibir mucha correspondencia electrónica
2. interesar: grupos de noticias
3. gustar: enviar mensajes de texto
4. molestar: buscadores muy lentos *(slow)*
5. interesar: sitios web comerciales
6. gustar: chatear con personas en otros países
7. importar: recibir e-mails de personas desconocidas

6 Encuesta Haz una encuesta con tus compañeros de clase. Pregúntales si les gustan las cosas y actividades indicadas. Después, con la clase entera, comparen los resultados para ver cuáles son los gustos y preferencias de todos los estudiantes.

_____ ¿los juegos interactivos o los juegos tradicionales?
_____ ¿los textos digitales o los libros?
_____ ¿las clases en la universidad o las clases virtuales?
_____ ¿estudiar en la biblioteca o estudiar en un café?
_____ ¿escuchar música cuando estudias o estudiar sin música?
_____ ¿ver películas en la computadora o ver películas en el televisor?

7 La tecnología Pregúntales a seis compañeros qué les gusta de la tecnología y qué les molesta. Escribe un resumen sobre los resultados.

MODELO   *¿Cuáles son tres cosas que te gustan de la tecnología?*
   ¿Cuáles son tres cosas que te molestan?

Describing yourself and others and expressing conditions and locations: The verb **estar** and the uses of **ser** and **estar**

© Cengage Learning 2013

Estoy muy **aburrida** con tu cuento trágico.

Cómo usarlo

You already know that the verb **ser** is translated as *to be* in English. You have already used the verb **estar**, which is also translated as *to be*, in expressions such as **¿Cómo estás?** While both these Spanish verbs mean *to be*, they are used in different ways.

1. Use **estar** . . .

- to express location of people, places, or objects.

La profesora Suárez **está** en la biblioteca.	*Professor Suárez **is** in the library.*
Los libros **están** en la mesa.	*The books **are** on the table.*

- to talk about a physical condition.

—¿Cómo **está** usted?	*How **are** you?*
—**Estoy** muy bien, gracias.	*I'm well, thank you.*
—Yo **estoy** un poco cansada.	*I'm a little tired.*

- to talk about emotional conditions.

El señor Albrega **está** un poco nervioso hoy.	*Mr. Albrega **is** a little nervous today.*
Estoy muy ocupada esta semana.	*I'm very busy this week.*

2. Use **ser** . . .

- to identify yourself and others.

Soy Ana y ésta **es** mi hermana Luisa.	*I'm Ana and this **is** my sister Luisa.*

- to indicate profession.

Pablo Picasso **es** un artista famoso.	*Pablo Picasso **is** a famous artist.*

- to describe personality traits and physical features.

Somos altos y delgados.	*We **are** tall and thin.*
Somos estudiantes buenos.	*We **are** good students.*

- to give time and date.

Es la una. Hoy **es** miércoles.	*It **is** one o'clock. Today **is** Wednesday.*

- to indicate nationality and origin.

—**Eres** española, ¿no?	*You **are** Spanish, right?*
—Sí, **soy** de España.	*Yes, I **am** from Spain.*

- to express possession with **de**.

Este celular **es de Anita.**	*This **is** Anita's cell phone.*

- to give the location of an event.

La fiesta **es** en la residencia estudiantil.	*The party **is** in the dorm.*

Notice that expressing the location of people, places, and things (other than events) requires the use of **estar. Ser** is used only to indicate *where an event will take place.*

1. Here are the forms of the verb **estar** in the present indicative tense.

estar *(to be)*			
yo	**estoy**	nosotros / nosotras	**estamos**
tú	**estás**	vosotros / vosotras	**estáis**
Ud. / él / ella	**está**	Uds. / ellos / ellas	**están**

2. In the **¡Imagínate!** section you learned some adjectives that are commonly used with **estar** to describe physical and emotional conditions.

aburrido(a)   nervioso(a)

cansado(a)   ocupado(a)

contento(a)   preocupado(a)

enfermo(a)   seguro(a)

enojado(a)   triste

furioso(a)

Don't forget that when you use adjectives with **estar,** as with any other verb, they need to agree with the person or thing they are describing in both gender and number.

Los estudiantes están preocupados por Miguel.

The students are worried about Miguel.

Elena está nerviosa a causa del examen.

Elena is nervous because of the exam.

ACTIVIDADES

8 **¿Dónde están?** Todos participan en diferentes actividades en diferentes lugares de la universidad. ¿Dónde están?

MODELO   Ricardo y Juana estudian. (Está / <u>Están</u>) en la biblioteca.

1. Javier toma un refresco. (Está / Estás) en la cafetería.
2. Mi compañero(a) de cuarto y yo descansamos. (Estoy / Estamos) en la residencia estudiantil.
3. Paula y Pedro navegan por Internet. (Estamos / Están) en el centro de computación.
4. La profesora Martínez lee una novela. (Estás / Está) en el parque.
5. Usted escribe en la pizarra. (Está / Están) en el salón de clase.
6. Nosotros escuchamos el audio de la clase de español. (Estoy / Estamos) en el centro de comunicaciones.
7. Teresa levanta pesas. (Está / Están) en el gimnasio.
8. Tú compras un libro para la clase de filosofía. (Estás / Está) en la librería.

9 **¿Cómo están?** Tú y varias personas están en las siguientes situaciones. Usa **estar** + adjetivo para describir cómo están. Usa adjetivos de la lista.

Adjetivos: aburrido(a), cansado(a), contento(a), enfermo(a), enojado(a), nervioso(a), ocupado(a), preocupado(a), triste

MODELO Sales bien en el examen de francés, tomas el sol por la tarde, cenas con tu mejor amigo(a) y alquilas un video que te gusta mucho.
Estoy contento(a).

1. Tienes una entrevista con el director de la universidad para un trabajo que necesitas.
2. Carlos tiene una infección y tiene que ir al hospital.
3. Marta y Mario no tienen nada *(nothing)* que hacer *(to do)* —no hay nada interesante en la tele y su computadora no funciona.
4. Compras una nueva computadora. Llegas a casa y cuando tratas de usarla, no funciona. La tienda de computadoras no abre hasta el lunes.
5. Tú y tu familia tienen mucho que hacer. Entre los estudios, el trabajo, los deportes, la familia y los amigos, no hay suficiente tiempo en el día para hacerlo todo.
6. Elena practica deportes por la mañana, trabaja en la biblioteca por la tarde y estudia por la noche. Cuando llega a casa, descansa.
7. La tarea de matemáticas es muy difícil —Martín no comprende las instrucciones. Es muy tarde para llamar a un amigo. Tiene que entregar la tarea muy temprano por la mañana.
8. El abuelo *(grandfather)* de Pedro y Delia está muy enfermo. Pedro y Delia lo visitan en el hospital.

10 **Yo soy…** Completa las oraciones con la forma correcta de **ser** o **estar**.

MODELO Yo _____ estudiante. _____ en clase.
Yo soy estudiante. Estoy en clase.

1. El señor Ortega _____ muy ocupado.
   _____ en la oficina.
2. Nosotros _____ divertidos.
   _____ contentos ahora.
3. Rogelio _____ profesor.
   _____ alto y delgado.
4. Alejandro y yo _____ de Barcelona.
   _____ aquí en Estados Unidos por un año.
5. Pedro y Arturo _____ enfermos.
   _____ en el hospital.
6. Esta computadora _____ de Lucía.
   Lucía _____ una estudiante muy trabajadora.

11 **¿Ser o estar?** Trabaja con un(a) compañero(a) de clase para completar las oraciones. Lean las oraciones y juntos decidan si se debe usar **ser** o **estar**. Escriban la forma correcta del verbo. Luego, escriban por qué se usa **ser** o **estar**.

MODELO *Soy* María Hernández Catina.
razón *(reason):* identidad

Razones: característica física, característica de personalidad, estado físico, estado temporáneo, fecha, hora, identidad, lugar de un evento, nacionalidad, posesión, posición *(location)*, profesión

1. ¿Cómo _____ usted, profesor Taboada? razón:
2. Yo _____ un poco cansado hoy. razón:
3. Isabel _____ de España. razón:
4. ¿Dónde _____ la biblioteca? razón:
5. Mi padre _____ profesor de lenguas. razón:
6. Hoy _____ miércoles, el 22 de octubre. razón:
7. Nati _____ alta, delgada y tiene el pelo castaño. razón:
8. Esta semana Leonardo _____ muy ocupado. razón:
9. Este libro, ¿ _____ de la profesora? razón:
10. ¿Dónde _____ la clase de filosofía? razón:

12 **¡Pobre Mónica!** Trabaja con un(a) compañero(a) de clase. Miren el dibujo y juntos escriban una descripción de Mónica y de la situación en general. Traten de usar **ser** o **estar** en cada oración y de escribir por lo menos cinco oraciones.

In Spanish-speaking countries, **martes 13,** or Tuesday the 13th, rather than Friday the 13th, is considered an unlucky day.

© Cengage Learning 2013

Sonrisas

© Cengage Learning 2013

Comprensión En tu opinión, ¿cuáles de los siguientes adjetivos describen al hombre rubio? Y al hombre moreno?

- ¿Quién está…?

  aburrido / cansado / contento / enfermo / furioso / nervioso / ocupado / preocupado / seguro / triste

- ¿Quién es…?

  activo / antipático / cómico / cuidadoso / divertido / egoísta / extrovertido / impaciente / introvertido / perezoso / serio / simpático / tonto

Gramática útil 3

Talking about everyday events: Stem-changing verbs in the present indicative

Cómo usarlo

In **Chapters 1** and **2** you learned the present indicative forms of regular **-ar, -er,** and **-ir** verbs in Spanish. There are other Spanish verbs that use the same endings as regular **-ar, -er,** and **-ir** verbs in this tense, but they also have a small change in their stem. (Remember that the stem is the part of the infinitive that is left after you remove the **-ar / -er / -ir** ending.)

¡Pobre Beto! **Siento** tu frustración.

—¿Qué **piensas** de este MP3 portátil?	*What **do you think** of this MP3 player?*
—Me gusta, pero **prefiero** éste.	*I like it, but I **prefer** this one.*
—¿Verdad? Bueno, ¿por qué no le **pides** el precio al dependiente?	*Really? Well, why don't **you ask** the sales clerk the price?*

Cómo formarlo

1. There are three categories of stem-changing verbs in the present indicative.

	o → ue: encontrar (to find)	e → ie: preferir (to prefer)	e → i: pedir (to ask for)
yo	enc**ue**ntro	pref**ie**ro	p**i**do
tú	enc**ue**ntras	pref**ie**res	p**i**des
Ud. / él / ella	enc**ue**ntra	pref**ie**re	p**i**de
nosotros / nosotras	encontramos	preferimos	pedimos
vosotros / vosotras	encontráis	preferís	pedís
Uds. / ellos / ellas	enc**ue**ntran	pref**ie**ren	p**i**den

2. Note that the stem changes in all forms except the **nosotros / nosotras** and **vosotros / vosotras** forms.

3. Remember, all the endings for the present indicative are the same for these verbs as for the other regular verbs you've learned: **-o, -as, -a, -amos, -áis, -an** for **-ar** verbs; **-o, -es, -e, -emos / -imos, -éis / -ís, -en** for **-er** and **-ir** verbs. The only thing that is different here is the change in the stem.

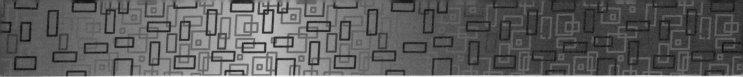

4. Here are some commonly used Spanish verbs that experience a stem change in the present indicative tense.

e → ie

cerrar	*to close*
comenzar (a)	*to begin (to)*
empezar (a)	*to begin (to)*
entender	*to understand*
pensar de	*to think (of), have an opinion about*
pensar en	*to think about, to consider*
perder	*to lose*
preferir	*to prefer*
querer	*to want, to love*
sentir	*to feel*

o → ue

contar	*to tell, to relate; to count*
dormir	*to sleep*
encontrar	*to find*
jugar*	*to play*
poder	*to be able to*
sonar	*to ring, to go off (phone, alarm clock, etc.)*
soñar (con)	*to dream (about)*
volver	*to return*

e → i

pedir	*to ask for something*
repetir	*to repeat*
servir	*to serve*

*Jugar is the only **u → ue** stem-changing verb in Spanish. It's grouped with the **o → ue** verbs, because its change is most similar to those.

ACTIVIDADES

13 **En la clase de computación** Estás en la clase de computación. Escoge la forma correcta del verbo entre paréntesis para describir lo que hacen todos.

1. Yo (pido / pide) el número de teléfono del nuevo estudiante.
2. La profesora (repite / repiten) las instrucciones de la actividad.
3. Nosotros (sirvo / servimos) refrescos después de la clase.
4. Él (prefiere / prefieren) usar los mensajes de texto para comunicarse con su familia.
5. Tú (encontramos / encuentras) la clase muy difícil.
6. Ellos (piden / pedimos) la dirección electrónica de la universidad.
7. Nosotras (preferimos / prefieren) ir a un café con wifi después de clase.
8. Yo (encuentras / encuentro) la clase muy divertida.

14 **¿Entiendes?** Tú tienes que presentar el nuevo sistema de software a un grupo diverso de asistentes administrativos. Les preguntas si entienden cómo hacer ciertas cosas con los nuevos programas. Tu compañero(a) te contesta.

MODELO ¿_____ (ustedes) cómo instalar el programa antivirus? (sí)
Tú: *¿Entienden cómo instalar el programa antivirus?*
Compañero(a): *Sí, entendemos cómo instalar el programa antivirus.*

1. ¿ _____ (ustedes) cómo abrir la aplicación? (no)
2. ¿ _____ (usted) cómo archivar los documentos al disco duro? (sí)
3. ¿ _____ (tú) cómo funciona el buscador? (no)
4. ¿ _____ (ellos) cómo cortar la conexión a Internet? (sí)
5. ¿ _____ (ustedes) cómo entrar en los foros? (no)
6. ¿ _____ (tú) cómo pedir apoyo técnico (*tech support*)? (sí)

15 **¿A qué hora vuelves?** Un amigo te pregunta cuándo vuelven a casa tú, tus amigos y varios miembros de tu familia. Escucha la pregunta y escribe la respuesta correcta en una oración completa. Estudia el modelo.

Track 12

MODELO Ves: 10:30 A.M.
Escuchas: *¿A qué hora vuelves de la clase de computación?*
Escribes: *Vuelvo de la clase de computación a las diez y media de la mañana.*

1. 4:00 P.M.   4. 8:00 P.M.
2. 1:00 A.M.   5. 7:00 P.M.
3. 3:15 P.M.   6. 11:30 A.M.

16 **En la clase de español** Todos los estudiantes en la clase de español están en medio de alguna actividad. Di lo que hace cada persona.

MODELO Olga (no entender las instrucciones)
Olga no entiende las instrucciones.

1. Joaquín (cerrar el texto digital)
2. Iris (perder su lugar en el capítulo)
3. Paulo (dormir en su escritorio)
4. Lisa (empezar a hacer la tarea)
5. Arturo (pensar en las vacaciones)
6. Andrés y Marta (jugar en la computadora)
7. Roberto y Humberto (querer ir al gimnasio)
8. Ingrid (preferir hacer la tarea en la computadora)
9. Francisco (no poder abrir la aplicación)
10. la profesora (volver a repetir la tarea)
11. yo (pedir el número de la página de la lectura)
12. yo (repetir la pregunta)

> **Volver a** + *infinitive* means to go back and do something, or to do it over.

17 **Trucos para tecnófobos** Con un(a) compañero(a) miren el anuncio de un programa de televisión sobre trucos para las personas que no saben mucho de tecnología. Después, contesten las preguntas a continuación.

¿Eres tecnófobo?

¡En este show puedes aprender 50 cosas fáciles para ayudarte con todos tus aparatos! ¿Quieres saber más? Pues, ¡a ver!
Canal 22, 19:30

© Cengage Learning 2013

cosas: *things*

1. ¿Cuántas cosas fáciles pueden hacer con estos trucos *(tricks)*?
2. ¿Prefieren aprender a usar los trucos o piensan que son una pérdida *(waste)* de tiempo?
3. ¿Pueden usar sus celulares para hacer otras funciones? ¿Cuáles?
4. ¿Tienen todos estos aparatos? ¿Quieren comprar otros aparatos electrónicos? ¿Por qué sí o no?

18 **¿Quieres ir?** Pregúntale a tu compañero(a) si quiere hacer una actividad contigo. Él o ella te dice que prefiere hacer otra cosa.

Actividades: ir a tomar un refresco, ver un video, estudiar en la biblioteca, mirar television, navegar por Internet, tomar el sol, visitar a amigos, bailar, ¿…?

MODELO Tú: *¿Quieres ver un video?*
Compañero(a): *No, prefiero jugar un juego interactivo.*

19 **La vida universitaria** ¿Es la vida del estudiante muy difícil hoy en día? Con tres compañeros de clase, contesten las siguientes preguntas sinceramente. Basándose en las respuestas de sus compañeros, decidan juntos si la vida universitaria produce mucho estrés para el estudiante. Presenten su conclusión a la clase.

1. ¿Sientes mucho estrés? ¿Por qué?
2. ¿A qué hora vuelves a la residencia estudiantil de la universidad?
3. ¿A qué hora duermes? ¿Dónde duermes? ¿Cuántas horas duermes por noche? ¿Duermes lo suficiente?
4. ¿Juegas videojuegos? ¿Juegos interactivos? ¿Juegos en la red? ¿Cuánto tiempo pasas a diario jugando estos juegos?
5. ¿Pierdes tus llaves *(keys)* con frecuencia? ¿Tus gafas *(glasses)*? ¿Tu dinero *(money)*? ¿Tu tarea? ¿Tus libros? ¿Tus cuadernos? ¿Tu mochila?
6. ¿Piensas mucho en el futuro? ¿Puedes imaginar tu futuro?

20 **Los hábitos del universitario** Haz una gráfica como la de abajo. Usa las frases indicadas para crear preguntas. (Si quieres, puedes escribir tus propias preguntas.) Luego, hazles las preguntas a diez compañeros de clase. Según sus respuestas, apunta el número de estudiantes en la columna apropiada. Luego, escribe una descripción de tus resultados.

Frases para las preguntas	Número de estudiantes
dormir más de seis horas por noche:	6
no dormir más de seis horas por noche:	4
preferir hablar por teléfono para comunicarse:	
preferir escribir e-mail para comunicarse:	
preferir enviar un mensaje de texto para comunicarse:	
jugar un deporte:	
jugar videojuegos:	
sentir mucho estrés:	
no sentir mucho estrés:	
pensar en su futuro todos los días:	
no pensar en su futuro todos los días:	
encontrar la vida universitaria difícil:	
encontrar la vida universitaria fácil:	
¿...?	

MODELO *Seis estudiantes duermen más de seis horas por noche.*
Cuatro estudiantes no duermen más de seis horas por noche.

21 **Mi blog** Escribe un perfil personal para tu blog en Internet. Describe tus características físicas, tu personalidad, tus clases preferidas, tus hábitos en la universidad, tus emociones y lo que te gusta, molesta o interesa, etc. Ponle a tu descripción todo el detalle que puedas.

Gramática útil 4

Describing how something is done: Adverbs

The magazine *Muy interesante* runs an annual contest to award prizes to top Spanish innovators in a variety of fields. This is a profile of one of them. Can you find the **-mente** adverb and guess its meaning in English?

Personalidades famosas

Carla Royo-Villanova

Fundadora de Carla Bulgaria Roses Beauty

"Para mi innovar es una filosofia de vida. Procuro innovar en cada momento profesional y personal y asi no caer nunca en la rutina. Que cada dĺa sea diferente. La idea original de mi empresa fue precisamente gracias a ese espiritu innovador que me caracteriza".

« Anterior   Siguiente »

Slide of Carla Royo Villanova from *Muy Interestante*, http://premioinnova.muyinteresante.es/index.php. Used with permission from Gruner y Jahr and Carla Royo Villanova.

Cómo usarlo

When you want to say how an activity is carried out (slowly, thoroughly, generally, etc.), you use an adverb.

Generalmente, prefiero usar una contraseña secreta.	***Generally***, *I prefer to use a secret password.*
Escribo más **rápido** / **rápidamente** en computadora que con bolígrafo.	*I write more **rapidly** on the computer than I do with a pen.*
Este programa es **muy** lento.	*This program is **very** slow.*

Cómo formarlo

LO BÁSICO

An adverb is a word that modifies a verb, an adjective, or another adverb. (Sometimes adjectives can also be used as adverbs—for example, *fast*). *Generally, rapidly,* and *very* are all adverbs. You can identify an adverb by asking the question, *"How?"*

1. To form an adverb from a Spanish adjective, it is often possible to add the ending **-mente** to the adjective: **fácil → fácilmente**. If the adjective ends in an **-o**, change it to **-a** before adding **-mente: rápido → rápidamente**.

Lento and **rápido** can also be used with **muy** for the same effect: **Esta computadora se conecta a Internet muy rápido / muy lento / rápidamente / lentamente.**

2. Here are some frequently used Spanish adjectives that can be turned into **-mente** adverbs.

fácil *(easy)*	→ **fácilmente**
difícil *(difficult)*	→ **difícilmente**
lento *(slow)*	→ **lentamente**
rápido *(fast)*	→ **rápidamente**

3. The following **-mente** adverbs are also useful to talk about your routine and what you normally do.

frecuentemente	*frequently*	**normalmente**	*normally*
generalmente	*generally*		

4. Here are some other common Spanish adverbs.

bastante	*somewhat, rather*	Este sistema es **bastante** lento.
bien	*well*	Tu computadora funciona **bien**.
demasiado	*too much*	Navego **demasiado** por Internet.
mal	*badly*	¡Mi cámara web funciona muy **mal**!
mucho	*a lot*	Me gustan **mucho** los juegos interactivos.
muy	*very*	Guardo archivos **muy** frecuentemente.
poco	*little*	Chateo **poco** por Internet.

> Remember, adverbs can be used to modify other adverbs, so it's perfectly acceptable to use **muy** with **frecuentemente** or **mal**, for example!

ACTIVIDADES

22 ¿Cómo? Escucha a Miriam mientras describe su vida a una amiga.
Track 13 Completa sus oraciones. Escoge el adjetivo más lógico del grupo y conviértelo en un adverbio añadiendo el sufijo **-mente**.

Adjetivos: constante, cuidadoso, directo, fácil, frecuente, general, inmediato, lento, normal, paciente, rápido, tranquilo.

1. Puedes instalar el programa antivirus _____.
2. Yo chateo por Internet _____.
3. Hay algunos sitios web que funcionan _____.
4. _____, navego por Internet dos o tres horas por día.
5. Con este módem interno, puedo hacer una conexión _____.
6. Instalo los programas de software en mi computadora _____.
7. Tengo tarea _____.
8. Los domingos prefiero pasar el día _____.

23 ¿Cómo te sientes? Averigua *(Find out)* cómo se sienten tus compañeros de clase en ciertas situaciones. Hazles las siguientes preguntas a varios compañeros y apunta sus respuestas. Luego, dale los resultados de tu encuesta a la clase.

¿Cómo te sientes cuando...
1. vas a tener un examen?
2. tu computadora no funciona bien?
3. recibes la cuenta *(bill)* de tu teléfono celular?
4. la batería de tu teléfono no funciona?
5. pierdes los archivos de tu tarea?
6. ¿...?

Posibles respuestas

bien	bastante nervioso (triste, preocupado, etc.)
mal	demasiado nervioso (cansado, furioso, etc.)
muy bien	no me afecta
muy mal	¿...?

¡Explora y exprésate!

España

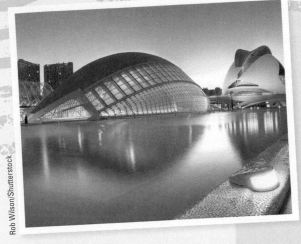

Rob Wilson/Shutterstock

Información general ▶

Nombre oficial: Reino de España

Población: 40.548.753

Capital: Madrid (f. siglo X) (3.300.000 hab.)

Otras ciudades importantes: Barcelona
(1.600.000 hab.), Valencia (840.000 hab.),
Sevilla (710.000 hab.), Toledo (85.000 hab.)

Moneda: euro

Idiomas: castellano (oficial), catalán, vasco,
gallego

Mapa de España: Apéndice D

Spain is often seen as one big culture when, in fact, it is the amalgamation of former kingdoms and separate regions. Many of these are autonomous states and have separate languages and/or dialects, and distinct cultural customs. Spanish is referred to as "castellano" in areas where there is an additional native language. Typically these are bilingual zones.

Vale saber…

- El Imperio español fue *(was)* el primer imperio global y uno de los más grandes en toda la historia mundial. En su apogeo *(peak)*, España tenía territorios en todos los continentes menos Antártida.

- España ha producido muchos artistas ilustres. En la literatura, se distingue Miguel de Cervantes, escritor de *El ingenioso hidalgo Don Quijote de la Mancha*, que se considera la primera novela moderna. En las artes, los grandes maestros de la pintura española incluyen a El Greco, Diego de Velázquez y Francisco de Goya. En el siglo *(century)* XX, Pablo Picasso, Joan Miró y Salvador Dalí son los innovadores más importantes del arte moderno.

- La influencia árabe en la arquitectura del siglo VIII, construida por los colonizadores musulmanes comúnmente llamados "los moros", es evidente por todo el sur de España, en particular en Granada, Córdoba y Sevilla.

Buika, artista universal

Paul White/AP Images

Concha Buika, conocida profesionalmente como Buika, es cantante española, hija de ecuatoguineanos y una maravillosa estudiante de todos los estilos musicales del mundo. Boleros, flamenco, jazz, funk, soul y el ritmo africano todos forman parte de su obra musical. Además, le fascinan los ritmos electrónicos y dice que para ella sus 'joyas' *(jewels)* son los aparatos electrónicos que utiliza para hacer música. Con sus ritmos globales y su uso de la tecnología, Buika es una artista universal que rompe *(breaks)* todas las barreras.

>> En resumen

La información general

1. ¿Qué país fue *(was)* el primer imperio global?
2. ¿En qué continentes tenía *(had)* España territorios?
3. ¿Quién es el autor de la primera novela moderna?
4. ¿Quiénes son los grandes maestros de la pintura española?
5. ¿Quiénes son los artistas españoles que se consideran innovadores del arte moderno?
6. ¿Qué tres ciudades españolas tienen una influencia árabe en su arquitectura?

El tema de la música electrónica

1. ¿De dónde son los padres de Buika?
2. ¿Qué estilos musicales incorpora Buika en su obra musical?
3. ¿Qué considera Buika sus 'joyas'?
4. ¿Qué hace de Buika una artista universal?

⊕ ¿QUIERES SABER MÁS?

En la tabla que empezaste al principio del capítulo, añade toda la información que ya sabes en la columna **Lo que aprendí.** Escoge uno o dos de los temas que escribiste en la columna **Lo que quiero aprender,** o uno o dos de los temas a continuación para investigar en línea. Prepárate para compartir la información con la clase.

Palabras clave: el Imperio español; la Guerra Civil español; la influencia musulmana; Pedro Almodóvar; Penélope Cruz; Rafael Nadal

⊕ **Tú en el mundo hispano** Para explorar oportunidades de usar el español para estudiar o hacer trabajos voluntarios o aprendizajes en España, sigue los enlaces en el sitio web de **www.cengagebrain.com.**

🎵 **Ritmos del mundo hispano** Sigue los enlaces en **www.cengagebrain.com** para escuchar música de España.

A leer

>> **Antes de leer**

ESTRATEGIA

Using format clues to aid comprehension

In **Chapter 3,** you looked at the visuals that accompanied an article to get an idea of its content. It is also very helpful to look at an article's format. The headline, a section title, and any kind of highlighted or boxed text (often called sidebars) can give you a general idea of the article's content.

1 Mira el artículo en la página 153. ¿Cuántas de las siguientes claves *(clues)* de formato puedes identificar en el artículo? Basándote en esas claves, ¿de qué trata el artículo?

- título de sección
- título de artículo
- texto del lado *(sidebar)*
- citas *(quotations)*
- fotos
- ilustraciones o gráficos

2 Ahora lee el artículo en la página 153 y busca las ideas principales.

>> **Después de leer**

3 Di si las siguientes oraciones son **ciertas (C)** o **falsas (F)**.

1. _____ Este artículo habla de una plataforma tecnológica de hardware.
2. _____ Tuenti es un sitio exclusivo.
3. _____ Muchas de las personas que trabajan para Tuenti son jóvenes.
4. _____ Para Tuenti, la privacidad no es muy importante.
5. _____ Todas las personas que trabajan para Tuenti son españoles.

4 Contesta las preguntas con un(a) compañero(a).

1. ¿Puedes usar Tuenti con tu celular?
2. Según Tuenti, ¿cuántas personas usan el sitio web cada día?
3. ¿Cuáles son las nacionalidades de los cofundadores?
4. ¿Cuántas invitaciones recibe cada nuevo usuario?
5. ¿Dónde está la oficina de Tuenti?
6. ¿Qué significa Tuenti?
7. En tu opinión, ¿puede tener éxito *(be successful)* un sitio como Tuenti en Estados Unidos?

LECTURA

Sólo con invitación

¿Qué es Tuenti?

Tuenti es una red social española que es uno de los sitios web más populares del país. Es la creación de dos españoles, Felix Ruiz y Joaquín Ayuso, y dos norteamericanos, Zaryn Dentzel y Kenny Bentley. Y, a diferencia de otras redes sociales como Facebook, es necesario recibir una invitación personal antes de poder juntarse[1] a esta comunidad virtual.

> **"Si no eres tú mismo, no eres nadie[2] en Tuenti"**
> **—Zaryn Dentzel, uno de los cofundadores de Tuenti**

¿Por qué requiere Tuenti una invitación?

Según Dentzel, "Anteponemos[3] la privacidad de nuestro público al crecimiento sin control[4]. De ese modo cuando entras en la red ya tienes, al menos, un amigo".

Esta decisión resulta en una exclusividad bastante inflexible. Cada nuevo usuario recibe sólo tres invitaciones — ¡así que tiene que pensarlo bien antes de usarlas!

Unos datos sobre Tuenti

- El nombre es una abreviatura de "tu entidad".
- Está basado en Madrid.
- La edad media de las personas que trabajan para Tuenti es de 24 años. Ellos son de más de quince países diferentes.

 **tuenti**

¿Qué es Tuenti?

Tuenti es una plataforma social privada, a la que se accede únicamente por invitación. Cada día la usan millones de personas para comunicarse entre ellas y compartir información.

Social
Conéctate, comparte y comunícate con tus amigos, compañeros de trabajo y familia.

 Local
Descubre servicios locales y participa con las marcas que realmente te importan.

Móvil
Accede a Tuenti desde tu móvil en tiempo real, estés donde estés.

únicamente: *only* **marcas:** *brands*

[1]*to join* [2]*no one* [3]*We give preference to* [4]**al...:** *over uncontrolled growth*

A escribir

ESTRATEGIA

Prewriting—Narrowing your topic

After you choose a topic for a piece of writing, but before you begin the writing process, you need to narrow your topic to fit the scope of your written piece. For example, in this section, you will write a note to a friend who is interested in technology. Since most notes are short, you don't want to choose a huge topic to cover.

One way to narrow a topic is to take it and ask yourself questions about it. For example, if your general topic is "computers," ask, "What kind of computer?" You might answer, "A laptop." The next question might be, "Why do you want a laptop?" The answer might be, "Because I like to be able to take it with me." You could then ask, "Where do you want to use your laptop?" with the answer, "At the coffee shop down the corner with free wifi." Once you have progressed through a series of narrowing questions like this, you have narrowed your topic from "computers" to "ways having a laptop can help you save money."

1 Piensa en dos o tres temas generales que puedes usar para escribir a un(a) amigo(a) que es muy aficionado(a) *(a big fan)* a la tecnología. Un ejemplo de un tema general puede ser **las computadoras**, **el Internet**, etc.

2 Go back to the list of topics you created in **Actividad 1**. Ahora, elige *(choose)* uno de los temas y practica la técnica de la **Estrategia** para hacer el tema más específico.

3 Ahora, lee el mensaje modelo a continuación donde Magali habla de sus clases y tarea relacionadas con la tecnología y también de sus planes para el fin de semana. ¿Contiene su mensaje palabras o frases que puedes usar en tu composición? Si hay, apúntalas. Si necesitas otras palabras que no sabes *(you don't know)*, búscalas en un diccionario bilingüe antes de escribir.

Hola, ¿cómo estás?

Buscar mensaje 🔍   **+ Nuevo mensaje**

◄ **Volver a Mensajes** | **Marcar como no leído** | **Denunciar correo no deseado** | **Eliminar**   ▲ ▼

Entre Tú y Magali Fulanita

Magali Fulanita 19 de enero, 18:00

Hola, ¿Cómo estás? Todo va bien aquí.☺ Tengo muchos planes para el fin de semana. Primero, voy a trabajar un poco en la computadora.
Tengo que crear la plantilla *(template)* de un sitio web para mi clase de diseño gráfico. ¡Sólo podemos usar los tres colores principales! Muy fácil, ¿verdad? ☺ Bueno, a mí me gustan mucho los colores vivos – el rojo, el amarillo… Entonces, ¡va a ser un programa brillante! Después de trabajar en la computadora, voy a salir el sábado con Laila y Marta. (¿Por qué no vienes?) Y el domingo tengo tarea para la clase de programación. Así que voy a estar muy ocupada… y un poco cansada! ☹
Bueno, ¡escríbeme pronto para decirme tus noticias!

Un abrazo, Magali

Respuesta

Responder

Composición

4 Ahora, escribe un borrador *(rough draft)* de tu mensaje. Incluye información sobre el tema que desarrollaste *(that you developed)* en las **Actividades 1** y **2**. También debes incluir un poco de información personal para tu amigo(a), como en el mensaje modelo. Trata de escribir rápidamente, sin preocuparte *(without worrying)* demasiado por los errores.

Después de escribir

5 Mira tu borrador otra vez. Usa la siguiente lista para revisarlo *(to revise it)*.

- ¿Tiene tu mensaje toda la información necesaria? ¿Está bien organizado?
- ¿Corresponden los sujetos de las oraciones a los verbos?
- ¿Corresponden las formas de los artículos, los sustantivos y los adjetivos?
- ¿Usas correctamente **ser** y **estar**, los verbos con cambio en la raíz *(stem)* y los verbos como **gustar**?
- ¿Hay errores de puntuación o de ortografía *(spelling)*?

Vocabulario

La tecnología *Technology*

El hardware *hardware*

La computadora *computer*
el altoparlante *speaker*
el cable *cable*
el disco duro *hard drive*
la memoria flash / el pendrive *flash drive*
el módem externo *external modem*
el micrófono *microphone*
el monitor *monitor*
el puerto de USB *USB port*
el ratón *mouse*

La computadora portátil *Laptop computer*
los audífonos *earphones*
el módem interno *internal modem*
la impresora *printer*
el lector de CD-ROM o DVD *CD-ROM / DVD drive*
la pantalla *screen*
la tecla *key*
el teclado *keyboard*

El software *Software*
la aplicación *application*
los archivos *files*
el archivo PDF *PDF attachment*
el ícono del programa *program icon*
el juego interactivo *interactive game*
el programa antivirus *antivirus program*
el programa de procesamiento de textos *word processing program*

Funciones de la computadora *Computer functions*
archivar *to file*
bajar / descargar *to download*
conectar *to connect*
enviar *to send*
funcionar *to function*
grabar *to record*
guardar *to save*
hacer clic / doble clic *to click / double-click*
instalar *to install*
subir / cargar *to upload*

Los colores *Colors*

amarillo(a) *yellow*
anaranjado(a) *orange*
azul *blue*
blanco(a) *white*
café / marrón *brown*
gris *gray*

morado(a) *purple*
negro(a) *black*
rojo(a) *red*
rosa / rosado(a) *pink*
verde *green*

Las emociones *Emotions*

aburrido(a) *bored*
cansado(a) *tired*
contento(a) *happy*
enfermo(a) *sick*
enojado(a) *angry*
furioso(a) *furious*

nervioso(a) *nervous*
ocupado(a) *busy*
preocupado(a) *worried*
seguro(a) *sure*
triste *sad*

Aparatos electrónicos *Electronic devices*

el asistente electrónico *electronic notebook*
la cámara digital *digital camera*
la cámara web *webcam*
el MP3 portátil *portable MP3 player*
el reproductor / grabador de discos compactos *CD player / burner*

el reproductor / grabador de DVD *DVD player / burner*
la tableta *tablet computer*
el teléfono inteligente / smartphone *smartphone*
la videocámara *videocamera*

Funciones de Internet *Internet functions*

acceder *to access*
el blog *blog*
el buzón electrónico *electronic mailbox*
el buscador *search engine*
chatear *to chat online*
el ciberespacio *cyberspace*
la conexión *the connection*
hacer una conexión *to get online*
cortar la conexión *to get offline, disconnect*
la contraseña *password*
el correo electrónico / e-mail *e-mail*
en línea *online*

el enlace *link*
el foro *forum*
el grupo de conversación *chat room*
el grupo de noticias *newsgroup*
la página web *web page*
el proveedor de acceso *Internet provider*
la red mundial *World Wide Web*
la red social *social networking site*
el sitio web *website*
el (la) usuario(a) *user*
el wifi *wifi, wireless connection*

Verbos como *gustar*

encantar *to like a lot*
fascinar *to fascinate*
importar *to be important to someone; to mind*

interesar *to interest, to be interesting*
molestar *to bother*

Otros verbos*   ~~Stem changers~~

cerrar (ie) *to close*
comenzar (ie) *to begin*
contar (ue) *to tell, to relate; to count*
dormir (ue) *to sleep*
empezar (ie) *to begin*
encontrar (ue) *to find*
entender (ie) *to understand*
jugar (ue) *to play*
pedir (i) *to ask for something*
pensar (ie) de *to think, have an opinion about*
pensar (ie) en *to think about, to consider*

perder (ie) *to lose*
poder (ue) *to be able to*
preferir (ie) *to prefer*
querer (ie) *to want; to love*
repetir (i) *to repeat*
sentir (ie) *to feel*
servir (i) *to serve*
sonar (ue) *to ring, to go off (phone, alarm clock, etc.)*
soñar (ue) con *to dream (about)*
volver (ue) *to return*

Adjetivos

difícil *difficult*
fácil *easy*

lento *slow*
rápido *fast*

Adverbios

difícilmente *with difficulty*
fácilmente *easily*
frecuentemente *frequently*
generalmente *generally*
lentamente *slowly*
normalmente *normally*
rápidamente *rapidly*

bastante *somewhat, rather*
bien *well*
demasiado *too much*
mal *badly*
mucho *a lot*
muy *very*
poco *little*

*Starting here, stem-changing verbs will be indicated in vocabulary lists with the stem change in parentheses.

Repaso y preparación

>> Repaso del Capítulo 4

Complete these activities to check your understanding of the new grammar points in **Chapter 4** before you move on to **Chapter 5**.

The answers to the activities in this section can be found in **Appendix B**.

Gustar with nouns and other verbs like gustar (p. 134)

1 Completa las oraciones con un pronombre de objeto indirecto y escoge la forma correcta del verbo indicado.

1. A ellos _____ (gusta / gustan) los blogs.
2. A mí _____ (encanta / encantan) mi teléfono inteligente.
3. A él _____ (molesta / molestan) perder acceso a Internet.
4. A nosotros _____ (interesa / interesan) los foros sobre la tecnología.
5. A ti no _____ (importa / importan) cambiar tu contraseña frecuentemente.
6. A usted _____ (gusta / gustan) el nuevo programa antivirus.

The verb estar and the uses of ser and estar (p. 138)

2 Completa las oraciones con una forma de **ser** o **estar**.

1. Oye, Marcos ¿ _____ enojado?
2. Nosotros _____ en la biblioteca.
3. Yo _____ estudiante.
4. Ellos _____ altos y rubios.
5. ¡Tengo examen! _____ muy nervioso.
6. Ella no puede dormir. _____ cansada.
7. Hoy _____ miércoles.
8. El celular _____ de Marisa.
9. Mi computadora _____ en mi mochila.
10. Mis amigos _____ españoles.
11. La fiesta _____ en el café.
12. Los altoparlantes _____ en la mesa.

Stem-changing verbs in the present indicative (p. 143)

3 Haz oraciones completas con los sujetos y verbos indicados.

1. tú / dormir mucho
2. yo / cerrar la computadora portátil
3. ella / entender las instrucciones
4. nosotras / jugar el juego interactivo
5. usted / repetir la contraseña
6. ellos / querer un MP3 portátil
7. yo / poder instalar el programa
8. nosotros / preferir ir a un café con wifi

Adverbs (p. 148)

4 Escoge un adjetivo de la lista, cámbialo a un adverbio con **-mente** y úsalo para completar una de las siguientes oraciones.

Adjetivos: fácil, general, lento, rápido

1. No me gusta escribir. Escribo muy _____.
2. ¡Está computadora es fantástica! Funciona muy _____.
3. _____ me gusta navegar en Internet, pero no me gusta este sitio web.
4. Ella aprende nuevos programas muy _____. No son difíciles para ella.

Preparación para el Capítulo 5

The present indicative of regular -ar, -er, and -ir verbs (Chapters 2 and 3)

5 Completa las oraciones del anuncio (*advertisement*) con la forma correcta del verbo indicado.

Complete these activities to review some previously learned grammatical structures that will be helpful when you learn the new grammar in **Chapter 5**.

Be sure to reread **Chapter 4: Gramática útil 2** and **3** before moving on to the new **Chapter 5** grammar sections.

¡Súper rápido, súper ligero!
Y esta semana, ¡una súper oferta!

El Incre-Libre 2020
_____ (deber) ser tu
nueva computadora si tú...

- _____ (enviar) o_____ (recibir) archivos grandes por e-mail,
- _____ (grabar) muchos videos o _____(instalar) programas de software que requieren mucha memoria,
- _____ (llevar) tu portátil siempre contigo y_____ (trabajar) con ella en

muchos sitios, ...ésta es la computadora para ti.

Nuestros clientes _____(hablar) de su satisfacción con el Incre-Libre:

"¡Esta computadora_____(funcionar) muy rápidamente! Yo_____(bajar) y _____
(subir) archivos a mi sitio web todos los días sin problema."

–Pilar Torres García, diseñadora de sitios web

"¡El Incre-Libre no_____(pesar—*to weigh*) nada! Voy a un café, _____ (sacar) la
computadora de mi mochila, _____(acceder) a Internet y _____(leer) las noticias
del mundo. No importa dónde estoy."

–Javier Salazar Rojas, profesor

"Los altoparlantes son increíbles. Cuando mi hermanos y yo_____(usar) la computadora
para mirar videos, ellos siempre _____(comentar) la calidad del audio."

–Marcos Villarreal Barrios, estudiante

iEsta semana, nosotros _____(ofrecer) el Incre-Libre por sólo 1.200 euros!

Es nuestra portátil más popular – _____(vender) casi 100 de ellas cada semana.

**¡Si quieres una, _____(deber) actuar AHORA! Nuestros expertos en la computación
personal están listos para atenderles.**

capítulo 5 ¿Qué tal la familia?

Stephen Simpson/Getty Images

RELACIONES FAMILIARES

En el mundo hispanohablante, las relaciones familiares son un aspecto muy importante de la identidad personal.

¿Es tu familia una parte importante de tu vida diaria? ¿Cuánto tiempo pasas con miembros de tu familia en una semana? ¿En un mes?

Communication

By the end of this chapter you will be able to

- talk about and describe your family
- talk about professions
- describe daily routines
- indicate ongoing actions

Un viaje por El Salvador y Honduras

Estos países centroamericanos comparten una frontera y una costa pacífica. Honduras también tiene una costa atlántica. Los dos tienen un clima tropical.

País / Área	Tamaño y fronteras	Sitios de interés
El Salvador 20.720 km²	un poco más pequeño que Massachusetts; fronteras con Guatemala y Honduras	el bosque lluvioso *(rain forest)* del Parque Nacional Montecristo; los volcanes de Izalco, Santa Ana y San Vicente; las ruinas mayas de Joya de Cerén; las playas *(beaches)* del Pacífico
Honduras 111.890 km²	un poco más grande que Tennessee; fronteras con El Salvador, Guatemala y Nicaragua	las ruinas mayas de Copán, las islas de la Bahía, la arquitectura colonial de Tegucigalpa y San Pedro Sula, el bosque tropical de la región de la Mosquitia

¿Qué sabes? Di si las siguientes oraciones son ciertas **(C)** o falsas **(F)**.

1. Estos dos países tienen más o menos el mismo *(same)* tamaño.
2. Hay ruinas mayas en Honduras, pero no en El Salvador.
3. El Salvador tiene muchos volcanes.
4. Hay ejemplos de arquitectura colonial en Honduras.

Lo que sé y lo que quiero aprender Completa la tabla del **Apéndice A**. Escribe algunos datos que **ya sabes** sobre estos países en la columna **Lo que sé**. Después, añade algunos temas que **quieres aprender** a la columna **Lo que quiero aprender**. Guarda la tabla para usarla otra vez en la sección **¡Explora y exprésate!** en la página 187.

Cultures

By the end of this chapter you will have explored

- facts about Honduras and El Salvador
- a unique course of study in Honduras
- a financial cooperative in El Salvador
- careers where knowledge of Spanish is helpful
- the Afro-Hispanic **garífuna** culture of Honduras

¡Imagínate!

▶ >> **Vocabulario útil 1**

ANILÚ: Son fotos de mi **familia**.

DULCE: ¿De veras? ¿En la computadora?

ANILÚ: Sí, mi **hermanito** Roberto tiene una cámara digital.
Saca fotos de la familia y me las manda por Internet.

In Spanish, the masculine plural **hermanos** can mean both *brothers* (all males) and *brothers and sisters / siblings* (both males and females).

To refer to a couple, use **la pareja**. For example: **Es una pareja muy elegante.** Also, to ask about someone's partner, you can say: **¿Quién es la pareja de Juan?** Or: **Su pareja es doctor.**

Notice that **parientes** is a false cognate: it does *not* mean *parents;* it means *family members.* **Los padres** is the correct term for *parents.*

In some countries, the **-astro(a)** ending might be viewed as pejorative, and speakers might refer to **la esposa de mi padre** instead of **mi madrastra.** Be conscious of these nuances.

>> **La familia nuclear**

la madre (mamá) *mother*
el padre (papá) *father*
los padres *parents*
la esposa *wife*
el esposo *husband*
la hija *daughter*
el hijo *son*
la hermana (mayor) *(older) sister*
el hermano (menor) *(younger) brother*

la tía *aunt*
el tío *uncle*
la prima *female cousin*
el primo *male cousin*
la sobrina *niece*
el sobrino *nephew*
la abuela *grandmother*
el abuelo *grandfather*
la nieta *granddaughter*
el nieto *grandson*

>> **La familia política**

la suegra *mother-in-law*
el suegro *father-in-law*
la nuera *daughter-in-law*
el yerno *son-in-law*
la cuñada *sister-in-law*
el cuñado *brother-in-law*

>> **Otros parientes**

la madrastra *stepmother*
el padrastro *stepfather*
la hermanastra *stepsister*
el hermanastro *stepbrother*
la media hermana *half-sister*
el medio hermano *half-brother*

In Spanish, diminutives are common. You form the diminutive by adding **-ito** or **-ita** to a noun: **hermano → hermanito**. (Other diminutives are formed by adding **-cito / -cita: coche → cochecito**.)

A diminutive is used: 1) to indicate that something or someone is small, or younger. **Una casita** is a small house; **una hermanita** is a younger sister. 2) to express love or fondness. For example, Anilú probably refers to her grandmother as **abuelita** to indicate that she loves her dearly.

To express affection, Spanish speakers also use nicknames. In the video, **Anilú** is a nickname for Ana Luisa, **Beto** for Roberto, and **Chela** for Graciela.

ACTIVIDADES

1 **Los parientes** Completa las oraciones con la respuesta correcta para describir las relaciones entre los parientes de Anilú. Usa el árbol genealógico (*family tree*) de Anilú para identificar las relaciones.

1. Rodrigo es _____ de Adela.
   a. el esposo b. el suegro c. el tío
2. Tomás y Rafael son _____.
   a. hermanas b. primos c. hermanos
3. Sonia es _____ de Anilú.
   a. la tía b. la prima c. la hermanastra
4. Roberto es _____ de Rosa.
   a. el sobrino b. el nieto c. el yerno
5. Gloria es _____ de Rodrigo y Adela.
   a. la suegra b. la hija c. la nieta
6. Adela es _____ de Amelia.
   a. la madrastra b. la cuñada c. la suegra

Arturo Villa González y Beatriz Vega Chapa de Villa — Rodrigo Guzmán Corona y Adela Flores Romero de Guzmán

Carlos — Irene — Amelia — Pedro — Hernán — Rosa

Tomás — Rafael — Gloria — Anilú — Roberto — Alberto — Sonia

© Cengage Learning 2013

2 **La familia de Anilú** Con un(a) compañero(a) de clase, háganse preguntas sobre el árbol genealógico (*family tree*) de Anilú de la **Actividad 1.** Túrnense nombrando la persona y diciendo cuál es su relación con Anilú.

MODELO Compañero(a): *¿Quién es Beatriz Vega Chapa?*
        Tú: *Es la abuela de Anilú.*

3 **El árbol genealógico** Dibuja el árbol genealógico de tu familia. Empieza con tus abuelos y sigue con el resto de tu familia. Luego, en grupos de tres, intercambien sus árboles y háganse preguntas sobre sus familias.

MODELO Tú: *¿Tom es tu hermano?*
        Compañero(a): *Sí, es mi hermano menor. Tiene quince años y es muy divertido.*
        Tú: *¿Quién es Elisa?*
        Compañero(a): *Es mi sobrina. Es la hija de mi hermana mayor.*

4 **Mi familia** Escribe un párrafo corto sobre cada miembro de tu familia nuclear. Para cada individuo, di quién es, cómo se llama y cuántos años tiene. Incluye algunas características físicas y también unas de personalidad. Luego, en grupos de tres, lean sus descripciones al grupo. El grupo te hace preguntas sobre cada miembro de tu familia y tú contestas.

Notice that two surnames are given for Anilú's grandparents. In some Spanish-speaking countries, the first surname is the father's, and the second one is the mother's. Anilú's full name is Anilú Guzmán Villa. If she marries someone whose first surname is Rodríguez, Anilú may add it to become Anilú Guzmán Villa de Rodríguez, or Sra. Rodríguez. This tradition is changing, however, and in many Spanish-speaking countries women do not change their names.

DULCE: ¿Quién es este señor?

ANILÚ: Es mi papá. Se enoja cuando Roberto le saca fotos. No le gusta salir en fotos. Dice que se ve muy gordo.

DULCE: ¿Qué hace tu papá?

ANILÚ: Es **arquitecto**. Diseña edificios para negocios.

When describing someone's profession, don't use an article as we would in English: **Es abogada** translates as *She is a lawyer.*

El policía means a single policeman. **La policía** can mean a single policewoman or the entire police force. You have to extract the correct meaning from context. Other professions whose meaning depends on the context and the article are: **el químico / la química, el físico / la física, el músico / la música, el matemático / la matemática, el guardia / la guardia.**

La mujer policía is also used for a single policewoman.

>> **Las profesiones y las carreras**

la abogada

el periodista

la médica

la artista

el bombero

la carpintera

la policía

el plomero

el arquitecto

el actor / la actriz *actor / actress*
el (la) asistente *assistant*
el (la) camarero(a) *waiter / waitress*
el (la) cocinero(a) *cook, chef*
el (la) contador(a) *accountant*
el (la) dentista *dentist*
el (la) dependiente *salesclerk*
el (la) director(a) de social media *director of social media*
el (la) diseñador(a) gráfico(a) *graphic designer*
el (la) dueño(a) de... *owner of. . .*
el (la) enfermero(a) *nurse*

el (la) gerente de... *manager of. . .*
el hombre / la mujer de negocios *businessman / businesswoman*
el (la) ingeniero(a) *engineer*
el (la) maestro(a) *teacher*
el (la) mecánico(a) *mechanic*
el (la) peluquero(a) *barber / hairdresser*
el (la) programador(a) *programmer*
el (la) secretario(a) *secretary*
el (la) trabajador(a) *worker*
el (la) veterinario(a) *veterinarian*

As of this printing, no established translation for social media has been agreed upon by Spanish speakers. Most simply use the English "social media."

ACTIVIDADES

5 **¿Qué hace?** Escoge la profesión más lógica para cada persona.

1. Alejandro trabaja en un hospital. Es…
2. Catalina trabaja en el teatro. Es…
3. Pedro trabaja en un restaurante. Es…
4. El señor Cortez trabaja en una escuela secundaria *(high school)*. Es…
5. Amelia trabaja en el centro de computación. Es…
6. Irene trabaja en un hospital para animales. Es…

a. cocinero(a)
b. veterinario(a)
c. enfermero(a)
d. actor / actriz
e. maestro(a)
f. programador(a)

6 **Quiere ser…** Tú y tu compañero(a) hablan de varios amigos. Tú le dices a tu compañero(a) qué es lo que estudia esa persona y tu compañero(a) te dice qué quiere ser esa persona.

MODELO   medicina
Tú: *Marcos estudia medicina.*
Compañero(a): *Quiere ser médico.*

1. contabilidad
2. administración de empresas
3. ingeniería
4. informática
5. diseño gráfico
6. arte
7. pedagogía
8. periodismo

7 **Presentaciones** Estás en la fiesta de un amigo. Él te presenta a varios miembros de su familia. Lee sus presentaciones. Luego, para cada persona, indica cuál es su relación con el narrador y su profesión.

1. Quiero presentarte a Antonio. Él es el hijo de mi tía Rosa. Antonio trabaja en el Hospital Garibaldi. Ayuda a las personas enfermas.

   Nombre: Antonio   *Relación:* _____ *Profesión:* _____

2. Te presento a Miranda. Miranda es la hija de mi tío Ricardo. Miranda enseña francés en el Colegio Del Valle.

   Nombre: Miranda   *Relación:* _____ *Profesión:* _____

3. Mira, te presento a Olga. Olga trabaja para el periódico *El Universal*. Olga es la esposa de mi hermano.

   Nombre: Olga   *Relación:* _____ *Profesión:* _____

4. Quiero presentarte a César. César es el hijo de mi hermano. César trabaja en una pizzería después del colegio.

   Nombre: César   *Relación:* _____ *Profesión:* _____

5. Éste es Raúl. Raúl es el hermano de mi padre. Él diseña casas y edificios.

   Nombre: Raúl   *Relación:* _____ *Profesión:* _____

6. Te presento al señor Domínguez, el padre de mi esposa. Él escribe software para una compañía multinacional.

   Nombre: señor Domínguez   *Relación:* _____ *Profesión:* _____

8 **¿Qué quieres ser?** En grupos de tres, hablen sobre sus planes para el futuro.

MODELO Tú: *¿Qué profesión te interesa?*
Compañero(a): *¿A mí? Yo quiero ser director de social media.*
Tú: *¿Dónde quieres trabajar?*
Compañero(a): *Quiero trabajar aquí, en Los Ángeles.*

9 **El español y las profesiones** En Estados Unidos, hay muchas oportunidades profesionales para personas que hablan español. Aquí hay algunas carreras que utilizan el español.

- abogado(a)
- académico(a)
- enfermero(a)
- intérprete
- médico(a)

- periodista
- policía
- profesor(a) o maestro(a) de español
- secretario(a) bilingüe
- trabajador(a) social

Con un(a) compañero(a) de clase, contesten las siguientes preguntas.

1. ¿Te interesa alguna de estas carreras? ¿Por qué? ¿Crees que poder hablar español es importante para tu futuro?

2. En Europa, los estudiantes de colegio aprenden inglés y muchas veces otro idioma además de su lengua nativa. ¿Crees que es buena idea? ¿Por qué? ¿Crees que los estadounidenses deben aprender otro idioma además del inglés? ¿Por qué?

¡Fíjate!   Las profesiones y el mundo

Gracias a la tecnología, el mundo va cambiando *(is changing)* muy rápido. Algunas profesiones que no existían ayer, existen hoy. Antes, más profesiones eran locales, es decir, consistían en lo que se podía hacer dentro de *(consisted of what could be done within)* la comunidad: policía, bombero, dentista, doctor, profesor. Ahora es posible elegir una profesión que puede tener un impacto global. ¿En qué campos existen profesiones internacionales?

Marvin Newman/Photolibrary

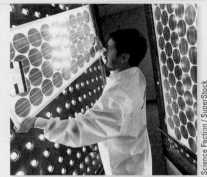

Science Faction / SuperStock

Asistencia sanitaria internacional	*International health care*
Banca internacional	*International banking*
Consultoría de negocios	*Consulting*
Derecho internacional	*International law*
Ingeniería multinacional	*International engineering*
Mercadotecnia internacional	*International marketing*
Política exterior	*Foreign policy*
Programas de conservación ambiental	*Environmental programs*
Servicios financieros	*Financial services*
Tecnología ambiental	*"Green" technology*
Telecomunicaciones	*Telecommunications*

Práctica   Ve a Internet y busca tres profesiones internacionales que te interesan. ¿En qué campo están? ¿Qué puedes hacer en tus estudios para empezar a prepararte para cada profesión?

With some professions, there is a lot of confusion about how to specify gender, especially for traditionally male professions like **piloto, bombero, ingeniero, general, mecánico, plomero**. The ambiguity is also due to the number of options for specifying gender. Some professions change the ending, like **el actor** and **la actriz; el maestro** and **la maestra; el alcalde** *(mayor)* and **la alcaldesa**. Other professions simply change the article, with no change to the noun, like **el gerente** and **la gerente, el dentista** and **la dentista**. Sometimes, the word **mujer** or **señora** is used to specify the gender: **la señora juez** *(judge)*, **la mujer policía**.

>> Vocabulario útil 3

ANILÚ: Mamá, ¿está Roberto por allí? Necesito hablar con él.

MAMÁ: No puede venir al teléfono. Se está bañando.

ANILÚ: ¿Está bañándose? ¿A esta hora?

MAMÁ: Acaba de regresar de su partido de fútbol. ¡Ay! ¡No hay ni **toallas** ni **jabón** en el baño! Me tengo que ir. Tengo que llevarle a tu hermano una toalla, el jabón y el **champú**…

>> **En el baño** *In the bathroom*

la toalla (de mano)

el cepillo de dientes

el champú

el desodorante

la máquina de afeitar

el jabón

la pasta de dientes

la rasuradora

el maquillaje

el peine

el cepillo

ACTIVIDADES

10 **¿Qué necesitan comprar?** Según la situación, ¿qué necesita comprar cada persona?

MODELO *Él necesita comprar champú.*

1.

2.

3.

4.

5.

6.

11 **El HiperMercado** Tú y tu hermano(a) ven un anuncio para el HiperMercado en el periódico. Tú le dices qué quieres comprar y él o ella te dice cuánto dinero necesitas para comprar ese artículo.

(**¡OJO!** *Dollars* = **dólares** y *cents* = **centavos**.)

MODELO Tú: *¿Quiero comprar un cepillo y un peine.*
Hermano(a): *Necesitas tres dólares y setenta y nueve centavos para comprar el cepillo y el peine.*

> Unlike grocery stores, which focus mostly on food items, **hipermercados** in Spanish-speaking countries are similar to supermarkets, but tend to sell an even wider range of household products.

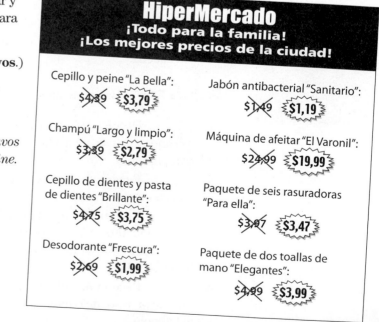

HiperMercado
¡Todo para la familia!
¡Los mejores precios de la ciudad!

Cepillo y peine "La Bella":
~~$4,39~~ **$3,79**

Jabón antibacterial "Sanitario":
~~$1,49~~ **$1,19**

Champú "Largo y limpio":
~~$3,39~~ **$2,79**

Máquina de afeitar "El Varonil":
~~$24,99~~ **$19,99**

Cepillo de dientes y pasta de dientes "Brillante":
~~$4,75~~ **$3,75**

Paquete de seis rasuradoras "Para ella":
~~$3,97~~ **$3,47**

Desodorante "Frescura":
~~$2,69~~ **$1,99**

Paquete de dos toallas de mano "Elegantes":
~~$4,99~~ **$3,99**

A ver

ESTRATEGIA

Listening for the main idea

A good way to organize your viewing of authentic video is to focus on getting the main idea of the segment (or of each of its parts). Don't try to understand every word; just try to get the gist of each scene. Later, with the help of the textbook activities, some of the other details of the segment will emerge.

Antes de ver Mira las fotos a la izquierda *(on the left)*. Haz correspondencia entre *(Match)* las fotos y los diálogos.

ⓐ

ⓑ

ⓒ

_____ 1. Dulce: ¿Qué hace tu papá?
      Anilú: Es arquitecto. Diseña edificios para negocios.

_____ 2. Mamá: Bueno, pero siempre hay que hacer tiempo para llamar a tu mamá.
      Anilú: Sí, mamá, está bien. Perdóname.

_____ 3. Anilú: Mira, ven a ver.
      Dulce: ¿Qué es?

▶ **Ver** Ahora mira el video para el **Capítulo 5.** Trata de entender la idea principal de cada escena.

Después de ver Haz correspondencia entre las escenas y las ideas principales.

1. _____ **Escena 1:** Anilú está mirando *(is looking at)* la computadora.

2. _____ **Escena 2:** Anilú habla con su mama.

3. _____ **Escena 3:** Anilú y Dulce miran una foto en la impresora.

4. _____ **Escena 4:** Roberto llama a Anilú.

5. _____ **Escena 5:** Anilú mira la foto de la fiesta de cumpleaños del abuelo.

a. La mamá de Anilú dice que ella nunca la llama.

b. A Anilú no le gusta la foto pero Roberto cree que es muy cómica.

c. Roberto quiere saber *(to know)* si a Anilú le gustan las fotos.

d. Anilú dice *(says)* que tiene unas fotos digitales.

e. Ven una foto del papá de Anilú.

Voces del mundo hispano

En el video para este capítulo Mirna, José y Aura hablan de las profesiones y de sus familias. Lee las siguientes oraciones. Después mira el video una o más veces para decir si las oraciones son ciertas (**C**) o falsas (**F**).

1. Mirna estudia para ser diseñadora gráfica.
2. José ya es paralegal y estudia para ser abogado.
3. Una de las hermanas de Mirna trabaja en administración de empresas.
4. Aura tiene un hermano y dos hermanas.
5. Una hermana de Aura es contadora.
6. José tiene seis miembros de su familia en Estados Unidos.

Voces de Estados Unidos

Track 14

Gloria G. Rodríguez, fundadora de Avance

❝ Essentially, to be Hispanic is to value children . . . Rarely are children as welcomed and visible with adults as in the Latino culture. Indeed, los hijos son la riqueza de los padres, son nuestro gran tesoro. ❞

La doctora Gloria G. Rodríguez es fundadora de Avance, una organización nacional que ayuda a familias latinas pobres con niños pequeños. En su libro, *Raising Nuestros Niños: Bringing Up Latino Children in a Bicultural World*, Rodríguez explica la filosofía de Avance así:

Los padres tienen la esperanza y el deseo, hope and desire, that their children succeed, and that they feel un gran orgullo, a great sense of pride, when they do. Esta esperanza y orgullo de los padres, this hope and pride, become tremendous driving forces for Latino parents (p. 3).

Esta méxicoamericana de orígenes muy pobres es ganadora de muchos premios y reconocimientos por su labor con familias hispanas.

¿Y tú? ¿Es importante tu familia en tu vida estudiantil? ¿Qué papel juega la familia en la educación de los niños?

¡Prepárate!

Describing daily activities: Irregular-yo verbs in the present indicative, saber vs. conocer, and the personal a

Cómo usarlo

1. You have already learned the present indicative tense of many verbs. These include regular **-ar, -er,** and **-ir** verbs (**hablar, comer, vivir,** etc.), some irregular verbs (**ser, tener, ir**), and some stem-changing verbs (**pensar, poder, dormir,** etc.).

2. Now you will learn some verbs that are regular in all forms of the present indicative except the **yo** form. Like other verbs in the present indicative tense, these verbs can be used to say what you routinely do, what you are doing at the moment, or what you plan to do in the future.

Todos los días **salgo** para la universidad a las ocho.	*Every day **I leave** for the university at 8:00.*
Ahora mismo, **pongo** mis libros en la mochila y **digo** "hasta luego" a mi compañera de cuarto.	*Right now, **I put / I'm putting** my books in my backpack and **I say / I'm saying**, "See you later" to my roommate.*
Esta noche, **traigo** mis libros a casa otra vez y **hago** la tarea.	*Tonight, **I bring / I'll bring** my books home again and **I do / I'll do** my homework.*

Cómo formarlo

Irregular-yo verbs

Many irregular-**yo** verbs in the present indicative fall into several recognizable categories. Others have to be learned individually.

1. -go endings:

hacer	*to make; to do*	**hago**, haces, hace, hacemos, hacéis, hacen
poner	*to put*	**pongo**, pones, pone, ponemos, ponéis, ponen
salir	*to leave, to go out (with)*	**salgo**, sales, sale, salimos, salís, salen
traer	*to bring*	**traigo**, traes, trae, traemos, traéis, traen

2. -zco endings:

conducir	*to drive; to conduct*	**conduzco**, conduces, conduce, conducimos, conducís, conducen
conocer	*to know a person; to be familiar with*	**conozco**, conoces, conoce, conocemos, conocéis, conocen
traducir	*to translate*	**traduzco**, traduces, traduce, traducimos, traducís, traducen

Conducir is used more frequently in Spain to talk about driving. In most of Latin America, the verbs **manejar** and **guiar** (both regular -ar verbs) are used. (**Guiar** uses an accent on the i in these forms: **guío, guías, guía, guían.**)

3. Other irregular-**yo** verbs:

dar	*to give*	**doy**, das, da, damos, dais, dan
oír	*to hear*	**oigo**, oyes, oye, oímos, oís, oyen
saber	*to know a fact;* *to know how to*	**sé**, sabes, sabe, sabemos, sabéis, saben
ver	*to see*	**veo**, ves, ve, vemos, veis, ven

Note that **oír** requires a **y** in the **tú, él / ella / Ud.,** and **ellos / ellas / Uds.** forms.

4. Two irregular-**yo** verbs (-**go** verbs) with a stem change:

decir	*to say, to tell*	**digo**, dices, dice, decimos, decís, dicen
venir	*to come, to attend*	**vengo**, vienes, viene, venimos, venís, vienen

5. Remember that most of these verbs are irregular only in the **yo** form. Otherwise, they follow the rules for regular -**ar**, -**er**, and -**ir** verbs that you have already learned. **Oír** uses the regular endings but includes a spelling change: the addition of **y** to all forms except the **yo** form. **Decir** and **venir** also have a stem change in addition to the irregular-**yo** form, but they still use -**ir** present-tense endings.

Saber vs. conocer

Saber and **conocer** both mean *to know*. It's important to know when to use each one.

- Use **saber** to say that you know a fact or information, or that you know how to do something.

Eduardo **sabe** hablar alemán, jugar tenis y bailar flamenco. Además **sabe** dónde están todos los restaurantes buenos de la ciudad.	*Eduardo **knows how** to speak German, play tennis, and dance flamenco. He also **knows** where all the good restaurants in the city are.*

- Use **conocer** to say that you know a person or are familiar with a thing.

—¿**Conocen** a Sandra?	*Do you **know** Sandra?*
—No, pero **conocemos** a su hermana.	*No, but we **know** her sister.*
—¿**Conoces** bien Tegucigalpa?	*Do you **know** Tegucigalpa well?*
—Sí, pero no **conozco** las otras ciudades de Honduras.	*Yes, but I don't **know** the other cities in Honduras.*

The personal a

When you use **conocer** to say that you know a person, notice that you use the preposition **a** before the noun referring to the person. This preposition is known as the personal **a** in Spanish and it must be used whenever a person receives the action of any verb (not just **conocer**). It has no equivalent in English.

Conocemos **a** Nina y **a** Roberto.	*We know Nina and Roberto.*
¿Ves **a** tus amigos frecuentemente?	*Do you see your friends frequently?*

© Cengage Learning 2013

Algún día vas a tener hijos y entonces vas a **saber** cómo es.

One way to remember the difference between **saber** and **conocer** is that **saber** is usually followed by either a verb or a phrase, while **conocer** is often followed by a noun and is never followed by an infinitive.

The personal **a** can also be used with pets: **Adoro a mi perro.**

In **Chapter 3** you learned that a + **el** = **al**. The personal **a** is no exception: **Veo al profesor.**

ACTIVIDADES

1 **¿Sí o no?** Lee las oraciones y decide si requieren la **a** personal o no. Añade la **a** personal si es necesaria o marca con una **X** si no es necesaria.

1. Veo _____ mis hermanos todos los días.
2. Hago mi tarea con _____ ellos.
3. Les digo las noticias de casa _____ ellos también.
4. Oigo _____ sus comentarios sobre la universidad.
5. Conozco _____ muchos de sus amigos.
6. Conduzco el auto cuando visito _____ mi familia.

2 **La mamá de Anilú** La mamá de Anilú le describe un día normal a una amiga. Da su descripción desde su punto de vista *(viewpoint)*.

1. salir del trabajo a las cinco
2. generalmente, traer trabajo a casa
3. cuando llego a casa, venir muy cansada
4. hacer la cena *(dinner)* a las siete
5. poner la mesa *(set the table)* antes de hacer la cena
6. cuando la cena está preparada, decir "todo está listo"
7. conocer a mis hijos muy bien
8. saber que tengo que llamarlos varias veces
9. por fin, oír a los niños apagar la tele
10. dar las gracias por otro día más o menos normal

3 **¿Sabes…?** Con un(a) compañero(a), formen preguntas con las siguientes frases. Túrnense para hacerse las preguntas. Luego, inventen nuevas preguntas usando el verbo en cada frase y háganse esas preguntas.

MODELO conducir para llegar a la universidad
    Tú: *¿Conduces para llegar a la universidad?*
    Compañero(a): *No, no conduzco para llegar a la universidad.*
    Tú: *¿Conduces todos los días?*
    Compañero(a): *No, conduzco tres días por semana.*

1. conocer al (a la) presidente de la universidad
2. dar tu contraseña a tus amigos
3. decir siempre la verdad
4. hacer la tarea puntualmente
5. saber escribir programas para los teléfonos inteligentes
6. salir frecuentemente con amigos
7. traducir poemas del inglés al español
8. traer la computadora portátil a la clase
9. venir cansado(a) o aburrido(a) de las clases
10. ver televisión por la mañana, la tarde o la noche

4 **¿Saber o conocer?** Con un(a) compañero(a), túrnense para hacer las siguientes preguntas. La persona que hace las preguntas tiene que decidir entre los verbos **saber** o **conocer**.

MODELO ¿(Saber / Conocer / Conocer a) hablar español?
Tú: *¿Sabes hablar español?*
Compañero(a): *Sí, sé hablar español.*

1. ¿(Saber / Conocer / Conocer a) el (la) compañero(a) de cuarto de…?
2. ¿(Saber / Conocer / Conocer a) Nueva York, París o Londres?
3. ¿(Saber / Conocer / Conocer a) tocar el violín?
4. ¿(Saber / Conocer / Conocer a) Honduras?
5. ¿(Saber / Conocer / Conocer a) preparar comida hondureña o salvadoreña?

5 **Sé y conozco** Escribe cinco cosas que **sabes** hacer. Luego escribe el nombre de cinco personas o lugares que **conoces**. Intercambia tu lista con un(a) compañero(a). Tu compañero(a) tiene que informarle a la clase lo que tú **sabes** y **conoces** y tú tienes que hacer lo mismo con la lista de tu compañero(a).

MODELO Tu lista: *Sé jugar tenis.*
Conozco a muchas personas que juegan tenis.
Tu compañero(a): *Javier sabe jugar tenis.*
Conoce a muchas personas que juegan tenis.

6 **Cuestionario** Primero, escribe tus respuestas a las preguntas. Luego, en grupos de tres, háganse las preguntas del siguiente cuestionario. Si quieren, pueden añadir algunas preguntas al cuestionario. Cada uno en el grupo debe contestar cada pregunta.

1. **Tu horario**
   ¿Cuándo haces ejercicio?
   ¿Cuándo haces la tarea?

2. **Tu vida social**
   ¿Sales por la noche? ¿Adónde vas?
   ¿Con quién sales los fines de semana?

3. **Tu medio de transporte preferido**
   ¿Tienes coche? ¿Conduces a la universidad?
   ¿Conduces todos los días o usas otro medio de transporte?

4. **Tu tiempo libre**
   ¿Sabes jugar algún deporte?
   ¿Sabes tocar un instrumento? ¿Cuál?

5. **¿Conoces el mundo?**
   ¿Conoces los países de Latinoamérica? ¿Cuáles?
   ¿Conoces África o Asia?

Gramática útil 2

Describing daily activities: Reflexive verbs

Ya es hora de
despertarse
a una nueva
clase de hotel
de negocios.

Hotel Calidad Ejecutiva
www.calidadejecutiva.com 1-800-444-4444
7800 Avenida Norte, San Salvador 2901-8720

This ad for a business
hotel in El Salvador
uses a reflexive verb.
What is it and what
does it mean?

The reflexive pronoun and
verb must always match
the subject of the
sentence: **Nosotros nos
bañamos, Ellos se afeitan,
Mateo se lava,** etc.

Cómo usarlo

1. So far, you have learned to use Spanish verbs to say what actions people are doing or to describe people and things.

Elena **habla** por teléfono.	*Elena **talks** on the phone.*
Tu hermano **está** cansado.	*Your brother **is** tired.*

2. Spanish has another category of verbs, called *reflexive* verbs, where the action of the verb *reflects back* on the person who is doing the action. When you use reflexive verbs in Spanish, they are often translated in English as *with* or *to myself, yourself, himself, herself, ourselves, yourselves, themselves.*

Lidia **se maquilla.**	*Lidia **puts makeup on (herself).***
Antes de ir a clase, yo **me ducho,** **me visto** y **me peino.**	*Before going to class, **I shower, get dressed,** and **comb my hair.***

3. Notice how a reflexive verb is always used with a reflexive pronoun. These pronouns always match the subject of the sentence. The action of the verb *reflects back* on the person when the pronoun is used.

Yo me acuesto a las once.	*I go to bed (put myself to bed) at eleven.*
Tú te despiertas a las diez los fines de semana.	*You get up (wake yourself up) at ten on the weekends.*
Nosotros nos bañamos antes de salir de casa.	*We bathe (ourselves) before we leave the house.*
Ellos se afeitan todos los días.	*They shave (themselves) every day.*

4. Most reflexive verbs can also be used without the reflexive pronoun to express non-reflexive actions, that is, actions that are performed on someone other than oneself.

Mateo **se baña** todos los días.	*Mateo **bathes** every day.*
Mateo **baña** a su perro.	*Mateo **bathes (washes)** his dog.*

5. Reflexive pronouns can also be used to indicate *reciprocal actions.*

Leo y Ali **se cortan** el pelo.	*Leo and Ali **cut each other's** hair.*

Cómo formarlo

LO BÁSICO

- A *reflexive verb* is one in which the action described reflects back on the subject.
- A *reflexive pronoun* is a pronoun that refers back to the subject of the sentence. English reflexive pronouns are *myself, herself, ourselves,* etc.

1. You conjugate reflexive verbs the same way you would any other verb. The only difference is that you must always include the reflexive pronoun.

2. Here is the reflexive verb **lavarse** conjugated in the present indicative tense.

lavarse *(to wash oneself)*	
yo	**me lavo**
tú	**te lavas**
Ud. / él / ella	**se lava**
nosotros(as)	**nos lavamos**
vosotros(as)	**os laváis**
Uds. / ellos / ellas	**se lavan**

3. The only difference in the way that reflexive and non-reflexive verbs are conjugated is the addition of the reflexive pronoun to the verb form. Verbs that are irregular or stem-changing when used non-reflexively have the same irregularities or stem changes when used with a reflexive pronoun.

Me despierto a las seis y media. *I wake (myself) up at 6: 30.*
Despierto a mi esposo a las siete. *I wake my husband up at 7: 00.*

4. When you use a reflexive verb in its infinitive form, the reflexive pronoun may attach at the end of the infinitive (most commonly) or go at the beginning of the entire verb phrase.

Voy a acostarme a las once. OR: **Me voy a acostar** a las once.
Necesito acostarme a las once. **Me necesito acostar** a las once.
Tengo que acostarme a las once. **Me tengo que acostar** a las once.

Notice that with **gustar** (and similar verbs), the reflexive pronoun *must* be attached at the end of the infinitive.

Me gusta acostarme a las once.

> Remember that when you use a reflexive verb as an infinitive, you still need to change the pronoun to match the subject of the sentence: **Voy a acostarme a las once, pero tú vas a acostarte a medianoche.**

5. Here are some common reflexive verbs, many of which refer to daily routine. Many reflexive verbs have a stem change, which is indicated in parenthesis.

acostarse (ue) *to go to bed*	**levantarse** *to get up*
afeitarse *to shave oneself*	**maquillarse** *to put on makeup*
bañarse *to take a bath*	**peinarse** *to brush / comb one's hair*
cepillarse el pelo *to brush one's hair*	**ponerse (la ropa)** *to put on (clothing)*
cepillarse los dientes *to brush one's teeth*	**prepararse** *to get ready*
despertarse (ie) *to wake up*	**quitarse (la ropa)** *to take off (clothing)*
ducharse *to take a shower*	**secarse el pelo** *to dry one's hair*
lavarse *to wash oneself*	**sentarse (ie)** *to sit down*
lavarse el pelo *to wash one's hair*	**vestirse (i)** *to get dressed*
lavarse los dientes *to brush one's teeth*	

6. Some Spanish verbs are used with reflexive pronouns to emphasize a change in state or emotion. Spanish has many more verbs that are used this way than English does. Note that some of these verbs (**casarse, comprometerse,** etc.) are usually used to express reciprocal actions, due to the nature of their meaning.

casarse *to get married*	**irse** *to leave, to go away*
comprometerse *to get engaged*	**pelearse** *to have a fight*
despedirse (i) *to say goodbye*	**preocuparse** *to worry*
divertirse (ie) *to have fun*	**quejarse** *to complain*
divorciarse *to get divorced*	**reírse (i)** *to laugh*
dormirse (ue) *to fall asleep*	**relajarse** *to relax*
enamorarse *to fall in love*	**reunirse** *to meet, to get together*
enfermarse *to get sick*	**separarse** *to separate*

7. Here are some common words and phrases to use with these verbs.

a veces *sometimes*	**siempre** *always*
antes *before*	**todas las semanas** *every week*
después *after*	**todos los días** *every day*
luego *later*	**...veces al día /** *. . . times a day /*
nunca *never*	**por semana** *per week*

ACTIVIDADES

MODELO

🔊 **7** **Necesito…** Para vernos y sentirnos bien, todos tenemos que hacer ciertas cosas antes o después de participar en ciertas actividades. Escucha las descripciones y escoge el dibujo que le corresponde a cada descripción.

Track 15

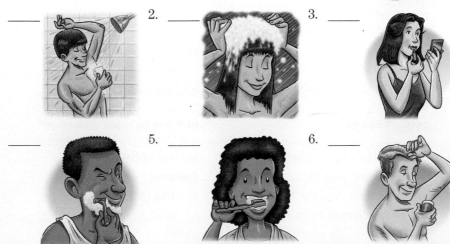

1. _____   2. _____   3. _____

4. _____   5. _____   6. _____

8 **De visita** Estás de visita en la casa de tu compañero(a) y quieres saber más de la rutina diaria de él o ella y de su familia. Hazle las preguntas de la lista y si quieres, también inventa otras.

MODELO Tú: *¿A qué hora (acostarse) tus padres?*
Tú: *¿A qué hora se acuestan tus padres?*
Compañero(a): *Mis padres se acuestan a las diez o las once de la noche.*

1. ¿Tú (lavarse) el pelo todos los días?
2. ¿Cuántas veces por semana (afeitarse) tu abuelo?
3. ¿(Despertarse) tarde o temprano tu madre?
4. ¿(Ducharse) por la mañana o por la noche tu hermano?
5. ¿(Maquillarse) tu hermana antes de salir para la universidad?
6. ¿A qué hora (acostarse) tu compañero(a) de cuarto?
7. ¿A qué hora (levantarse) tu padre?
8. ¿(Peinarse) antes de salir para el colegio tu primo?
9. ¿Cuántas veces por día (lavarse) los dientes tú y tus hermanos?

9 **La telenovela** Miguel y Marta son los protagonistas de una telenovela famosa. Tú eres el (la) guionista *(script writer)* y tienes que escribir una descripción del desarrollo de su relación. Sigue el modelo.

MODELO divertirse en la fiesta de unos amigos
Miguel y Marta se divierten en la fiesta de unos amigos.

1. enamorarse después de un mes
2. comprometerse después de un año
3. casarse en la casa de los padres de Marta
4. pelearse frecuentemente
5. quejarse mucho a sus amigos
6. separarse por seis meses
7. divorciarse después de dos años de matrimonio
8. despedirse en el aeropuerto
9. irse a diferentes regiones del país
10. por fin reunirse

10 **Preguntas personales** Tú y tu compañero(a) quieren saber más sobre sus vidas. Háganse las siguientes preguntas. Luego, inventen cinco preguntas más que usen los verbos de la rutina diaria o los otros verbos reflexivos en las páginas 177–178.

1. ¿A qué hora te acuestas durante la semana? ¿Los fines de semana?
2. ¿A qué hora te levantas durante la semana? ¿Los fines de semana?
3. ¿Te preocupas mucho por tus estudios?
4. ¿Cuántas veces por semana te reúnes con tus amigos?
5.–9. ¿...?

Gramática útil 3

Describing actions in progress: The present progressive tense

Cómo usarlo

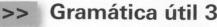

Las fotos. ¿**Estás viendo** las fotos?

1. The present progressive tense is used in Spanish to describe actions that are in progress at the moment of speaking. It is equivalent to the *is / are + -ing* structure in English.

En este momento **estamos llamando** a los abuelos.	*Right now, **we are calling** the (our) grandparents.*
Están comiendo ahora.	***They are eating** right now.*

2. Note that the present progressive tense is used *much* more frequently in English than it is in Spanish. Whereas in English it is used to describe future plans, in Spanish the present indicative or the **ir** + **a** + infinitive structure is used instead.

Salimos con la familia este viernes.	***We are going out** with the family this Friday.*
Vamos a salir con la familia este viernes.	***We are going to go out** with the family this Friday.*

3. Use the present progressive in Spanish only to describe actions in which people are engaged at the moment. Do not use it to describe routine ongoing activities (use the present indicative), to describe generalized action (use the infinitive), or to describe future actions.

Right now:	No puedo hablar. **Estamos estudiando.**	*I can't talk. **We're studying** (right now).*
BUT:		
Routine:	**Estudio** español, biología, historia e informática.	***I am studying / I study** Spanish, biology, history, and computer science.*
Generalized action:	**Estudiar** es importante.	***Studying** is important.*
Future:	**Estudio** con Mario el lunes.	***I will study** with Mario on Monday.*

Cómo formarlo

LO BÁSICO

A *present participle* is the verb form that expresses a continuing or ongoing action. In English, present participles end in *-ing: laughing, reading.*

1. Form the present progressive tense by using the present indicative forms of the verb **estar** (which you learned in **Chapter 4**) and the present participle.

> **estoy / estás / está / estamos / estáis / están** + present participle

2. Here's how to form the present participle of regular **-ar, -er**, and **-ir** verbs.

-ar verbs	-er / -ir verbs
Remove the **-ar** from the infinitive and add **-ando**.	Remove the **-er** / **-ir** from the infinitivo and add **-iendo**.
caminar → **caminando**	ver → **viendo**
	escribir → **escribiendo**

Estamos caminando al centro.   *We're walking downtown.*
Estoy viendo la televisión.   *I'm watching television.*
Chali **está escribiendo** su trabajo.   *Chali is writing her paper.*

3. A few present participles are irregular.

leer: **leyendo**   oír: **oyendo**

4. All **-ir** stem-changing verbs show a stem change in their present participle as well.

e → i			
despedirse	**despidiéndose**	reírse	**riéndose**
divertirse	**divirtiéndose**	repetir	**repitiendo**
pedir	**pidiendo**	servir	**sirviendo**
o → u			
dormir	**durmiendo**	morir	**muriendo**

5. As you may have noticed in the list above, to form the present participle of reflexive verbs, you may attach the reflexive pronoun to the end of the present participle, or place it before the entire verb phrase, the same as when you use reflexive verbs in the infinitive. Note that when the pronoun is attached, the new present participle form requires an accent to maintain the correct pronunciation.

Lina **está levantándose** ahora mismo. /   *Lina is getting up right now.*
Lina **se está levantando** ahora mismo.

Estoy divirtiéndome mucho. /   *I'm having a lot of fun.*
Me estoy divirtiendo mucho.

🔊
Track 16

11 Preparaciones La familia González va a una boda *(wedding)* y todos están preparándose. Escucha la conversación telefónica de un miembro de la familia y escoge la oración que dice qué está haciendo cada persona mencionada.

MODELO _____ La prima está peinándose. / _____ La prima está riéndose.

1. _____ El padre está vistiéndose. / _____ El padre está afeitándose.

2. _____ La madre está duchándose. / _____ La madre está bañándose.

3. _____ El hermano está lavándose los dientes. / _____ El hermano está lavándose las manos.

4. _____ La hermana está secándose el pelo. / _____ La hermana está sentándose.

5. _____ Los abuelos están vistiéndose. / _____ Los abuelos están bañándose.

6. _____ Las tías están cepillándose el pelo. / _____ Las tías están maquillándose.

12 ¿Qué están haciendo? Básandote en los dibujos, pregúntale a un(a) compañero(a) qué está haciendo la persona del dibujo. Menciona la profesión de la persona también.

MODELO camarero (servir la comida)
Tú: *¿Qué está haciendo el camarero?*
Compañero(a): *Está sirviendo la comida.*

1. la profesora 2. la médica 3. la directora de social media 4. el cocinero 5. la asistente 6. la actriz

© Cengage Learning 2013

13 ¡Imagínense! Trabaja con un(a) compañero(a) de clase. Juntos hagan una lista de diez personas famosas. Luego, digan qué (en su opinión) están haciendo en este momento. Escriban por lo menos dos frases para cada persona. ¡Sean creativos!

14 ¡Chismosos! Ahora, intercambien sus frases de la **Actividad 13** con las de otra pareja. Juntos escriban una columna de chismes *(gossip)* para una revista semanal. Traten de escribir de una manera interesante y descriptiva. Pueden incluir dibujos de las personas, si quieren.

Sonrisas

👥 **Expresión** Trabaja con un(a) compañero(a) de clase para imaginar cómo es el día de un(a) presidente de una compañía internacional (o de otra profesión). ¿Cuál es su rutina diaria? Hagan un horario de un día típico.

MODELO *Son las ocho de la mañana. Está preparándose para una reunión.*

Honduras

Robert English/Shutterstock

Información general ▶

Nombre oficial: República de Honduras

Población: 7.989.415

Capital: Tegucigalpa (f. 1762) (1.200.000 hab.)

Otras ciudades importantes: San Pedro Sula (640.000 hab.), El Progreso (90.000 hab.)

Moneda: lempira

Idiomas: español (oficial), idiomas amerindios

Mapa de Honduras: Apéndice D

Christian Wilkinson/Shutterstock

Vale saber...

- Honduras tiene una gran historia de pueblos indígenas, entre ellos los lencas, los garífunas, los miskitos, los chortis, los pech, los tolupanes, los tawahkas y los mayas.

- En su cuarto y último viaje al Nuevo Mundo, Cristóbal Colón llega a las costas de Honduras en 1502. La conquista española de Honduras empieza dos décadas después, bajo órdenes de Hernán Cortés, y termina en 1537, con la muerte *(death)* de Lempira, guerrero héroe de orígenes maya-lenca.

- Copán, un centro gubernamental y ceremonial de la antigua civilización maya, se encuentra a orillas *(is located on the shores)* del río Copán, cerca de la frontera con Guatemala. Se considera uno de los sitios arqueológicos más importantes del Período Clásico.

- Honduras basa su economía en la agricultura, especialmente en las plantaciones de banana, cuya comercialización empezó *(began)* en 1889 con la fundación de Standard Fruit Company.

El Salvador

Información general

Nombre oficial: República de El Salvador

Población: 6.052.064

Capital: San Salvador (f. 1524) (400.000 hab.)

Otras ciudades importantes: San Miguel (250.000 hab.), Santa Ana (250.000 hab.)

Moneda: dólar estadounidense

Idiomas: español (oficial), náhuatl, otras lenguas amerindias

Mapa de El Salvador: Apéndice D

Alvaro Calero/iStockphoto

Vale saber...

- El Salvador es el país más pequeño de Centroamérica pero el más denso en población.
- Durante la época precolombina, El Salvador fue habitado por los pipiles y los lencas.
- Joya de Cerén, un Monumento de la Humanidad de la UNESCO en El Salvador, es un descubrimiento de gran importancia. Es un pueblo *(town)* entero sepultado en el siglo VII por una erupción volcánica. Como una Pompeya americana, Joya de Cerén es de inestimable valor arqueológico e histórico.
- Entre 1980 y 1990, El Salvador vivió en guerra civil. Durante esos años, muchos salvadoreños emigraron a Estados Unidos.

Luis Galdamez/Reuters/Landov

La mecatrónica

Courtesy of Unitec

En la Universidad Tecnológica Centroamericana (Unitec) de Honduras, puedes hacer la licenciatura en Mecatrónica, un curso de estudio que combina la mecánica, la electrónica y la informática. ¿Qué aprendes si estudias mecatrónica? Cómo diseñar y construir productos mecatrónicos, como los instrumentos médicos, las cámaras fotográficas, los 'chips' que automatizan a las máquinas, aparatos biomédicos y productos innovadores en varios campos como la bioingeniería. ¿Tienes aptitud para la mecatrónica?

COMEDICA, una cooperativa médica

Hace cuatro décadas *(four decades ago)*, once médicos salvadoreños deciden hacer algo revolucionario para pagar sus costos educativos. Con 100 colones de cada uno, abren una cooperativa para obtener crédito y ahorrar *(save)*. Hoy día, COMEDICA cuenta con $27.12 millones. Entre sus clientes hay médicos, odontólogos, psicólogos, químicos, farmacéuticos y enfermeros. Muchos médicos han adquirido *(have gotten)* sus casas, sus vehículos, equipo para sus clínicas y también sus estudios posgrados con la ayuda de COMEDICA. Los once médicos ilustran el dicho "¡Sí se puede!"

Photo Courtesy of COMEDICA

>> En resumen

La información general

Di a qué país o países se refiere cada oración.

1. Un sitio arqueológico muy importante se encuentra en este país.
2. Las plantaciones de banana son una parte importante de la economía de este país.
3. Es el país más pequeño de Centroamérica.
4. Lempira es un gran héroe de este país.
5. El pueblo indígena de los lencas habita este país.
6. Este país pasó por *(underwent)* una guerra civil que duró *(lasted)* diez años.

El tema de las profesiones

1. ¿Qué áreas de estudio combina la mecatrónica?
2. ¿Qué productos aprendes a diseñar y construir en la mecatrónica?
3. ¿Quién empezó *(started)* la cooperativa COMEDICA?
4. ¿Qué dicho ilustra las acciones de los once médicos salvadoreños?

¿QUIERES SABER MÁS?

Revisa y rellena la tabla que empezaste al principio del capítulo. Luego, escoge un tema para investigar en línea y prepárate para compartir la información con la clase. También puedes escoger de las palabras clave a continuación o en **www.cengagebrain.com**.

Palabras clave: (Honduras) los mayas, Lempira, los garífunas, los Miskito, José Antonio Velásques**; (El Salvador)** Tazumal, Acuerdos de Paz de Chapultepec, Óscar Arnulfo Romero, Claribel Alegría

Tú en el mundo hispano Para explorar oportunidades de usar el español para estudiar o hacer trabajos voluntarios o aprendizajes en Honduras y El Salvador, sigue los enlaces en **www.cengagebrain.com**.

Ritmos del mundo hispano Sigue los enlaces en **www.cengagebrain.com** para escuchar música de Honduras y El Salvador.

A leer

ESTRATEGIA

Skimming for the main idea

When reading authentic materials, it's more important to focus on getting the main idea than to understand every word. Skimming is a reading strategy that helps you get the main idea of each paragraph. When you skim, you read quickly, looking for key words and phrases. Together, these techniques give you the main idea of each paragraph.

1 Mira la información sobre la cultura garífuna y completa las oraciones a continuación.

Jim Whitmers

Los garífunas son de ascendencia africana, arauaca e indio-caribe. Sus antepasados, exiliados de la isla de San Vicente en 1797, viajaron *(they traveled)* a la costa Atlántica de Belice y Honduras y a las islas de Barlovento de Nicaragua. Viven allí y en otras regiones cercanas *(close)* con la mayor parte de su cultura intacta, incluso su música y arte tradicionales.

1. La cultura garífuna tiene aproximadamente (150 / 220 / 250) años.
2. Los garífunas son de origen (africano / español / inglés).
3. Los garífunas todavía tienen su propia (país / cultura / presidente).

2 Trabaja con un(a) compañero(a) para hacer correspondencia entre las frases de la lectura a la izquierda y sus equivalentes en inglés a la derecha. Usen los cognados en negrilla *(boldface)* como guía.

1. _____ a las **culturas** que los rodeaban
2. _____ querían que los dejaran en **paz**
3. _____ están **separados** por fronteras **nacionales**
4. _____ se mantienen… **unidos**
5. _____ los **antecesores** han legado
6. _____ han permanecido fieles a su **pasado**

a. *the **ancestors** have left to them*
b. *they maintain themselves **united***
c. *they are **separated** by **national** borders*
d. *have remained faithful to their **past***
e. *to the **cultures** that surround them*
f. *they wanted to be left in **peace***

3 Ahora lee rápidamente el siguiente artículo sobre la cultura garífuna de Centroamérica. Presta atención en particular a las frases en negrilla. Éstas son importantes para entender la sección. Después de cada sección, vas a tener la oportunidad de ver si entiendes bien las ideas principales.

LECTURA

La cultura garífuna

Durante siglos[1] los garífunas, que constituyen un **grupo étnico disperso a lo largo de las costas de cinco países, se han mantenido apartados**[2] de los demás pueblos[3]. Desde el principio, sus antepasados **no buscaron**[4] **conquistar ni asimilarse a las culturas** que los rodeaban. Sólo querían que los dejaran en paz.

    Aunque están separados por fronteras nacionales, los garífunas se mantienen no obstante unidos en su determinación por preservar su cultura, rica en influencias africanas y americanas.

Esteban Felix/AP Images

¿Cierto o falso?

1. Los garífunas querían *(wanted to)* asimilarse a otras culturas.

2. La cultura garífuna es rica en influencias europeas.

Las comunidades garífunas **conservan celosamente**[5] **su arte, su música, sus artesanías y sus creencias religiosas**, que en conjunto[6] constituyen una forma de vida muy particular. Los antecesores han legado a los garífunas su **música característica, que incorpora canciones y ritmos africanos y americanos**, y un **expresivo lenguaje** que contiene elementos arauacos y caribes—los idiomas originales de los indios caribes—y yoruba, una lengua proveniente de África Occidental. Los garífunas **han permanecido fieles a su pasado**.

¿Cierto o falso?

3. Mantener las tradiciones del arte, de la música y de las creencias religiosas es muy importante para los garífunas.

4. La música garífuna tiene elementos africanos y europeos.

5. La lengua garífuna tiene elementos de lenguas caribes y de una lengua africana.

A través de[7] los siglos, los garífunas sin duda han mantenido el fuego[8] de su vida cultural. En la actualidad, **la libre práctica de sus antiguas tradiciones asegura el conocimiento de su singular historia** y contribuye a acrecentar[9] la riqueza cultural de los países que los albergan[10], compartiendo las sagradas creencias y las ricas expresiones artísticas de sus orgullosos[11] antepasados.

¿Cierto o falso?

6. En realidad, los garífunas no pueden conservar sus tradiciones antiguas.

7. Los garífunas hacen contribuciones culturales a los países donde viven.

Check yourself: 1. F 2. F 3. C 4. F 5. C 6. F 7. C

---

[1]centuries [2]**se...:** *they kept themselves separate* [3]*grupos étnicos* [4]**no...:** *did not seek to* [5]*jealously* [6]**en...:** *como un grupo* [7]**A...:** *Across, Throughout* [8]*fire* [9]*to strengthen, increase* [10]**los...:** *shelter them* [11]*proud*

Excerpt from "Los fuertes lazos ancestrales," from *Américas*, Vol. 43, No. 1, 1991. Reprinted from *Américas* magazine, the official publication of the Organization of American States (OAS), published bimonthly in identical English and Spanish editions. Used with permission.

4 Ahora que entiendes las ideas principales de las secciones del artículo, trabaja con un(a) compañero(a) de clase. Lean los párrafos otra vez y luego contesten las siguientes preguntas.

1. ¿Dónde viven los garífunas?
2. ¿Cómo es la lengua garífuna?
3. ¿Cómo es la música garífuna?

5 Lee rápidamente la siguiente información sobre los garífunas en Estados Unidos y con un(a) compañero(a), contesten las preguntas a continuación.

Text: © Cengage Learning 2013
Poster: Ivan Moreira

Hay comunidades de garífunas en Estados Unidos también. Una de las más grandes y activas está en y cerca de *(near)* la Ciudad de Nueva York—es la población más grande de garífunas fuera de Centroamérica. La organización Garifuna Coalition USA, Inc. promueve la cultura garífuna de Nueva York y sirve como centro de información sobre sus eventos, noticias y celebraciones.

Todos los años la Coalición organiza el Mes de la Herencia Garífuna y presenta premios *(awards)* a las personas que han promovido *(have promoted)* la cultura garífuna y sus intereses en Estados Unidos. Recientemente organizó una campaña para educar a los garífunas de su comunidad sobre la importancia de identificarse como garífuna en los formularios del Censo 2010.

1. ¿Dónde hay una población grande de garífunas en Estados Unidos?
2. ¿Qué hace la Coalición?
3. ¿De qué trata *(What is it about)* una campaña reciente de la Coalición?

6 En grupos de tres o cuatro estudiantes, identifiquen uno o dos grupos culturales de Estados Unidos o de otros países que mantienen sus tradiciones y costumbres diferentes de las de sus países de residencia. En su opinión, ¿es la preservación de tradiciones y costumbres una consecuencia del aislamiento? ¿Hay beneficios de mantenerse aislados? ¿Hay desventajas *(disadvantages)*?

Antes de escribir

ESTRATEGIA

Writing—Creating a topic sentence

On page 189, you looked for the main idea, which is usually expressed by the topic sentence. A good paragraph contains a topic sentence and supporting details. When you write, focus on the information you want to convey and write a topic sentence for each paragraph that summarizes its key idea.

1 Con un(a) compañero(a) de clase, miren el artículo en la página 189. Analicen cada párrafo para identificar la oración que mejor presente la idea principal del párrafo. Ésta es la **oración temática** *(topic sentence)*.

MODELO **Párrafo 1:** *Durante siglos los garífunas, que constituyen un grupo étnico disperso a lo largo de las costas de cinco países, se han mantenido apartados de los demás pueblos.*

2 Vas a escribir unas oraciones temáticas para una composición de tres párrafos sobre tu profesión futura. Piensa en los tres párrafos que vas a usar y escribe una oración temática para cada uno.

> For extra help narrowing your topic, refer to the **A escribir** section in **Chapter 4**.

MODELO **Tema:** *Las profesiones*
Aspecto específico del tema: *Mi profesión del futuro*
Párrafo 1: (Description of the profession)
Oración temática: *Me interesa el diseño gráfico.*
Párrafo 2: (Reason you want to have this profession)
Oración temática: *Me gusta dibujar y trabajar en la computadora.*
Párrafo 3: (What you need to do to prepare yourself for this profession)
Oración temática: *Para prepararme, necesito tomar una combinación de cursos de diseño gráfico, de arte y de computación.*

Composición

3 Ahora, usa las tres oraciones temáticas que escribiste para la **Actividad 2** y escribe una composición de tres párrafos sobre tu profesión futura.

Después de escribir

4 Mira tu borrador otra vez. Usa la siguiente lista para revisarlo.

- ¿Tienen tus oraciones temáticas toda la información necesaria?
- ¿Corresponden los sujetos de las oraciones a los verbos correctos?
- ¿Corresponden las formas de los artículos, los sustantivos y los adjetivos?
- ¿Usas correctamente los verbos reflexivos y los verbos irregulares?
- ¿Hay errores de puntuación o de ortografía?

Vocabulario

La familia *The family*

La familia nuclear *The nuclear family*
la madre (mamá) *mother*
el padre (papá) *father*
los padres *parents*
la esposa *wife*
el esposo *husband*
la hija *daughter*
el hijo *son*
la hermana (mayor) *(older) sister*
el hermano (menor) *(younger) brother*
la tía *aunt*
el tío *uncle*
la prima *female cousin*
el primo *male cousin*
la sobrina *niece*
el sobrino *nephew*
la abuela *grandmother*
el abuelo *grandfather*
la nieta *granddaughter*
el nieto *grandson*

La familia política *In-laws*
la suegra *mother-in-law*
el suegro *father-in-law*
la nuera *daughter-in-law*
el yerno *son-in-law*
la cuñada *sister-in-law*
el cuñado *brother-in-law*

Otros parientes *Other relatives*
la madrastra *stepmother*
el padrastro *stepfather*
la hermanastra *stepsister*
el hermanastro *stepbrother*
la media hermana *half-sister*
el medio hermano *half-brother*

Las profesiones y carreras *Professions and careers*

el (la) abogado(a) *lawyer*
el (la) asistente *assistant*
el actor / la actriz *actor / actress*
el (la) arquitecto(a) *architect*
el (la) artista *artist*
el (la) bombero(a) *firefighter*
el (la) camarero(a) *waiter / waitress*
el (la) carpintero(a) *carpenter*
el (la) cocinero(a) *cook, chef*
el (la) contador(a) *accountant*
el (la) dentista *dentist*
el (la) dependiente *salesclerk*
el (la) director(a) de social media
  director of social media
el (la) diseñador(a) gráfico(a)
  graphic designer
el (la) dueño(a) de... *owner of . . .*

el (la) enfermero(a) *nurse*
el (la) gerente de... *manager of . . .*
el hombre / la mujer de negocios *businessman / businesswoman*
el (la) ingeniero(a) *engineer*
el (la) maestro(a) *teacher*
el (la) mecánico(a) *mechanic*
el (la) médico(a) *doctor*
el (la) peluquero(a) *barber / hairdresser*
el (la) periodista *journalist*
el (la) plomero(a) *plumber*
el (la) policía *policeman / policewoman*
el (la) programador(a) *programmer*
el (la) secretario(a) *secretary*
el (la) trabajador(a) *worker*
el (la) veterinario(a) *veterinarian*

En el baño *In the bathroom*

el cepillo *hairbrush*
el cepillo de dientes *toothbrush*
el champú *shampoo*
el desodorante *deodorant*
el jabón *soap*
el maquillaje *makeup, cosmetics*

la máquina de afeitar *electric razor*
la pasta de dientes *toothpaste*
el peine *comb*
la rasuradora *razor*
la toalla *towel*
la toalla de mano *hand towel*

Verbos con la forma **yo** irregular

conducir (-zc) *to drive; to conduct*
conocer (-zc) *to know a person; to be familiar with*
dar (doy) *to give*
decir (-g) (i) *to say, to tell*
hacer (-g) *to make; to do*
oír (oigo) *to hear*

poner (-g) *to put*
saber (sé) *to know a fact; to know how to*
salir (-g) *to leave; to go out (with)*
traducir (-zc) *to translate*
traer (-go) *to bring*
venir (-g) (ie) *to come*
ver (veo) *to see*

Verbos reflexivos

Acciones físicas *Physical actions*
acostarse (ue) *to go to bed*
afeitarse *to shave oneself*
bañarse *to take a bath*
cepillarse el pelo *to brush one's hair*
cepillarse los dientes *to brush one's teeth*
despertarse (ie) *to wake up*
dormirse (ue) *to fall asleep*
ducharse *to take a shower*
lavarse *to wash oneself*
lavarse el pelo *to wash one's hair*
lavarse los dientes *to brush one's teeth*
levantarse *to get up*
maquillarse *to put on makeup*
peinarse *to brush / comb one's hair*
ponerse (la ropa) *to put on (clothing)*
prepararse *to get ready*
quitarse (la ropa) *to take off (clothing)*
secarse el pelo *to dry one's hair*
sentarse (ie) *to sit down*
vestirse (i) *to get dressed*

Estados / emociones *States / emotions*
casarse *to get married*
comprometerse *to get engaged*
despedirse (i) *to say goodbye*
divertirse (ie) *to have fun*
divorciarse *to get divorced*
enamorarse *to fall in love*
enfermarse *to get sick*
irse *to leave, to go away*
pelearse *to have a fight*
preocuparse *to worry*
quejarse *to complain*
reírse (i) *to laugh*
relajarse *to relax*
reunirse *to meet, to get together*
separarse *to get separated*

Otros verbos

bañar *to swim; to give someone a bath*
despertar (ie) *to wake someone up*
lavar *to wash*
levantar *to raise, to lift*

manejar *to drive*
quitar *to take off*
secar *to dry something*
vestir (i) *to dress someone*

Otras palabras y expresiones

a veces *sometimes*
antes *before*
después *after*
luego *later*
nunca *never*

siempre *always*
todas las semanas *every week*
...veces al día / por semana *. . . times a day / per week*

Repaso y preparación

Complete these activities to check your understanding of the new grammar points in **Chapter 5** before you move on to **Chapter 6**.

The answers to the activities in this section can be found in **Appendix B**.

Irregular-**yo** verbs (p. 172)

1 Completa la encuesta con las formas correctas de los verbos indicados. Después indica si las oraciones son ciertas **(Sí)** o falsas **(No)** para ti.

Yo...	Sí	No	Yo...	Sí	No
1. ...(saber) hablar francés.			4. ...(hacer) mi tarea todos los días.		
2. ...(conocer) a una persona famosa.			5. ...(salir) todas las noches.		
3. ...(conducir) todos los días.			6. ...(ver) a familia todas las semanas.		

Saber vs. conocer (p. 173)

2 Mira cada cosa o actividad y di si la persona indicada **sabe** o **conoce** cada una. Escribe oraciones completas y no olvides usar la **a** personal cuando sea necesario.

1. tú / Buenos Aires
2. ellos / jugar golf
3. yo / todas las respuestas
4. usted / mis primos
5. nosotras / el chef
6. ella / cocinar bien

Reflexive verbs (p. 176)

3 Completa las oraciones con las formas correctas de los verbos indicados.

1. Martina _____ (maquillarse) todos los días.
2. Frecuentemente yo _____ (acostarse) muy tarde.
3. Ustedes _____ (reunirse) todos los miércoles.
4. ¿Tú _____ (levantarse) temprano o tarde?
5. Nosotros nunca _____ (enfermarse).
6. Ellos _____ (pelearse) casi todos los días.

The present progressive tense (p. 180)

4 Haz una oración para decir qué está haciendo cada persona en este momento. Usa las actividades de la lista y sigue el modelo.

MODELO Tú eres actriz.
        Estás maquillándote.

Actividades: escribir un artículo, hablar con un paciente, maquillarse, pintar, preparar la comida, servir la comida, trabajar en la computadora

1. Ella es médica.
2. Yo soy periodista.
3. Ellos son cocineros.
4. Nosotros somos artistas.
5. Usted es camarera.
6. Él es secretario.

Preparación para el Capítulo 6

Adjective agreement (Chapter 2)

5 Tu amigo habla de su familia. Completa sus comentarios con las formas correctas de los adjetivos indicados.

Complete these activities to review some previously learned grammatical structures that will be helpful when you learn the new grammar in **Chapter 6**.

Be sure to reread **Chapter 5: Gramática útil 1** before moving on to the new **Chapter 6** grammar sections.

Tengo una familia 1. _____ (grande). Pero todas las personas son muy 2. _____ (extrovertido). Mis hermanas son bastante 3. _____ (simpático) pero mi hermanito es un poco 4. _____ (tonto). Mis primos normalmente están 5. _____ (contento) pero hoy están muy 6. _____ (nervioso). Mis abuelos son 7. _____ (viejo) y muy 8. _____ (divertido). Me gustan mucho mis familiares y estoy 9. _____ (triste) que no puedo ver a mi familia más frecuentemente.

The present indicative of regular -ar verbs (Chapter 2), regular -er and -ir verbs (Chapter 3), and stem-changing verbs (Chapter 4)

6 Escribe oraciones completas con las formas correctas de los verbos indicados.

1. mi tío / lavar su auto todas las semanas
2. mis abuelos / no dormir mucho
3. mis primas / preferir estudiar en la residencia estudiantil
4. mi hermano y yo / correr en el parque los sábados
5. tú / manejar todos los días
6. mi madre / vestir a mi hermanita por las mañanas
7. yo / mirar una película
8. mi madre y yo / vivir en un apartamento grande

The verb estar (Chapter 4)

7 Di dónde están las personas indicadas.

MODELO   *yo / café*
         Yo estoy en el café.

1. la mujer de negocios / oficina
2. tú y yo / salón de clase
3. el Doctor Méndez / hospital
4. los programadores / centro de computación
5. la policía / parque
6. yo / biblioteca
7. los cocineros / restaurante
8. tú / gimnasio

Reference Materials

Appendix A: KWL Chart

Lo que sé	Lo que quiero saber	Lo que aprendí

Capítulo 1 (pp. 40–41)

Act. 1: 1. la 2. X 3. la 4. X 5. X 6. X 7. unos 8. una 9. los

Act. 2: 1. Tú 2. Nosotros 3. Yo 4. es 5. son 6. somos

Act. 3: 1. Hay dos chicas. 2. Hay un hombre. 3. Hay una mujer. 4. No hay niño. 5. No hay computadora. 6. No hay mochila. 7. Hay una serpiente. 8. No hay elefante.

Act. 4: 1. tienes 2. tiene 3. tengo 4. tenemos 5. tienen 6. tienes

Act. 5: 1. tengo que 2. tienen que 3. tenemos que 4. tiene que 5. tienes que 6. tienen que

Act. 6: *Answers will vary depending on current year.*
1. Tú tienes... años. 2. Ellos tienen... años. 3. Usted tiene... años. 4. Ella tiene... años. 5. Yo tengo... años. 6. Nosotros tenemos... años. 7. Ustedes tienen... años. 8. Tú y yo tenemos... años.

Capítulo 2 (pp. 80–81)

Act. 1: 1. Esteban y Carolina caminan. 2. Usted pinta. 3. Loreta levanta pesas. 4. Yo saco fotos. 5. Nosotros tomamos el sol. 6. Tú cocinas. 7. Ustedes hablan por teléfono. 8. Tú y yo patinamos.

Act. 2: 1. A mí me gusta estudiar. 2. A ti te gusta mirar televisión. 3. A usted le gusta visitar a amigos. 4. A nosotras nos gusta pintar. 5. A ustedes les gusta practicar deportes.

Act. 3: 1. Gretchen y Rolf son alemanes. Son muy sinceros. 2. Brigitte es francesa. Es muy divertida. 3. Nosotras somos españolas. Somos simpáticas. 4. Yo soy estadounidense. Soy muy generosa. 5. Usted es japonesa. Es muy interesante. 6. Tú eres italiano. Eres muy activo.

Act. 4: 1. las 2. El 3. la 4. unos 5. la 6. una 7. un 8. la 9. la 10. las

Act. 5: 1. f, es 2. d, es 3. a, es 4. g, son 5. b, somos 6. e, eres 7. c, soy

Capítulo 3 (pp. 118–119)

Act. 1: 1. qué 2. Por qué 3. Cuál 4. cuándo 4. Cuántas 5. Quién

Act. 2: 1. escribe 2. debemos 3. como 4. viven 5. lee

Act. 3: 1. mis 2. tus 3. nuestra 4. sus 5. sus 6. mi

Act. 4: 1. voy, van 2. va, vamos 3. vas

Act. 5: 1. A mí me gusta leer. 2. A nosotros nos gusta comer. 3. A ustedes les gusta bailar. 4. A ti te gusta cocinar. 5. A él le gusta patinar. 6. A mí me gusta cantar.

Act. 6: 1. estudia 2. cocina 3. toca 4. canta 5. levantan 6. practican 7. miramos 8. alquilamos 9. trabajo 10. visito 11. paso

Act. 7: 1. Rogelio y Mauricio son muy egoístas. 2. Tú eres muy impaciente. 3. Nosotros somos muy perezosos. 4. Yo soy muy activo(a). 5. Sandra es muy generosa. 6. Néstor y Nicolás son muy tímidos.

Capítulo 4 (pp. 158–159)

Act. 1: 1. les gustan 2. me encanta 3. le molesta 4. nos interesan 5. te importa 6. le gusta

Act. 2: 1. estás 2. estamos 3. soy 4. son 5. Estoy 6. Está 7. es 8. es 9. está 10. son 11. es 12. están

Act. 3: 1. Tú duermes mucho. 2. Yo cierro la computadora portátil. 3. Ella entiende las instrucciones. 4. Nosotras jugamos el juego interactivo. 5. Usted repite la contraseña. 6. Ellos quieren un MP3 portátil. 7. Yo puedo instalar el programa. 8. Nosotros preferimos ir a un café con wifi.

Act. 4: 1. lentamente 2. rápidamente 3. Generalmente 4. fácilmente

Act. 5: debe, envias, recibes, grabas, instalas, llevas, trabajas, hablan, funciona, bajo, subo, pesa, saco, accedo, leo, usamos, comentan, ofrecemos, vendemos, debes

Capítulo 5 (pp. 194–195)

Act. 1: *Answers will vary for **Sí/No** column.* 1. Sé 2. Conozco 3. Conduzco 4. Hago 5. Salgo 6. Veo

Act. 2: 1. Tú conoces Buenos Aires. 2. Ellos saben jugar golf. 3. Yo sé todas las respuestas. 4. Usted conoce a mis primos. 5. Nosotras conocemos al chef. 6. Ella sabe cocinar bien.

Act. 3: 1. se maquilla 2. me acuesto 3. se reunen 4. te levantas 5. nos enfermamos 6. se pelean

Act. 4: 1. Ella está hablando con un paciente. 2. Yo estoy escribiendo un artículo. 3. Ellos están preparando la comida. 4. Nosotros estamos pintando. 5. Usted está sirviendo la comida. 6. Él está trabajando en la computadora.

Act. 5: 1. grande 2. extrovertidas 3. simpáticas 4. tonto 5. contentos 6. nerviosos 7. viejos 8. divertidos 9. triste

Act. 6: 1. Mi tío lava su auto todas las semanas. 2. Mis abuelos no duermen mucho. 3. Mis primas prefieren estudiar en la residencia estudiantil. 4. Mi hermano y yo corremos en el parque los sábados. 5. Tú manejas todos los días. 6. Mi madre viste a mi hermanita por las mañanas. 7. Yo miro una película. 8. Mi madre y yo vivimos en un apartamento grande.

Act. 7: 1. La mujer de negocios está en la oficina. 2. Tú y yo estamos en el salón de clase. 3. El Doctor Méndez está en el hospital. 4. Los programadores están en el centro de computación. 5. La policía está en el parque. 6. Yo estoy en la biblioteca. 7. Los cocineros están en el restaurante. 8. Tú estás en el gimnasio.

Capítulo 6 (pp. 228–229)

Act. 1: El perro está lejos del auto. 2. El perro está delante del auto. 3. El perro está detrás del auto. 4. El perro está debajo del auto. 5. El perro está dentro del auto. 6. El perro está entre los autos.

Act. 2: 1. Vengan, pierdan 2. Ponga, Hable 3. Haga, Llame

Act. 3: 1. Siempre, 2. También, 3. algunos 4. nada 5. algo 6. nadie

Act. 4: 1. estos, ésos 2. aquella, ésta 3. esos, aquéllos 4. esta, ésa 5. aquellas, éstas 6. este, ése

Act. 5: 1. salgo 2. traigo 3. Pongo 4. conduzco 5. veo 6. conozco 7. Oigo 8. hago 9. digo 10. sé

Act. 6: 1. te preparas 2. me acuesto 3. nos preocupamos 4. se están divirtiendo / están divirtiéndose 5. se quejen 6. Siéntese, relájese

Capítulo 7 (pp. 266–267)

Act. 1: 1. montaste 2. leyó 3. compartí 4. navegamos 5. corrieron

Act. 2: 1. Tú y yo fuimos... 2. Marilena estuvo... 3. Yo hice... 4. Guille y Paulina dijeron... 5. Mis padres condujeron... 6. Tú tradujiste...

Act. 3: 1. ¿Los perros? Tú los lavaste. 2. ¿El surfing? Victoria lo hizo. 3. ¿La pelota (de golf)? Yo no la encontré. 4. ¿Las mochilas? Nosotros las perdimos. 5. ¿Los refrescos? Ustedes no los bebieron. 6. ¿Las pesas? Esteban y Federico no las levantaron.

Act. 4: 1. pongas, Ten, lee 2. Pon, siéntate, salgas

Act. 5: 1. quieren 2. me divierto 3. se visten 4. pueden 5. duermo 6. pides

Act. 6: 1. A mí me gusta remar. 2. A usted le gusta nadar. 3. A ti te gustan esos esquíes. 4. A ellos les gusta el boxeo. 5. A nosotros nos gusta pescar. 6. A ella le gusta la nieve. 7. A ti te gusta entrenarte. 8. A mí me gustan las vacaciones. 9. A nosotros nos gusta la primavera.

Act. 7: 1. sé 2. conozco 3. saben 4. podemos 5. pueden 6. conocemos 7. quiero 8. puedo

Capítulo 8 (pp. 304–305)

Act. 1: 1. Supe 2. hicimos 3. sugirió 4. preferí 5. sirvió 6. dijo 7. quiso 8. pudo 9. tuvo 10. pidió 11. puso 12. anduvimos 13. Nos reímos 14. nos divertimos 15. nos despedimos 16. dijimos

Act. 2: 1. nos 2. te 3. les 4. me 5. le

Act. 3: 1. tantos, como 2. más, que 3. menos, que 4. tan, como 5. el más 6. más

Act. 4: 1. compraste 2. vi 3. estuvo 4. trajo 5. fuimos 6. dieron 7. hiciste 8. escribió

Act. 5: 1. Delfina lo compró. 2. Diego y Eduardo no la compraron. 3. Tú no los compraste. 4. Yo los compré. 5. Nosotros las compramos. 6. Usted no lo compró.

Act. 6: 1. Yo me puse un abrigo. 2. Ellos se pusieron unas sandalias. 3. Tú te pusiste un chaleco. 4. Nosotros nos pusimos unos jeans. 5. Ella se puso una bufanda. 7. Ustedes se pusieron un impermeable.

Capítulo 9 (pp. 344–345)

Act. 1: 1. La señora Muñoz preparaba unas galletas. 2. Yo freía un huevo. 3. Nosotros pelábamos zanahorias para una ensalada. 4. Manolito ponía la mesa. 5. Sarita y Carmela picaban cebollas para una sopa. 6. Tú hervías agua para preparar el té.

Act. 2: 1. Eran 2. quería 3. llegué 4. vi 5. estaba 6. tenía 7. me senté 8. empezamos 9. hablábamos 10. dijo 11. exclamé 12. sabía 13. Me despedí 14. salí 15. Estaba 16. quería

Act. 3: 1. Ábrenosla. 2. Cuéceselos. 3. No me lo compres. 4. No se lo calientes. 5. Pásanosla. 6. No se la prepares.

Act. 4: 1. come 2. venden 3. hablan 4. sirve 5. cierra 6. duerme

Act. 5: 1. Los manteles son rojos. 2. El flan es bueno. 3. Las almejas están frescas. 4. El café está caliente. 5. La carne está frita. 6. Los huevos son blancos. 7. El pescado está crudo. 8. El té está frío. 9. La limonada es dulce. 10. Los platos están limpios. 11. La langosta es cara. 12. Las fresas son baratas.

Act. 6: 1. mi 2. tus 3. nuestro 4. sus 5. sus 6. su 7. sus 8. su 9. nuestras 10. tus

Act. 7: 1. hiciste 2. hago 3. hizo 4. hicieron 5. hacemos

Capítulo 10 (pp. 376–377)

Act. 1: 1. ¿La aspiradora? No es tuya. Es suya. 2. ¿Las licuadoras? No son suyas. Son mías. 3. ¿Las planchas? No son nuestras. Son suyas. 4. ¿La tostadora? No es mía. Es suya. 5. ¿Los microondas? No son suyos. Son nuestros. 6. ¿El lavaplatos? No es suyo. Es tuyo.

Act. 2: 1. Hace un año que Sarita no va de vacaciones. 2. Hace seis meses que ellos viven en esa casa. 3. Ellos limpiaron el baño hace dos semanas. 4. Hacía tres meses que Luis no podía trabajar en la casa. 5. Los abuelos vinieron de visita hace dos años.

Act. 3: 1. por 2. Para 3. Por 4. por 5. para 6. Por 7. para 8. para

Act. 4: 1. Lavo 2. Plancho 3. Barro 4. Sacudo 5. Hiervo 6. Riego 7. Sirvo 8. Vuelvo 9. pido 10. duermo

Act. 5: 1. Estoy 2. Conduzco 3. doy 4. digo 5. Oigo 6. Vengo 7. Veo 8. Sé 9. Pongo 10. Tengo

Act. 6: 1. laves 2. planches 3. saques 4. pases 5. pongas 6. uses 7. trapees 8. sacudas 9. comas 10. insistas

Appendix C: Spanish Verbs

Regular Verbs

Simple Tenses

Infinitive	Past participle / Present participle	Indicative					Subjunctive	
		Present	Imperfect	Preterite	Future	Conditional	Present	Imperfect*
cantar *to sing*	cantado cantando	canto cantas canta cantamos cantáis cantan	cantaba cantabas cantaba cantábamos cantabais cantaban	canté cantaste cantó cantamos cantasteis cantaron	cantaré cantarás cantará cantaremos cantaréis cantarán	cantaría cantarías cantaría cantaríamos cantaríais cantarían	cante cantes cante cantemos cantéis canten	cantara cantaras cantara cantáramos cantarais cantaran
correr *to run*	corrido corriendo	corro corres corre corremos corréis corren	corría corrías corría corríamos corríais corrían	corrí corriste corrió corrimos corristeis corrieron	correré correrás correrá correremos correréis correrán	correría correrías correría correríamos correríais correrían	corra corras corra corramos corráis corran	corriera corrieras corriera corriéramos corrierais corrieran
subir *to go up, to climb up*	subido subiendo	subo subes sube subimos subís suben	subía subías subía subíamos subíais subían	subí subiste subió subimos subisteis subieron	subiré subirás subirá subiremos subiréis subirán	subiría subirías subiría subiríamos subiríais subirían	suba subas suba subamos subáis suban	subiera subieras subiera subiéramos subierais subieran

*In addition to this form, another one is less frequently used for all regular and irregular verbs: cantase, cantases, cantase, cantásemos, cantaseis, cantasen; corriese, corrieses, corriese, corriésemos, corrieseis, corriesen; subiese, subieses, subiese, subiésemos, subieseis, subiesen.

Commands

Person	Affirmative	Negative	Affirmative	Negative	Affirmative	Negative
tú	canta	no cantes	corre	no corras	sube	no subas
usted	cante	no cante	corra	no corra	suba	no suba
nosotros	cantemos	no cantemos	corramos	no corramos	subamos	no subamos
vosotros	cantad	no cantéis	corred	no corráis	subid	no subáis
ustedes	canten	no canten	corran	no corran	suban	no suban

Stem-Changing Verbs: *-ar* and *-er* Groups

Type of change in the verb stem	Subject	Indicative Present	Subjunctive Present	Commands Affirmative	Commands Negative	Other *-ar* and *-er* stem-changing verbs
-ar verbs e > ie pensar *to think*	yo	pienso	piense	—	—	atravesar *to go through, to cross;* cerrar *to close;* despertarse *to wake up;* empezar *to start;* negar *to deny;* sentarse *to sit down*
	tú	piensas	pienses	piensa	no pienses	
	él/ella, Ud.	piensa	piense	piense	no piense	
	nosotros/as	pensamos	pensemos	pensemos	no pensemos	
	vosotros/as	pensáis	penséis	pensad	no penséis	Nevar *to snow* is only conjugated in the third-person singular.
	ellos/as, Uds.	piensan	piensen	piensen	no piensen	
-ar verbs o > ue contar *to count, to tell*	yo	cuento	cuente	—	—	acordarse *to remember;* acostarse *to go to bed;* almorzar *to have lunch;* colgar *to hang;* costar *to cost;* demostrar *to demonstrate, to show;* encontrar *to find;* mostrar *to show;* probar *to prove, to taste;* recordar *to remember*
	tú	cuentas	cuentes	cuenta	no cuentes	
	él/ella, Ud.	cuenta	cuente	cuente	no cuente	
	nosotros/as	contamos	contemos	contemos	no contemos	
	vosotros/as	contáis	contéis	contad	no contéis	
	ellos/as, Uds.	cuentan	cuenten	cuenten	no cuenten	
-er verbs e > ie entender *to understand*	yo	entiendo	entienda	—	—	encender *to light, to turn on;* extender *to stretch;* perder *to lose*
	tú	entiendes	entiendas	entiende	no entiendas	
	él/ella, Ud.	entiende	entienda	entienda	no entienda	
	nosotros/as	entendemos	entendamos	entendamos	no entendamos	
	vosotros/as	entendéis	entendáis	entended	no entendáis	
	ellos/as, Uds.	entienden	entiendan	entiendan	no entiendan	
-er verbs o > ue volver *to return*	yo	vuelvo	vuelva	—	—	mover *to move;* torcer *to twist*
	tú	vuelves	vuelvas	vuelve	no vuelvas	
	él/ella, Ud.	vuelve	vuelva	vuelva	no vuelva	Llover *to rain* is only conjugated in the third-person singular.
	nosotros/as	volvemos	volvamos	volvamos	no volvamos	
	vosotros/as	volvéis	volváis	volved	no volváis	
	ellos/as, Uds.	vuelven	vuelvan	vuelvan	no vuelvan	

Stem-Changing Verbs: -ir Verbs

Type of change in the verb stem	Subject	Indicative		Subjunctive		Commands	
		Present	Preterite	Present	Imperfect	Affirmative	Negative
-ir verbs e > ie or i **Infinitive:** sentir *to feel* **Present participle:** sintiendo	yo	siento	sentí	sienta	sintiera	—	—
	tú	sientes	sentiste	sientas	sintieras	siente	no sientas
	él/ella, Ud.	siente	sintió	sienta	sintiera	sienta	no sienta
	nosotros/as	sentimos	sentimos	sintamos	sintiéramos	sintamos	no sintamos
	vosotros/as	sentís	sentisteis	sintáis	sintierais	sentid	no sintáis
	ellos/as, Uds.	sienten	sintieron	sientan	sintieran	sientan	no sientan
-ir verbs o > ue or u **Infinitive:** dormir *to sleep* **Present participle:** durmiendo	yo	duermo	dormí	duerma	durmiera	—	—
	tú	duermes	dormiste	duermas	durmieras	duerme	no duermas
	él/ella, Ud.	duerme	durmió	duerma	durmiera	duerma	no duerma
	nosotros/as	dormimos	dormimos	durmamos	durmiéramos	durmamos	no durmamos
	vosotros/as	dormís	dormisteis	durmáis	durmierais	dormid	no durmáis
	ellos/as, Uds.	duermen	durmieron	duerman	durmieran	duerman	no duerman

Other similar verbs: advertir *to warn;* arrepentirse *to repent;* consentir *to consent, pamper;* convertir(se) *to turn into;* divertir(se) *to amuse (oneself);* herir *to hurt, wound;* mentir *to lie;* morir *to die;* preferir *to prefer;* referir *to refer;* sugerir *to suggest*

Type of change in the verb stem	Subject	Indicative		Subjunctive		Commands	
		Present	Preterite	Present	Imperfect	Affirmative	Negative
-ir verbs e > i **Infinitive:** pedir *to ask for, to request* **Present participle:** pidiendo	yo	pido	pedí	pida	pidiera	—	—
	tú	pides	pediste	pidas	pidieras	pide	no pidas
	él/ella, Ud.	pide	pidió	pida	pidiera	pida	no pida
	nosotros/as	pedimos	pedimos	pidamos	pidiéramos	pidamos	no pidamos
	vosotros/as	pedís	pedisteis	pidáis	pidierais	pedid	no pidáis
	ellos/as, Uds.	piden	pidieron	pidan	pidieran	pidan	no pidan

Other similar verbs: competir *to compete;* despedir(se) *to say good-bye;* elegir *to choose;* impedir *to prevent;* perseguir *to chase;* repetir *to repeat;* seguir *to follow;* servir *to serve;* vestir(se) *to dress, to get dressed*

Verbs with Spelling Changes

	Verb type	Ending	Change	Verbs with similar spelling changes
1	buscar *to look for*	-car	• Preterite: yo busqué • Present subjunctive: busque, busques, busque, busquemos, busquéis, busquen	comunicar, explicar *to explain* indicar *to indicate*, sacar, pescar
2	conocer *to know*	*vowel* + -cer or -cir	• Present indicative: conozco, conoces, conoce, and so on • Present subjunctive: conozca, conozcas, conozca, conozcamos, conozcáis, conozcan	nacer *to be born*, obedecer, ofrecer, parecer, pertenecer *to belong*, reconocer, conducir, traducir
3	ven<u>c</u>er *to win*	*consonant* + -cer or -cir	• Present indicative: venzo, vences, vence, and so on • Present subjunctive: venza, venzas, venza, venzamos, venzáis, venzan	convencer, torcer *to twist*
4	leer *to read*	-eer	• Preterite: leyó, leyeron • Imperfect subjunctive: leyera, leyeras, leyera, leyéramos, leyerais, leyeran • Present participle: leyendo	creer, poseer *to own*
5	llegar *to arrive*	-gar	• Preterite: yo llegué • Present subjunctive: llegue, llegues, llegue, lleguemos, lleguéis, lleguen	colgar *to hang*, navegar, negar *to negate, to deny*, pagar, rogar *to beg*, jugar
6	escoger *to choose*	-ger or -gir	• Present indicative: escojo, escoges, escoge, and so on • Present subjunctive: escoja, escojas, escoja, escojamos, escojáis, escojan	proteger, *to protect*, recoger *to collect, gather*, corregir *to correct*, dirigir *to direct*, elegir *to elect, choose*, exigir *to demand*
7	seguir *to follow*	-guir	• Present indicative: sigo, sigues, sigue, and so on • Present subjunctive: siga, sigas, siga, sigamos, sigáis, sigan	conseguir, distinguir, perseguir
8	huir *to flee*	-uir	• Present indicative: huyo, huyes, huye, huimos, huís, huyen • Preterite: huí, huiste, huyó, huimos, huisteis, huyeron • Present subjunctive: huya, huyas, huya, huyamos, huyáis, huyan • Imperfect subjunctive: huyera, huyeras, huyera, huyéramos, huyerais, huyeran • Present participle: huyendo • Commands: huye (tú), huya usted, huyamos (nosotros), huid (vosotros), huyan (ustedes), (negative) no huyas (tú), no huya (usted), no huyamos (nosotros), no huyáis (vosotros), no huyan (ustedes)	concluir, contribuir, construir, destruir, disminuir, distribuir, excluir, influir, instruir, restituir, substituir
9	abrazar *to embrace*	-zar	• Preterite: yo abracé • Present subjunctive: abrace, abraces, abrace, abracemos, abracéis, abracen	alcanzar *to achieve*, almorzar, comenzar, empezar, gozar *to enjoy*, rezar *to pray*

Compound Tenses

Indicative

	Present perfect		Past perfect		Preterite perfect		Future perfect		Conditional perfect	
	he		había		hube		habré		habría	
	has		habías		hubiste		habrás		habrías	
	ha	cantado	había	cantado	hubo	cantado	habrá	cantado	habría	cantado
	hemos	corrido	habíamos	corrido	hubimos	corrido	habremos	corrido	habríamos	corrido
	habéis	subido	habíais	subido	hubisteis	subido	habréis	subido	habríais	subido
	han		habían		hubieron		habrán		habrían	

Subjunctive

	Present perfect		Past perfect	
	haya		hubiera	
	hayas		hubieras	
	haya	cantado	hubiera	cantado
	hayamos	corrido	hubiéramos	corrido
	hayáis	subido	hubierais	subido
	hayan		hubieran	

All verbs, both regular and irregular, follow the same formation pattern with **haber** in all compound tenses. The only thing that changes is the form of the past participle of each verb. (See the chart below for common verbs with irregular past participles.) Remember that in Spanish, no word can come between **haber** and the past participle.

Common Irregular Past Participles

Infinitive	Past participle	
abrir	**abierto**	*opened*
caer	caído	*fallen*
creer	creído	*believed*
cubrir	**cubierto**	*covered*
decir	**dicho**	*said, told*
descubrir	**descubierto**	*discovered*
escribir	**escrito**	*written*
hacer	**hecho**	*made, done*
leer	leído	*read*

Infinitive	Past participle	
morir	**muerto**	*died*
oír	oído	*heard*
poner	**puesto**	*put, placed*
resolver	**resuelto**	*resolved*
romper	**roto**	*broken, torn*
(son)reír	(son)reído	*(smiled) laughed*
traer	traído	*brought*
ver	**visto**	*seen*
volver	**vuelto**	*returned*

Reflexive Verbs

Regular and Irregular Reflexive Verbs: Position of the Reflexive Pronouns in the Simple Tenses

Infinitive	Present participle	Reflexive pronouns	Indicative					Subjunctive	
			Present	Imperfect	Preterite	Future	Conditional	Present	Imperfect
lavarse	lavándome	me	lavo	lavaba	lavé	lavaré	lavaría	lave	lavara
to wash	lavándote	te	lavas	lavabas	lavaste	lavarás	lavarías	laves	lavaras
oneself	lavándose	se	lava	lavaba	lavó	lavará	lavaría	lave	lavara
	lavándonos	nos	lavamos	lavábamos	lavamos	lavaremos	lavaríamos	lavemos	laváramos
	lavándoos	os	laváis	lavabais	lavasteis	lavaréis	lavaríais	lavéis	lavarais
	lavándose	se	lavan	lavaban	lavaron	lavarán	lavarían	laven	lavaran

Regular and irregular reflexive verbs: Position of the reflexive pronouns with commands

Person	Affirmative	Negative	Affirmative	Negative	Affirmative	Negative
tú	lávate	no te laves	ponte	no te pongas	vístete	no te vistas
usted	lávese	no se lave	póngase	no se ponga	vístase	no se vista
nosotros	lavémonos	no nos lavemos	pongámonos	no nos pongamos	vistámonos	no nos vistamos
vosotros	lavaos	no os lavéis	poneos	no os pongáis	vestíos	no os vistáis
ustedes	lávense	no se laven	pónganse	no se pongan	vístanse	no se vistan

Regular and irregular reflexive verbs: Position of the reflexive pronouns in compound tenses*

Indicative

Reflexive Pronoun	Present Perfect	Past Perfect	Preterite Perfect	Future Perfect	Conditional Perfect	Participle
me	he	había	hube	habré	habría	lavado
te	has	habías	hubiste	habrás	habrías	
se	ha	había	hubo	habrá	habría	puesto
nos	hemos	habíamos	hubimos	habremos	habríamos	
os	habéis	habíais	hubisteis	habréis	habríais	vestido
se	han	habían	hubieron	habrán	habrían	

Subjunctive

Reflexive Pronoun	Present Perfect	Past Perfect	Participle
me	haya	hubiera	lavado
te	hayas	hubieras	
se	haya	hubiera	puesto
nos	hayamos	hubiéramos	
os	hayáis	hubierais	vestido
se	hayan	hubieran	

*The sequence of these three elements—the reflexive pronoun, the auxiliary verb **haber,** and the present perfect form—is invariable and no other words can come in between.

Regular and irregular reflexive verbs: Position of the reflexive pronouns with conjugated verb + infinitive**

Indicative

Reflexive Pronoun	Present	Imperfect	Preterite	Future	Conditional	Infinitive
me	voy a	iba a	fui a	iré a	iría a	lavar
te	vas a	ibas a	fuiste a	irás a	irías a	
se	va a	iba a	fue a	irá a	iría a	poner
nos	vamos a	íbamos a	fuimos a	iremos a	iríamos a	
os	vais a	ibais a	fuisteis a	iréis a	iríais a	vestir
se	van a	iban a	fueron a	irán a	irían a	

Subjunctive

Reflexive Pronoun	Present	Imperfect	Infinitive
me	vaya a	fuera a	lavar
te	vayas a	fueras a	
se	vaya a	fuera a	poner
nos	vayamos a	fuéramos a	
os	vayáis a	fuerais a	vestir
se	vayan a	fueran a	

The reflexive pronoun can also be placed after the infinitive: voy a lavarme,** voy a poner**me,** voy a vestir**me,** and so on.
Use the same structure for the present and the past progressive: **me** estoy lavando / estoy lavándo**me; me** estaba lavando / estaba lavándo**me.**

Irregular Verbs
andar, caber, caer

Infinitive	Past participle / Present participle	Indicative						Subjunctive	
		Present	Imperfect	Preterite	Future	Conditional	Present	Imperfect
andar	andado	ando	andaba	anduve	andaré	andaría	ande	anduviera
to walk;	andando	andas	andabas	anduviste	andarás	andarías	andes	anduvieras
to go		anda	andaba	anduvo	andará	andaría	ande	anduviera
		andamos	andábamos	anduvimos	andaremos	andaríamos	andemos	anduviéramos
		andáis	andabais	anduvisteis	andaréis	andaríais	andéis	anduvierais
		andan	andaban	anduvieron	andarán	andarían	anden	anduvieran
caber	cabido	quepo	cabía	cupe	cabré	cabría	quepa	cupiera
to fit; to	cabiendo	cabes	cabías	cupiste	cabrás	cabrías	quepas	cupieras
have enough		cabe	cabía	cupo	cabrá	cabría	quepa	cupiera
space		cabemos	cabíamos	cupimos	cabremos	cabríamos	quepamos	cupiéramos
		cabéis	cabíais	cupisteis	cabréis	cabríais	quepáis	cupierais
		caben	cabían	cupieron	cabrán	cabrían	quepan	cupieran
caer	caído	caigo	caía	caí	caeré	caería	caiga	cayera
to fall	cayendo	caes	caías	caíste	caerás	caerías	caigas	cayeras
		cae	caía	cayó	caerá	caería	caiga	cayera
		caemcs	caíamos	caímos	caeremos	caeríamos	caigamos	cayéramos
		caéis	caíais	caísteis	caeréis	caeríais	caigáis	cayerais
		caen	caían	cayeron	caerán	caerían	caigan	cayeran

Commands

Person	andar		caber		caer	
	Affirmative	Negative	Affirmative	Negative	Affirmative	Negative
tú	anda	no andes	cabe	no quepas	cae	no caigas
usted	ande	no ande	quepa	no quepa	caiga	no caiga
nosotros	andemos	no andemos	quepamos	no quepamos	caigamos	no caigamos
vosotros	andad	no andéis	cabed	no quepáis	caed	no caigáis
ustedes	anden	no anden	quepan	no quepan	caigan	no caigan

dar, decir, estar

Infinitive	Past participle / Present participle	Indicative					Subjunctive	
		Present	Imperfect	Preterite	Future	Conditional	Present	Imperfect
dar *to give*	dado dando	doy das da damos dais dan	daba dabas daba dábamos dabais daban	di diste dio dimos disteis dieron	daré darás dará daremos daréis darán	daría darías daría daríamos daríais darían	dé des dé demos deis den	diera dieras diera diéramos dierais dieran
decir *to say, to tell*	dicho diciendo	digo dices dice decimos decís dicen	decía decías decía decíamos decíais decían	dije dijiste dijo dijimos dijisteis dijeron	diré dirás dirá diremos diréis dirán	diría dirías diría diríamos diríais dirían	diga digas diga digamos digáis digan	dijera dijeras dijera dijéramos dijerais dijeran
estar *to be*	estado estando	estoy estás está estamos estáis están	estaba estabas estaba estábamos estabais estaban	estuve estuviste estuvo estuvimos estuvisteis estuvieron	estaré estarás estará estaremos estaréis estarán	estaría estarías estaría estaríamos estaríais estarían	esté estés esté estemos estéis estén	estuviera estuvieras estuviera estuviéramos estuvierais estuvieran

Commands

Person	dar		decir		estar	
	Affirmative	Negative	Affirmative	Negative	Affirmative	Negative
tú	da	no des	di	no digas	está	no estés
usted	dé	no dé	diga	no diga	esté	no esté
nosotros	demos	no demos	digamos	no digamos	estemos	no estemos
vosotros	dad	no deis	decid	no digáis	estad	no estéis
ustedes	den	no den	digan	no digan	estén	no estén

haber*, hacer, ir

Infinitive	Past participle / Present participle	Indicative						Subjunctive	
		Present	Imperfect	Preterite	Future	Conditional		Present	Imperfect
haber* *to have*	habido habiendo	he has ha hemos habéis han	había habías había habíamos habíais habían	hube hubiste hubo hubimos hubisteis hubieron	habré habrás habrá habremos habréis habrán	habría habrías habría habríamos habríais habrían		haya hayas haya hayamos hayáis hayan	hubiera hubieras hubiera hubiéramos hubierais hubieran
hacer *do*	hecho haciendo	hago haces hace hacemos hacéis hacen	hacía hacías hacía hacíamos hacíais hacían	hice hiciste hizo hicimos hicisteis hicieron	haré harás hará haremos haréis harán	haría harías haría haríamos haríais harían		haga hagas haga hagamos hagáis hagan	hiciera hicieras hiciera hiciéramos hicierais hicieran
ir *to go*	ido yendo	voy vas va vamos vais van	iba ibas iba íbamos ibais iban	fui fuiste fue fuimos fuisteis fueron	iré irás irá iremos iréis irán	iría irías iría iríamos iríais irían		vaya vayas vaya vayamos vayáis vayan	fuera fueras fuera fuéramos fuerais fueran

*Haber also has an impersonal form, hay. This form is used to express "There is, There are." The imperative of haber is not used.

Commands

Person	hacer		ir	
	Affirmative	Negative	Affirmative	Negative
tú	haz	no hagas	ve	no vayas
usted	haga	no haga	vaya	no vaya
nosotros	hagamos	no hagamos	vamos	no vayamos
vosotros	haced	no hagáis	id	no vayáis
ustedes	hagan	no hagan	vayan	no vayan

jugar, oír, oler

Infinitive	Past participle / Present participle	Indicative					Subjunctive	
		Present	Imperfect	Preterite	Future	Conditional	Present	Imperfect
jugar *to play*	jugado / jugando	juego juegas juega jugamos jugáis juegan	jugaba jugabas jugaba jugábamos jugabais jugaban	jugué jugaste jugó jugamos jugasteis jugaron	jugaré jugarás jugará jugaremos jugaréis jugarán	jugaría jugarías jugaría jugaríamos jugaríais jugarían	juegue juegues juegue juguemos juguéis jueguen	jugara jugaras jugara jugáramos jugarais jugaran
oír *to hear, to listen*	oído / oyendo	oigo oyes oye oímos oís oyen	oía oías oía oíamos oíais oían	oí oíste oyó oímos oísteis oyeron	oiré oirás oirá oiremos oiréis oirán	oiría oirías oiría oiríamos oiríais oirían	oiga oigas oiga oigamos oigáis oigan	oyera oyeras oyera oyéramos oyerais oyeran
oler *to smell*	olido / oliendo	huelo hueles huele olemos oléis huelen	olía olías olía olíamos olíais olían	olí oliste olió olimos olisteis olieron	oleré olerás olerá oleremos oleréis olerán	olería olerías olería oleríamos oleríais olerían	huela huelas huela olamos oláis huelan	oliera olieras oliera oliéramos olierais olieran

Commands

Person	jugar Affirmative	jugar Negative	oír Affirmative	oír Negative	oler Affirmative	oler Negative
tú	juega	no juegues	oye	no oigas	huele	no huelas
usted	juegue	no juegue	oiga	no oiga	huela	no huela
nosotros	juguemos	no juguemos	oigamos	no oigamos	olamos	no olamos
vosotros	jugad	no juguéis	oíd	no oigáis	oled	no oláis
ustedes	jueguen	no jueguen	oigan	no oigan	huelan	no huelan

poder, poner, querer

Infinitive	Past participle / Present participle	Indicative Present	Imperfect	Preterite	Future	Conditional	Subjunctive Present	Imperfect
poder _to be able to, can_	podido / pudiendo	puedo	podía	pude	podré	podría	pueda	pudiera
		puedes	podías	pudiste	podrás	podrías	puedas	pudieras
		puede	podía	pudo	podrá	podría	pueda	pudiera
		podemos	podíamos	pudimos	podremos	podríamos	podamos	pudiéramos
		podéis	podíais	pudisteis	podréis	podríais	podáis	pudierais
		pueden	podían	pudieron	podrán	podrían	puedan	pudieran
poner* _to put_	puesto / poniendo	pongo	ponía	puse	pondré	pondría	ponga	pusiera
		pones	ponías	pusiste	pondrás	pondrías	pongas	pusieras
		pone	ponía	puso	pondrá	pondría	ponga	pusiera
		ponemos	poníamos	pusimos	pondremos	pondríamos	pongamos	pusiéramos
		ponéis	poníais	pusisteis	pondréis	pondríais	pongáis	pusierais
		ponen	ponían	pusieron	pondrán	pondrían	pongan	pusieran
querer _to want, to wish; to love_	querido / queriendo	quiero	quería	quise	querré	querría	quiera	quisiera
		quieres	querías	quisiste	querrás	querrías	quieras	quisieras
		quiere	quería	quiso	querrá	querría	quiera	quisiera
		queremos	queríamos	quisimos	querremos	querríamos	queramos	quisiéramos
		queréis	queríais	quisisteis	querréis	querríais	queráis	quisierais
		quieren	querían	quisieron	querrán	querrían	quieran	quisieran

*Similar verbs to poner: imponer, suponer.

Commands**

	poner		querer	
Person	Affirmative	Negative	Affirmative	Negative
tú	pon	no pongas	quiere	no quieras
usted	ponga	no ponga	quiera	no quiera
nosotros	pongamos	no pongamos	queramos	no queramos
vosotros	poned	no pongáis	quered	no queráis
ustedes	pongan	no pongan	quieran	no quieran

Note: The imperative of **poder is used very infrequently and is not included here.

saber, salir, ser

Infinitive	Past participle / Present participle	Indicative					Subjunctive	
		Present	Imperfect	Preterite	Future	Conditional	Present	Imperfect
saber *to know*	sabido sabiendo	sé sabes sabe sabemos sabéis saben	sabía sabías sabía sabíamos sabíais sabían	supe supiste supo supimos supisteis supieron	sabré sabrás sabrá sabremos sabréis sabrán	sabría sabrías sabría sabríamos sabríais sabrían	sepa sepas sepa sepamos sepáis sepan	supiera supieras supiera supiéramos supierais supieran
salir *to go out, to leave*	salido saliendo	salgo sales sale salimos salís salen	salía salías salía salíamos salíais salían	salí saliste salió salimos salisteis salieron	saldré saldrás saldrá saldremos saldréis saldrán	saldría saldrías saldría saldríamos saldríais saldrían	salga salgas salga salgamos salgáis salgan	saliera salieras saliera saliéramos salierais salieran
ser *to be*	sido siendo	soy eres es somos sois son	era eras era éramos erais eran	fui fuiste fue fuimos fuisteis fueron	seré serás será seremos seréis serán	sería serías sería seríamos seríais serían	sea seas sea seamos seáis sean	fuera fueras fuera fuéramos fuerais fueran

Commands

Person	saber		salir		ser	
	Affirmative	Negative	Affirmative	Negative	Affirmative	Negative
tú	sabe	no sepas	sal	no salgas	sé	no seas
usted	sepa	no sepa	salga	no salga	sea	no sea
nosotros	sepamos	no sepamos	salgamos	no salgamos	seamos	no seamos
vosotros	sabed	no sepáis	salid	no salgáis	sed	no seáis
ustedes	sepan	no sepan	salgan	no salgan	sean	no sean

sonreír, tener*, traer

Infinitive	Past participle / Present participle	Indicative					Subjunctive	
		Present	Imperfect	Preterite	Future	Conditional	Present	Imperfect
sonreír *to smile*	sonreído sonriendo	sonrío sonríes sonríe sonreímos sonreís sonríen	sonreía sonreías sonreía sonreíamos sonreíais sonreían	sonreí sonreíste sonrió sonreímos sonreísteis sonrieron	sonreiré sonreirás sonreirá sonreiremos sonreiréis sonreirán	sonreiría sonreirías sonreiría sonreiríamos sonreiríais sonreirían	sonría sonrías sonría sonriamos sonriáis sonrían	sonriera sonrieras sonriera sonriéramos sonrierais sonrieran
tener* *to have*	tenido teniendo	tengo tienes tiene tenemos tenéis tienen	tenía tenías tenía teníamos teníais tenían	tuve tuviste tuvo tuvimos tuvisteis tuvieron	tendré tendrás tendrá tendremos tendréis tendrán	tendría tendrías tendría tendríamos tendríais tendrían	tenga tengas tenga tengamos tengáis tengan	tuviera tuvieras tuviera tuviéramos tuvierais tuvieran
traer *to bring*	traído trayendo	traigo traes trae traemos traéis traen	traía traías traía traíamos traíais traían	traje trajiste trajo trajimos trajisteis trajeron	traeré traerás traerá traeremos traeréis traerán	traería traerías traería traeríamos traeríais traerían	traiga traigas traiga traigamos traigáis traigan	trajera trajeras trajera trajéramos trajerais trajeran

*Many verbs ending in -tener are conjugated like tener: contener, detener, entretener(se), mantener, obtener, retener.

Commands

Person	sonreír Affirmative	Negative	tener Affirmative	Negative	traer Affirmative	Negative
tú	sonríe	no sonrías	ten	no tengas	trae	no traigas
usted	sonría	no sonría	tenga	no tenga	traiga	no traiga
nosotros	sonriamos	no sonriamos	tengamos	no tengamos	traigamos	no traigamos
vosotros	sonreíd	no sonriáis	tened	no tengáis	traed	no traigáis
ustedes	sonrían	no sonrían	tengan	no tengan	traigan	no traigan

Infinitive	Past participle / Present participle	Indicative					Subjunctive	
		Present	Imperfect	Preterite	Future	Conditional	Present	Imperfect
valer *to be worth*	valido / valiendo	valgo	valía	valí	valdré	valdría	valga	valiera
		vales	valías	valiste	valdrás	valdrías	valgas	valieras
		vale	valía	valió	valdrá	valdría	valga	valiera
		valemos	valíamos	valimos	valdremos	valdríamos	valgamos	valiéramos
		valéis	valíais	valisteis	valdréis	valdríais	valgáis	valierais
		valen	valían	valieron	valdrán	valdrían	valgan	valieran
venir* *to come*	venido / viniendo	vengo	venía	vine	vendré	vendría	venga	viniera
		vienes	venías	viniste	vendrás	vendrías	vengas	vinieras
		viene	venía	vino	vendrá	vendría	venga	viniera
		venimos	veníamos	vinimos	vendremos	vendríamos	vengamos	viniéramos
		venís	veníais	vinisteis	vendréis	vendríais	vengáis	vinierais
		vienen	venían	vinieron	vendrán	vendrían	vengan	vinieran
ver *to see*	visto / viendo	veo	veía	vi	veré	vería	vea	viera
		ves	veías	viste	verás	verías	veas	vieras
		ve	veía	vio	verá	vería	vea	viera
		vemos	veíamos	vimos	veremos	veríamos	veamos	viéramos
		veis	veíais	visteis	veréis	veríais	veáis	vierais
		ven	veían	vieron	verán	verían	vean	vieran

*Similar verb to venir: prevenir

Commands

Person	valer Affirmative	valer Negative	venir Affirmative	venir Negative	ver Affirmative	ver Negative
tú	vale	no valgas	ven	no vengas	ve	no veas
usted	valga	no valga	venga	no venga	vea	no vea
nosotros	valgamos	no valgamos	vengamos	no vengamos	veamos	no veamos
vosotros	valed	no valgáis	venid	no vengáis	ved	no veáis
ustedes	valgan	no valgan	vengan	no vengan	vean	no vean

AMÉRICA DEL SUR

MAR CARIBE
OCÉANO ATLÁNTICO
BELICE
HONDURAS
NICARAGUA
Lago de Managua
Maracaibo
Barranquilla
Cartagena
Caracas
Lago de Maracaibo
Río Orinoco
EL SALVADOR
GUATEMALA
PANAMÁ
COSTA RICA
San Cristóbal
VENEZUELA
GUAYANA
Georgetown
Paramaribo
SURINAM
Cayena
Medellín
Boa Vista
GUAYANA FRANCESA
Bogotá
Cali
COLOMBIA
ECUADOR
ISLAS GALÁPAGOS
Quito
Guayaquil
Cuenca
Iquitos
Río Amazonas
AMAZONAS
PERÚ
LOS ANDES
Lima
Machu Picchu
Ayacucho
Cuzco
BOLIVIA
BRASIL
Brasilia
Lago Titicaca
La Paz
Santa Cruz
Sucre
Potosí
Río Paraná
Río de Janeiro
São Paulo
CHILE
LOS ANDES
PARAGUAY
Asunción
Iguazú
OCÉANO ATLÁNTICO
OCÉANO PACÍFICO
Río Uruguay
Córdoba
URUGUAY
Montevideo
Viña del Mar
Valparaíso
Santiago
Buenos Aires
ARGENTINA
Bahía Blanca
Río de la Plata
Concepción
Viedma
Malvinas (Br.)
Estrecho de Magallanes
TIERRA DEL FUEGO

ECUADOR

250 500 750 1,000 MILLAS
500 1,000 1,500 KILÓMETROS

NIGERIA
ÁFRICA
Malabo
CAMERÚN
GUINEA ECUATORIAL
GABÓN
ÁFRICA
MILLAS 500
KILÓMETROS 750

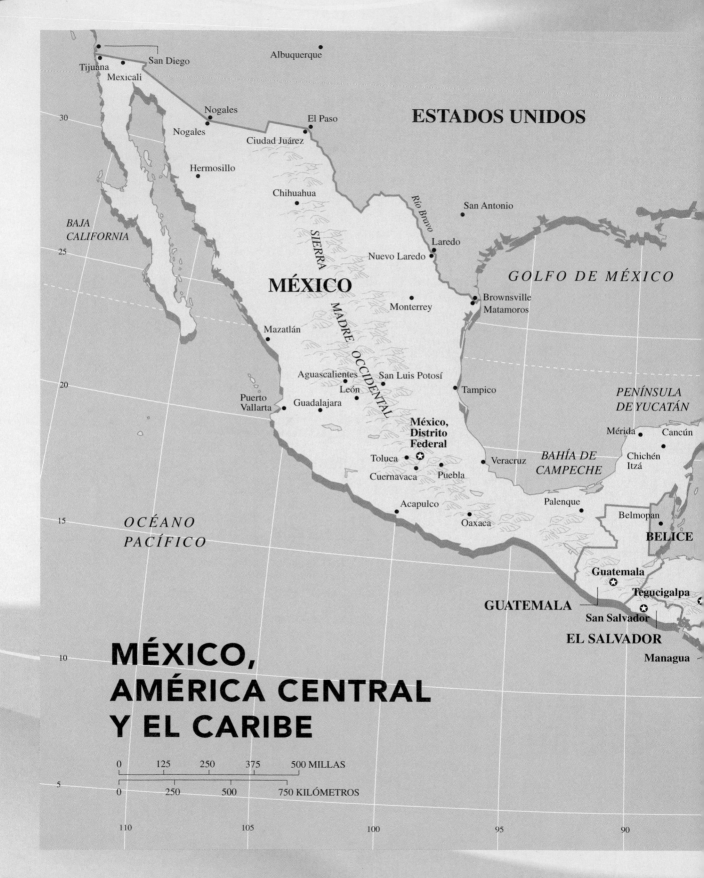

ESTADOS UNIDOS

Albuquerque

San Diego
Tijuana
Mexicali

Nogales
Nogales
El Paso
Ciudad Juárez

Hermosillo

Chihuahua

San Antonio

Río Bravo

Laredo

Nuevo Laredo

GOLFO DE MÉXICO

BAJA
CALIFORNIA

SIERRA

MÉXICO

MADRE OCCIDENTAL

Monterrey

Brownsville
Matamoros

Mazatlán

Aguascalientes
León
San Luis Potosí

Tampico

PENÍNSULA
DE YUCATÁN

Puerto
Vallarta
Guadalajara

México,
Distrito
Federal

Mérida
Cancún

BAHÍA DE
CAMPECHE

Chichén
Itzá

Toluca
Cuernavaca
Puebla

Veracruz

Acapulco

Palenque

Belmopan

Oaxaca

OCÉANO
PACÍFICO

BELICE

Guatemala

Tegucigalpa

GUATEMALA

San Salvador

EL SALVADOR

Managua

MÉXICO,
AMÉRICA CENTRAL
Y EL CARIBE

| 0 | 125 | 250 | 375 | 500 MILLAS |

| 0 | 250 | 500 | 750 KILÓMETROS |

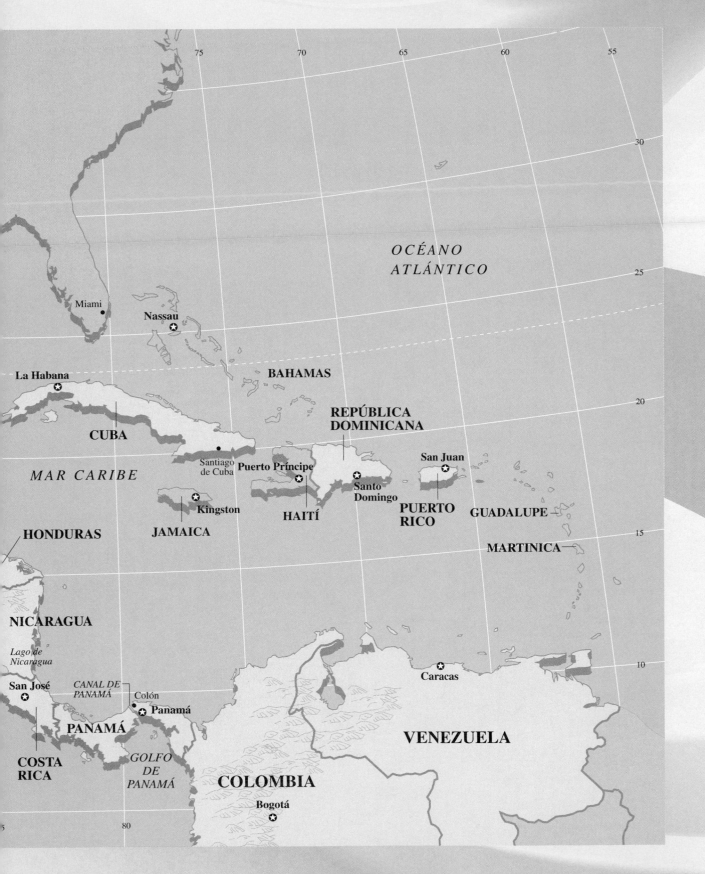

75 70 65 60 55

30

OCÉANO ATLÁNTICO

25

Miami

Nassau

BAHAMAS

20

La Habana

CUBA

REPÚBLICA DOMINICANA

San Juan

MAR CARIBE

Santiago de Cuba

Puerto Príncipe

Santo Domingo

PUERTO RICO

GUADALUPE

Kingston

HAITÍ

JAMAICA

HONDURAS

15

MARTINICA

NICARAGUA

Lago de Nicaragua

10

Caracas

San José

CANAL DE PANAMÁ

Colón

Panamá

PANAMÁ

VENEZUELA

COSTA RICA

GOLFO DE PANAMÁ

COLOMBIA

Bogotá

80

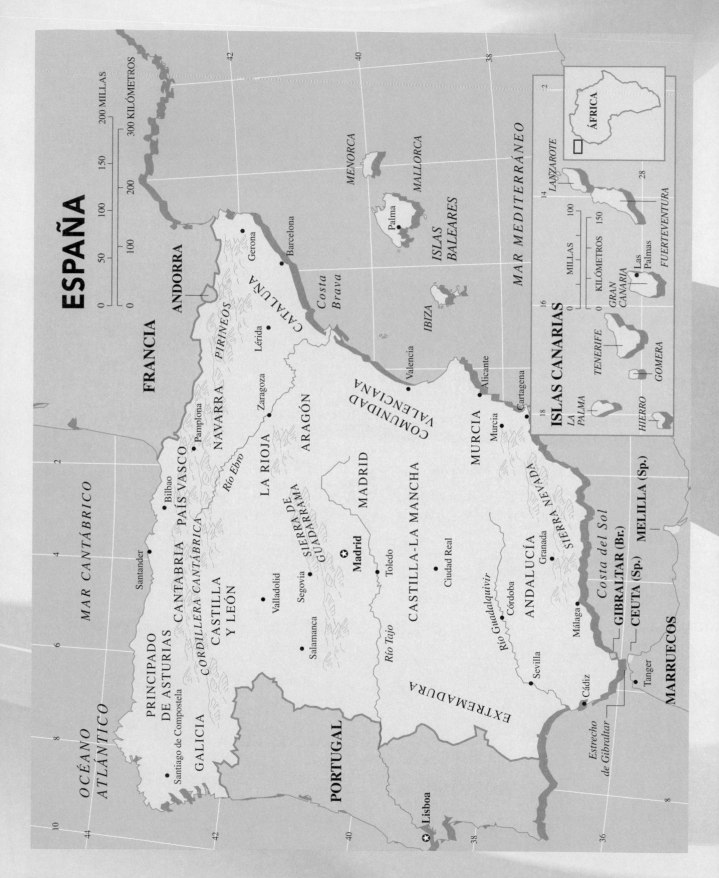

ESPAÑA

FRANCIA

ANDORRA

PIRINEOS

CATALUÑA

Gerona

Barcelona

Costa Brava

Lérida

NAVARRA

Pamplona

Río Ebro

Zaragoza

ARAGÓN

LA RIOJA

PAÍS VASCO

Bilbao

CANTABRIA

CORDILLERA CANTÁBRICA

Santander

MAR CANTÁBRICO

PRINCIPADO DE ASTURIAS

GALICIA

Santiago de Compostela

OCÉANO ATLÁNTICO

CASTILLA Y LEÓN

Valladolid

Segovia

Salamanca

SIERRA DE GUADARRAMA

MADRID

★ Madrid

Toledo

Río Tajo

CASTILLA-LA MANCHA

Ciudad Real

COMUNIDAD VALENCIANA

Valencia

Alicante

MURCIA

Murcia

Cartagena

SIERRA NEVADA

Granada

ANDALUCÍA

Córdoba

Río Guadalquivir

Sevilla

Málaga

Costa del Sol

Cádiz

EXTREMADURA

PORTUGAL

★ Lisboa

Estrecho de Gibraltar

GIBRALTAR (Br.)

CEUTA (Sp.)

MELILLA (Sp.)

MARRUECOS

Tánger

MENORCA

MALLORCA

Palma

ISLAS BALEARES

IBIZA

MAR MEDITERRÁNEO

ÁFRICA

ISLAS CANARIAS

LANZAROTE

FUERTEVENTURA

GRAN CANARIA

Las Palmas

TENERIFE

GOMERA

HIERRO

LA PALMA

MILLAS

KILÓMETROS

0   100   150

0   16   18   28

200 MILLAS

300 KILÓMETROS

0   50   100   150   200

0   100   200   300

2

40

42

38

36

4

6

8

10

44

42

40

38

Spanish–English Glossary

The vocabulary includes the active vocabulary presented in the chapters and many receptive words. Exceptions are verb conjugations, regular past participles, adverbs ending in **-mente,** superlatives, diminutives, and proper names of individuals and most countries. Active words are followed by a number that indicates the chapter in which the word appears as an active item. **P** refers to the opening pages that precede Chapter 1.

The gender of nouns is indicated except for masculine nouns ending in **-o** and feminine nouns ending in **-a.** Stem changes and spelling changes are shown for verbs, e.g., **dormir (ue, u); buscar (qu).**

The following abbreviations are used. Note that the *adj., adv.,* and *pron.* designations are used only to distinguish similar or identical words that are different parts of speech.

adj.	adjective	*fam.*	familiar	*irreg.*	irregular verb	*p.p.*	past participle
adv.	adverb	*form.*	formal	*m.*	masculine	*pron.*	pronoun
f.	feminine	*inf.*	infinitive	*pl.*	plural	*s.*	singular

A

a to; **~ cambio de** in exchange for; **~ nivel mundial** worldwide; **~ pesar de** in spite of; **~ pie** on foot, walking, 6; **~ través de** across, throughout

abogado(a) lawyer, 5

abrelatas eléctrico (*m. s.*) electric can opener, 10

abrigo coat, 8

abril April, 1

abrir to open, 3; **Abran los libros.** Open your books. P

abuelo(a) grandfather (grandmother), 5

abundancia abundance

aburrido(a) boring, 2; bored, 4

aburrimiento boredom

acabar de (+inf.) to have just (*done something*), 2

académico(a) academic

acceder to access, 4

accesorio accessory, 8

acción (*f.*) action, 5

aceite (*m.*) **de oliva** olive oil, 9

acero steel

aconsejar to advise, 10

acostarse (ue) to go to bed, 5

acrecentar (ie) to strengthen; to increase

actividad (*f.*) activity, P; **~ deportiva** sports activity, 7

activo(a) active, 2

actor (*m.*) actor, 5

actriz (*f.*) actress, 5

actualidad (*f.*): **en la ~** at the present time

acudir to go; to attend

adelantar to get ahead, to promote

adelante ahead

además besides

adinerado(a) rich, wealthy

adiós goodbye, 1

adivinar to guess; **Adivina.** Guess. P

administración (*f.*) **de empresas** business administration, 3

¿adónde? (to) where?

adquisición (*f.*) acquisition

aeropuerto airport, 6

afán (*m.*) desire

afeitarse to shave oneself, 5

afueras (*f. pl.*) outskirts, 10

agosto August, 1

agregar (gu) to add, 9

agrícola agricultural

agua (*f.*) (*but:* **el agua**) water; **~ dulce** fresh water; **~ mineral** sparkling water, 9

aguacate avocado, 9

ajedrez (*m.*) chess

ajo garlic, 9

al (a + el) to the, 3

albergar (gu) to shelter

albóndiga meatball

alcalde (alcaldesa) mayor

alcanzar (c) to achieve

alemán (alemana) German, 2

alemán (*m.*) German language, 3

alfabeto alphabet

alfombra rug, carpet, 10

algo something, 6

algodón (*m.*) cotton, 8

alguien someone, 6

algún, alguno(a)(s) some, any, 6

alistar to recruit; to enroll

allá over there, 6

allí there, 6

alma (*f.*) (*but:* **el alma**) soul

almacén (*m.*) store, 6

almeja clam, 9

almohada pillow

almuerzo lunch, 9

¿Aló? hello (*on the phone*), 1

alpinismo: practicar / hacer ~ to hike, to (mountain) climb, 7

alquilar videos / películas to rent videos / movies, 2

alquiler (*m.*) rent

alrededor de around

altitud (*f.*) altitude, height

altivo(a) arrogant

alto(a) tall, 2

altoparlante (*m., f.*) speaker, 4

altura height

amanecer (zc) to dawn

amante (*m., f.*) lover

amar to love

amarillo(a) yellow, 4

ambiente (*m.*) atmosphere; **medio ~** (*m.*) environment

ambigüedad (*f.*) ambiguity

ambos(as) both

amenaza threat

amigo(a) friend, P

amor (*m.*) love

anaranjado(a) orange (*in color*), 4

andar (*irreg.*) to walk, 8

anexo attachment

anfitrión (*m.*) host

anhelo wish, desire

anillo ring, 8

anoche last night, 7

anónimo(a) anonymous

Antártida Antarctica

anteayer the day before yesterday, 7

antecesor(a) ancestor

anteojos (*m. pl.*) eyeglasses

antepasado(a) ancestor

anteponer to give preference

antes before, 5

anticuado(a) antiquated, old-fashioned

antipático(a) unpleasant, 2

antros bar or club; the "in" place

anuncio personal personal ad

añadir to add, 9

año year, 3; ~ **pasado** last year, 7; **tener** (*irreg.*) ... ~ to be . . . years old, 1

apacible mild, gentle

apagar (gu) to turn off, 2

aparatos electrónicos electronics, 4

aparecer (zc) to appear

apariencia física physical appearance

apartamento apartment, 6

apenas scarcely

apetecer (zc) to long for

aplicación (*f.*) application, 4

apodo nickname

apoyar to support

apreciar to appreciate

aprender to learn, 3

aprendizaje (*m.*) learning

apropiado(a) appropriate

apto(a) apt, fit

apuntes (*m.*) notes, P

aquel / aquella(s) (*adj.*) those (over there), 6

aquél / aquélla(s) (*pron.*) those (over there), 6

aquí here, 6

árbol (*m.*) tree; ~ **genealógico** family tree

archivar to file, 4

archivo file, 4; ~ **PDF** PDF file, 4

arder to burn

arete (*m.*) earring, 8

argentino(a) Argentinian, 2

arquitecto(a) architect, 5

arquitectura architecture, 3

arreglar el dormitorio to straighten up the bedroom, 10

arroz (*m.*) **con pollo** chicken with rice, 9

arrugado(a) wrinkled

arte (*m.*) art, 3

artesanía handicrafts

artículo article, 1

artista (*m., f.*) artist, 5

asado(a) grilled

asco disgusting

asegurarse to make sure

asistente (*m., f.*) assistant, 5; ~ (*m.*) **electrónico** electronic notebook, 4

asistir a to attend, 3

aspiradora vacuum cleaner, 10

ataque (*m.*) attack

atardecer (*m.*) late afternoon

atún (*m.*) tuna, 9

audiencia audience

audífonos (*m. pl.*) earphones, 4

audio audio, P

auditorio auditorium, 6

aumentar to increase

aun even

aún yet (*in negative contexts*); still

australiano(a) Australian, 2

autobús: **en** ~ by bus, 6

automóvil: **en** ~ by car, 6

avenida avenue, 1

avergonzado(a) embarrassed

avergonzar (ue) (c) to embarrass

avión (*m.*) airplane; **en** ~ by airplane, 6

aviso warning

ayer yesterday, 3

ayuda help

ayudar to help, 8

azúcar (*m., f.*) sugar, 9; **caña de** ~ sugar cane

azul blue, 4

B

bacalao codfish, 9

bailar to dance, 2

baile (*m.*) dance, 3

bajar to get down from, to get off of (*a bus, etc.*), 6; to download, 4

bajo(a) short (*in height*), 2

balay large basket

baldosa paving stone

banco (commercial) bank, 6

bañador(a) bather

bañar to swim; to give someone a bath, 5; **bañarse** to take a bath, 5

baño bathroom, 10

barato: Es muy ~. It's very inexpensive. 8

barco boat

barrer el suelo / el piso to sweep the floor, 10

barrio neighborhood, 1; ~ **residencial** residential neighborhood, suburbs, 10; ~ **comercial** business district, 10

básquetbol (*m.*) basketball, 7

basta it is enough

bastante somewhat, rather, 4

Bastante bien. Quite well. 1

basura garbage, 10; **sacar la** ~ to take out the garbage, 10

basurero wastebasket

batir to beat; to break

beber to drink, 3

bebida beverage, 9

béisbol (*m.*) baseball, 7

belleza beauty

bello(a) beautiful

berro watercress

besar to kiss

bicicleta: en ~ on bicycle, 6; **montar en** ~ to ride a bike, 7

bien well, 4; ~, **gracias.** Fine, thank you. 1; **(no) muy** ~ (not) very well, 1

bienestar (*m.*) well-being

bienvenido(a) welcome

bilingüe bilingual

biología biology, 3

bistec (*m.*) steak, 6

blanco(a) white, 4

blog blog, 4

blusa blouse, 8

bocadillo sandwich, 9

boda wedding

bodegón (*m.*) tavern

bolígrafo ballpoint pen, P

boliviano(a) Bolivian, 2

bolsa purse, 8

bombero(a) fire fighter, 5

bondadoso(a) kind; good

bonito(a) pretty

bordado(a) embroidered, 8

borrador (*m.*) rough draft

bosquejo outline

bota boot, 8

botar to throw out

bote (*m.*) boat

boxeo boxing, 7

brazalete (*m.*) bracelet, 8

breve brief

bróculi (*m.*) broccoli, 9

broma joke

bueno(a) good, 2; **Buenas noches.** Good night. Good evening 1; **Buenas tardes.** Good afternoon. 1; **Buenos días.** Good morning. 1

bufanda scarf, 8

buscador (*m.*) search engine, 4

buscar (qu) to look for, 2

buzón (*m.*) **electrónico** electronic mailbox, 4

C

caballo: montar a ~ to ride horseback, 7

cable (*m.*) cable, 4

cabo end

cacao chocolate

cachemira cashmere

cadena chain, 8

caer (*irreg.*) to fall

café (*m.*) coffee, 9; (*adj.*) brown, 4

cafetería cafeteria, 3

caimán (*m.*) alligator (*cayman*)

cajero automático automated bank teller, ATM, 6

cajón (*m.*) large box; drawer

calcetín (*m.*) sock, 8

calculadora calculator, P

cálculo calculus, 3

caldo de pollo chicken soup, 9

calentar (ie) to heat, 9

calidad (*f.*) quality; **de buena (alta) ~** of good (high) quality, 8

calificación (*f.*) evaluation

calle (*f.*) street, 1

calor: Hace ~. It's hot., 7; **tener** (*irreg.*) **~** to be hot, 7

caluroso(a) warm

cama bed, 10; **hacer la ~** to make the bed, 10

cámara: ~ digital digital camera, 4; **~ web** webcam, 4

camarero(a) waiter (waitress), 5

camarón (*m.*) shrimp, 9

cambio change; exchange rate; **a ~ de** in exchange for

caminar to walk, 2

camisa shirt, 8

camiseta t-shirt, 8

campestre rural

campo: ~ de estudio field of study, 3; **~ de fútbol** soccer field, 6

caña de azúcar sugar cane

canadiense (*m., f.*) Canadian, 2

canasta basket

cancha soccer field, 6; **~ de tenis** tennis court, 6

canela cinnamon

cansado(a) tired, 4

cantante (*m., f.*) singer

cantar to sing, 2

capítulo chapter, P

característica trait; **~ de la personalidad** personality trait, 2; **~ física** physical trait, 2

Caribe (*m., f.*) Caribbean (sea)

cariño love, fondness, affection

carne (*f.*) meat, 9

cargar to upload, 4

carnicería butcher shop, 6

caro: Es (demasiado) caro(a). It's (too) expensive. 8

carpintero(a) carpenter, 5

carrera career, 5

carreta wooden cart

carro: en ~ by car, 6

carta: a la ~ à la carte, 9

cartera wallet, 8

cartón (*m.*) cardboard

casa house, 6

casarse to get married, 5

casco helmet

casero(a) homemade

castaño brown, 2

catarata waterfall

catorce fourteen, P

cebolla onion, 9

celebración (*f.*) celebration

celos: tener (*irreg.*) **~** to be jealous

celosamente jealously

celoso(a) jealous

cena dinner

cenar to eat dinner, 2

censo census

centavo cent

centro center; **~ comercial** mall, 6; **~ de computación** computer center, 3; **~ de comunicaciones** media center, 3; **~ de la ciudad** downtown, 10; **~ estudiantil** student center, 6

Centroamérica Central America

cepillarse el pelo to brush one's hair, 5

cepillo brush, 5; **~ de dientes** toothbrush, 5

cerca de close to, 6

cereal (*m.*) cereal, 9

cero zero, P

cerrar (ie) to close, 4; **Cierren los libros.** Close your books. P

cerveza beer, 9

chaleco vest, 8

champú (*m.*) shampoo, 5

chaparrón (*m.*) cloudburst, downpour

chaqueta jacket (*outdoor, non-suit coat*), 8

chatear to chat online, 4

Chau. Bye, Goodbye, 1

cheque (*m.*) check; **pagar con ~ / con ~ de viajero** to pay by check / with a traveler's check, 8

chévere terrific, great, cool (*Cuba, Puerto Rico*)

chico(a) boy (girl), P

chileno(a) Chilean, 2

chimenea fireplace, 10

chino Chinese language, 3

chino(a) Chinese, 2

chisme (*m.*) gossip

chismoso(a) gossiping

chompa sweater

chuleta de puerco pork chop, 6

ciberespacio cyberspace, 4

ciclismo cycling, 7

ciego(a) blind; **cita a ciegas** blind date

cien one hundred, P; **~ mil** one hundred thousand, 8

ciencias (*f. pl.*) science, 3; **~ políticas** political science, 3

científico(a) scientific

ciento uno one hundred and one, 8

cierto(a) certain

cinco five, P; **~ mil** five thousand, 8

cincuenta fifty, P

cine (*m.*)   cinema, 6
cinturón (*m.*)   belt, 8
cita   quotation; **~ a ciegas**   blind date
ciudad (*f.*)   city, 6
claridad (*f.*)   clarity
clase (*f.*)   class, P; **~ baja**   lower class
clic: hacer ~ / doble ~   to click / double click, 4
cliente (*m., f.*)   customer, 8
clóset (*m.*)   closet, 10
cobre (*m.*)   copper
cocer (-z) (ue)   to cook, 9
coche: en ~   by car, 6
cocina   kitchen, 10
cocinar   to cook, 2
cocinero(a)   cook, chef, 5
código   code
colectivo   bus
cólera   anger
collar (*m.*)   necklace, 8
colombiano(a)   Colombian, 2
colonia   neighborhood, 1
color (*m.*)   color, 4; **de un solo ~** solid (colored), 8
coma   comma
comedor (*m.*)   dining room, 10
comenzar (ie) (c)   to begin, 4
comer   to eat, 3; **darle de ~ al perro / gato**   to feed the dog / cat, 10
cómico(a)   funny, 2
comida   food, 6
comino   cumin, 9
¿cómo?   how? 3; **¿~ desea pagar?**   How do you wish to pay? 8; **¿~ es?**   What's he / she / it like? 2; **¿~ está (usted)?** (*s. form.*)   How are you? 1; **¿~ están (ustedes)?** (*pl.*) How are you? 1; **¿~ estás (tú)?** (*s. fam.*)   How are you? 1; **¿~ te / le / les va?**   How's it going with you? 1; **~ no.**   Of course. 6; **¿~ se dice…?**   How do you say . . . ? P; **¿~ se llama?** (*s. form.*)   What's your name? 1; **¿~ te llamas?** (*s. fam.*)   What's your name? 1
cómoda   dresser, 10
compañero(a) de cuarto   roommate, P
comparación (*f.*)   comparison, 8
compartir   to share, 3
competencia   competition, 7

competir (i, i)   to compete
complicidad (*f.*)   complicity
comportamiento   behavior
comprar   to buy, 2
compras: hacer las ~ to go shopping, 6
comprender   to understand, 3
comprensión (*f.*)   understanding
comprometerse   to get engaged, 5
computación (*f.*)   computer science, 3
computadora   computer, P; **~ portátil**   laptop computer, P
común   common
comunicación (*f.*) **pública**   public communications, 3
con   with
concordancia   agreement
concurso   contest
conducir (zc)   to drive, to conduct, 5
conectar   to connect, 4
conexión (*f.*)   connection, 4; **hacer una ~**   to go online, 4
confección (*f.*)   confection
conferencista (*m., f.*)   speaker
congelado(a)   frozen, 9
congelador   freezer, 10
conjunto   group; **en ~**   as a group
conmigo   with me, 8
conocer (zc)   to meet; to know a person, to be familiar with, 5
conseguir (i, i)   to get, to obtain, 8
contabilidad (*f.*)   accounting, 3
contado: al ~   in cash, 8
contador(a)   accountant, 5
contar (ue)   to tell, to relate, 4; to count; **~ con**   to be certain of
contento(a)   happy, 4
contestar   to answer; **Contesten.**   Answer. P
contigo   with you (*fam.*), 8
contracción (*f.*)   contraction, 3
contrario: al ~   on the contrary
contraseña   password, 4
conversación (*f.*)   conversation
convertir (ie, i)   to change
copa   wine glass, goblet, 9
coraje (*m.*)   courage
cordillera   mountain range
coreano(a)   Korean, 2
corregir (i, i) (j)   to correct
correo electrónico   e-mail, 4
correr   to run, 3 to mow the lawn, 10; **~ la conexión**   to go offline, 4

cortesía   courtesy, 4
cortina   curtain, 10
corto(a)   short (*in length*)
costarricense (*m., f.*)   Costa Rican, 2
cotidiano(a)   daily
crear   to create
creativo(a)   creative
crecimiento   growth
creer (en)   to believe (in); to think, 3
cronología   chronology
crucero   cruise ship
crudo(a)   raw, 9
cruzar (c)   to cross, 6
cuaderno   notebook, P
cuadra   (city) block, 6
cuadro   painting; print, 10
cuadros: a ~   plaid, 8
¿cuál?   what? which one? 3; **¿~ es tu / su dirección (electrónica)?** (*s. fam. / form.*)   What's your (e-mail) address? 1; **¿~ es tu / su número de teléfono?** (*s. fam. / form.*)   What is your phone number? 1
¿cuáles?   what? which ones? 3
cualquier   whatever
¿cuándo?   when? 3; **¿~ es tu cumpleaños?**   When is your birthday? 1
¿cuánto(a)?   how much? 3; **¿Cuánto cuesta(n)?**   How much does it (do they) cost? 8
¿cuántos(as)?   how many? 3
cuarenta   forty, P
cuarto   room, P; bedroom, 10
cuarto(a)   fourth, 10
cuate(a)   friend, buddy
cuatro   four, P
cuatrocientos(as)   four hundred, 8
cubano(a)   Cuban, 2
cuchara   spoon, 9
cucharada   tablespoonful, 9
cucharadita   teaspoonful, 9
cuchillo   knife, 9
cuenta   check, bill, 9
cuento de hadas   fairy tale
cuero   leather, 8
cuestionario   questionnaire
cuidado: tener (*irreg.*) **~**   to be careful, 7; **¡~!**   careful!
cuidadoso(a)   cautious, 2
culinario(a)   culinary

cultura culture
cuna cradle
cuñado(a) brother-in-law (sister-in-law), 5
curso básico basic course, 3
cuy (*m.*) guinea pig
cuyo(a) whose

D

dar (*irreg.*) to give, 5; **~ información personal** to give personal information, 1; **~ la hora** to give the time, 3; **~ un papel** to give (play) a role; **~le de comer al perro / gato** to feed the dog / cat, 10; **~le mucha dicha** to give one a lot of happiness
dato fact; piece of information
De nada. You're welcome. 1
debajo de below, underneath, 6
deber (*+ inf.*) should, ought to (*do something*), 2
décimo(a) tenth, 10
decir (*irreg.*) to say, to tell, 5; **~ cómo llegar** to give directions, 6; **~ la hora** to tell the time, 3; **Se dice...** It's said . . . , P
decoración (*f.*) decoration, 10
definido(a) definite, 1
dejar to leave, to stop, 2; **~ de** (*+ inf.*) to stop (*doing something*), 2
del (**de + el**) from the, of the, 3
delante de in front of, 6
delgado(a) thin, 2
demasiado(a) too much, 4
demostrar (ue) to demonstrate, to show
demostrativo(a) demonstrative, 6
dentista (*m., f.*) dentist, 5
dentro de inside of, 6; **~ la casa** inside the house, 10
dependiente (*m., f.*) salesclerk, 5
deporte (*m.*) sport, 7
derecha: a la ~ to the right, 6
derecho: (todo) ~ (straight) ahead, 6
desarrollar to develop
desayuno breakfast, 9
descalificar (qu) to disqualify
descalzo(a) barefoot
descansar to rest, 2
descargar to download, 4

descortés rude
describir to describe, 2
descubrir to discover, 3
descuento discount, 8
desear to want; to wish, 10
desempeñarse to manage; to work (as)
desengaño disillusionment
desilusión (*f.*) disappointment
desodorante (*m.*) deodorant, 5
despachar to dispatch; to wait on; to work (from a home office)
despacio (*adv.*) slowly; (*adj.*) slow
despedido(a) fired (*from a job*)
despedirse (i, i) to say good-bye, 1
despertar (ie) to wake someone up, 5; **despertarse (ie)** to wake up, 5
después after, 5
destacar (qu) to emphasize
detalle (*m.*) detail
detrás de behind, 6
día (*m.*) day, 3; **~ de la semana** day of the week, 3; **~ de las Madres** Mother's Day, 3; **todos los días** every day, 3
dialecto dialect
dibujo drawing, P
diccionario dictionary, P
dicha happiness
dicho saying
diciembre December, 1
diecinueve nineteen, P
dieciocho eighteen, P
dieciséis sixteen, P
diecisiete seventeen, P
diez ten, P; **~ mil** ten thousand, 8
diferencia difference
difícil difficult, 4
dinero money
director(a) de social media social media director, 5
dirección (*f.*) address
disco duro hard drive, 4
Disculpe. Excuse me. 4
diseñador(a) gráfico(a) graphic designer, 5
diseño design; **~ gráfico** graphic design, 3
disfrutar (la vida) to enjoy (life)
disponibilidad (*f.*) availability
dispuesto(a) willing

diversidad (*f.*) diversity
diversión (*f.*) amusement
divertido(a) fun, entertaining, 2
divertirse (ie, i) to have fun, 5
dividir to divide
divorciarse to get divorced, 5
doblar to turn, 6; to fold
doce twelve, P
docena dozen, 9
doctor(a) doctor
dólar (*m.*) dollar
domesticado(a) tame, tamed
domingo Sunday, 2
dominicano(a) Dominican, 2
don (doña) title of respect used with male (female) first name, 1
¿dónde? where? 3; **¿~ tienes la clase de... ?** Where does your . . . class meet? 3; **¿~ vives / vive?** (*s. fam. / form.*) Where do you live? 1
dondequiera: por ~ everywhere
dorado(a) golden, browned, 9
dormir (ue, u) to sleep, 4; **dormirse (ue, u)** to fall asleep, 5
dormitorio bedroom, 10; **~ estudiantil** dormitory, 6
dos two, P; **~ mil** two thousand, 8
doscientos(as) two hundred, 8
ducharse to take a shower, 5
duelo pain
dueño(a) owner, 5
dulce (*adj.*) sweet
duro(a) hard

E

economía economics, 3
ecuador (*m.*) equator
ecuatoriano(a) Ecuadoran, 2
edad (*f.*) age
edificio building, 6
educación (*f.*) education, 3
efectivo: en ~ in cash, 8
egoísta selfish, egotistic, 2
ejemplo example, 10; **por ~** for example, 10
ejercicio: hacer ~ to exercise, 7
el (*m.*) the, 1
él he, 1; him, 8
electricidad (*f.*) electricity
electrodoméstico appliance, 10
elefante (*m.*) elephant

ella   she, 1; her, 8

ellos(as)   they, 1; them, 8

e-mail (*m.*)   e-mail, P

embajador(a)   ambassador

emoción (*f.*)   emotion, 4

empapado(a)   drenched

emparejar   to match

empezar (ie) (c)   to begin, 4

empresas (*pl.*)   business

en   in, on, at; **~ autobús /
tren**   by bus / train, 6;
~ bicicleta   on bicycle,
6; **~ carro / coche /
automóvil**   by car,
6; **~ línea**   online, 4;
~ metro   on the subway, 6;
~ realidad   actually

enamorarse   to fall in love, 5

Encantado(a).   Delighted to meet
you. 1

encargado de   in charge of

encendida   burning, on fire

encima de   on top of, on, 6

encontrar (ue)   to find, 4

encuentro   encounter; meeting

encuesta   survey

enero   January, 1

enfatizar (c)   to emphasize

enfermarse   to get sick, 5

enfermero(a)   nurse, 5

enfermo(a)   sick, 4

enfrente de   in front of,
opposite, 6

enfriarse   to get cold, 9

engañar   to fool

engaño   hoax

enlace (*m.*)   link, 4

enojado(a)   angry, 4

ensalada   salad, 9; **~ de fruta**
fruit salad, 9; **~ de lechuga y
tomate**   lettuce and tomato
salad, 9; **~ de papa**   potato
salad, 9; **~ mixta**   tossed
salad, 9

ensayo   essay

enseñar   to teach

entender (ie)   to understand, 4

entonces   then

entre   between, 6

entregar (gu)   to turn in;
Entreguen la tarea.   Turn in
your homework. P

entrenador(a)   trainer

entrenarse   to train, 7

entresemana   during the week,
on weekdays, 3

entretener (*like* **tener**)   to
entertain

enviar   to send, 4

equilibro: poner en ~   to balance

equipo   team, 7

erupción (*f.*) **volcánica**   volcanic
eruption

escaleras (*f. pl.*)   stairs, 10

esclavo(a)   slave

escoger (j)   to choose

esconder   to hide

escribir   to write, 3; **Escriban en
sus cuadernos.**   Write in your
notebooks. P

escritorio   desk, P

escuchar   to listen; **~ música**   to
listen to music, 2; **Escuchen el
audio / el CD.**   Listen to the
tape / CD. P

escuela   school, 3

ese (esa) (*s. adj.*)   that, 6

ése (ésa) (*s. pron.*)   that one, 6

eso   that, 6; **por ~**   so, that's
why, 10

esos (esas) (*pl. adj.*)   those, 6

ésos (ésas) (*pl. pron.*)   those
(ones), 6

España   Spain

español (a)   Spanish, 2

español (*m.*)   Spanish
language, 3

espárragos (*m.pl.*)   asparagus, 9

especialidad de la casa   house
special, 9

especie (*f.*)   species

espejo   mirror, 10

esperanza   wish, hope

esperar   to hope, 10

esposo(a)   husband (wife), 5

esquí (*m.*)   ski, skiing;
~ acuático   water skiing, 7;
~ alpino   downhill skiing, 7

esquiar   to ski, 7

esquina   corner, 6

estación (*f.*)   season, 7
de trenes / autobuses   train /
bus station, 6

estacionamiento   parking lot, 6

estadio   stadium, 6

estadística   statistics, 3

estado   state, 5; **~ civil**   marital
status

Estados Unidos   United States

estadounidense (*m., f.*)   U. S.
citizen, 2

estampado(a)   print, 8

estancia   ranch

estar (*irreg.*)   to be, 1;

estatura   height (*of a person*)

este (esta) (*s. adj.*)   this, 6

éste (ésta) (*s. pron.*)   this one, 6

estilo   style

estos(as) (*pl. adj.*)   these, 6

éstos(as) (*pl. pron.*)   these
(ones), 6

estrategia   strategy

estudiante (*m., f.*)   student, P

estudiar   to study; **~ en la
biblioteca (en casa)**   to study
at the library (at home), 2;
**Estudien las páginas...
a...**   Study pages . . . to . . . P

estudio   studio, 3

estufa   stove, 10

etapa   era

Europa   Europe

evitar   to avoid

exhibir   to exhibit

exigir (j)   to demand

éxito   success

exótico(a)   exotic, strange

expresar preferencias   to
express preferences, 2

expresión (*f.*)   expression, 1

extrovertido(a)   extroverted, 2

F

fácil   easy, 4

falda   skirt, 8

falso(a)   false

familia   family;
~ nuclear   nuclear family, 5;
~ política   in-laws, 5

fantasía   fantasy

farmacia   pharmacy, 6

fascinar   to fascinate, 4

fatal   terrible, awful, 1

favor: por ~   please, 1

febrero   February, 1

fecha   date, 3; **¿A qué
~ estamos?**   What is today's
date? 3

felicidad (*f.*)   happiness

femenino(a)   feminine

feo(a)   ugly, 2

ferrocarril (*m.*)   railroad

filantrópico(a)   philanthropic

filosofía   philosophy, 3

fin (*m.*)   end; intention; **~ de
semana**   weekend, 2; **por ~**
finally, 9

final   final
financiero(a)   financial
física   physics, 3
físico(a)   physical, 5
flan (*m.*)   custard, 9
flor (*f.*)   flower
florecer (zc)   to flower, to flourish
flotador(a)   floating
fondo   background
fortaleza   fortress
foro   forum, 4
foto (*f.*)   photo, P; **sacar fotos**   to take photos, 2
francés (francesa)   French, 2
francés (*m.*)   French language, 3
frecuentemente   frequently, 4
freír (i, i)   to fry, 9
frente a   in front of, facing, opposite, 6
fresa   strawberry, 9
fresco(a)   fresh, 9; **Hace fresco.**   It's cool. 7
frijoles (*m.*) **(refritos)**   (refried) beans, 9
frío(a)   cold; **Hace frío.**   It's cold. 7; **tener** (*irreg.*) **frío**   to be cold, 7
frito(a)   fried, 9
frontera   border
fruta   fruit, 6
fuego   fire; **a ~ suave / lento**   at low heat, 9
fuente (*f.*)   source
fuera de   outside of, 6; **~ de la casa**   outside the house, 10
fuerte   strong, filling (*e.g., a meal*), 9
funcionar   to function, 4
funciones (*f. pl.*) **de la computadora**   computer functions, 4
fundador(a)   founder
fungir   to work
furioso(a)   furious, 4
fútbol (*m.*)   soccer, 7; **~ americano**   football, 7

G

gafas (*f. pl.*) **de sol**   sunglasses, 8
galleta   cookie, 9
galón (*m.*)   gallon, 9
ganadería   cattle, livestock
ganado   cattle
ganar   to win, 7

ganas: tener (*irreg.*) **~ de**   to have the urge to, to feel like, 7
garaje (*m.*)   garage, 10
gato(a)   cat, 2
gazpacho   cold tomato soup (*Spain*), 9
general: por lo ~   generally, 9
género   genre
generoso(a)   generous, 2
gente (*f.*)   people
geografía   geography, 3
gerente (*m., f.*)   manager, 5
gimnasio   gymnasium, 3
gobernador(a) (*m.*)   governor
golf (*m.*)   golf, 7
gordo(a)   fat, 2
gorra   cap, 8
gozar (c)   to enjoy
grabador (*m.*) **de discos compactos / DVD**   CD / DVD recorder, 4
grabar   to record, 4
gracias: Muchas ~.   Thank you very much. 1
grado   degree; **~ Celsio(s)**   Celsius degree, 7; **~ Fahrenheit**   Fahrenheit degree, 7
gráfica   graph
grande   big, great, 2
grano: al ~   to the point
gris   gray, 4
gritar   to shout, to scream
grito   scream
grupo   group; **~ de conversación**   chat room, 4; **~ de noticias**   news group, 4
guagua   bus (*Cuba, Puerto Rico*)
guante (*m.*)   glove, 8
guapo(a)   handsome, attractive, 2
guardar   to store; **~ la ropa**   put away the clothes, 10; to save, 4
guatemalteco(a)   Guatemalan, 2
guión (*m.*)   script
guionista (*m., f.*)   script writer
guisado   beef stew, 9
guisante (*m.*)   pea, 9
guitarra   guitar, 2
gustar: A mí / ti me / te gusta . . .   I / You like . . . , 2; **A . . . le gusta . . .**   He / She likes . . . , 2; **A . . . les gusta . . .**   They / You (*pl.*) like . . . , 2; **Me gustaría** (+ *inf.*) **. . .**   I'd like (+ *inf.*) . . . , 6

gusto   taste; **al ~**   to individual taste, 9; **El ~ es mío.**   The pleasure is mine. 1; **Mucho ~.**   My pleasure. 1; **Mucho ~ en conocerte.**   A pleasure to meet you. 1

H

haba (*f.*) (*but: el haba*)   bean
habichuela   green bean, 9
habitación (*f.*)   bedroom, 10
habitante (*m., f.*)   inhabitant
hablar por teléfono   to talk on the telephone, 2
hacer (*irreg.*)   to make, to do, 5; **Hace buen / mal tiempo.**   It's nice / bad weather. 7; **Hace calor / fresco / frío.**   It's hot / cool / cold. 7; **Hace sol / viento.**   It's sunny / windy. 7; **~ alpinismo**   to hike, 7; **~ caso**   to pay attention, to obey; **~ clic / doble clic**   to click / double click, 4; **~ ejercicio**   to exercise, 7; **~ el reciclaje**   to do the recycling, 10; **~ la cama**   to make the bed, 10; **~ las compras**   to go shopping, 6; **~ preguntas**   to ask questions, 3; **~ surfing**   to surf, 7; **~ una conexión**   to go online, 4; **Hagan la tarea para mañana.**   Do the homework for tomorrow. P
hambre (*f.*) (*but: el hambre*)   hunger; **tener** (*irreg.*) **~**   to be hungry, 7
hamburguesa   hamburger, 9; **~ con queso**   cheeseburger, 9
hardware (*m.*)   hardware, 4
harina   flour, 9
hasta   until; **~ luego.**   See you later, 1; **~ mañana.**   See you tomorrow. 1; **~ pronto.**   See you soon. 1
hay   there is, there are, 1
hecho   fact
hecho(a) (*p. p.*): **Está ~ de...**   It's made out of . . . , 8
helado de vainilla / chocolate   vanilla / chocolate ice cream, 9
herencia   heritage
hermanastro(a)   stepbrother (stepsister), 5

hermano(a) (menor, mayor) (younger, older) brother (sister), 5

hermoso(a) handsome, beautiful

hervido(a) boiled, 9

hervir (ie, i) to boil, 9

hierro iron

hijo(a) son (daughter), 5

hilo: al ~ stringed, 9

himno hymn

hispano(a) Hispanic

hispanohablante Spanish-speaking

historia history, 3

hockey (*m.*) **sobre hielo / hierba** ice / field hockey, 7

hogar (*m.*) home; **sin ~** homeless

hoja de papel sheet of paper, P

hola hello, 1

hombre (*m.*) man, P; **~ de negocios** businessman, 5

hondureño(a) Honduran, 2

honesto(a) honest

hora hour; time; **dar** (*irreg.*) **la ~** to give the time, 3; **decir la ~** to tell the time, 3

horario schedule

horno oven; **al ~** roasted (in the oven), 9

hospital (*m.*) hospital, 6

hoy today, 3; **~ es martes treinta.** Today is Tuesday the 30th. 3; **¿Qué día es ~?** What day is today? 3

huella footprint

huevo egg, 6; **~ estrellado** egg sunny-side up, 9; **~ revuelto** scrambled egg, 9

humanidades (*f. pl.*) humanities, 3

húmedo(a) humid

humilde humble

I

ícono del programa program icon, 4

identidad (*f.*) identity

idioma (*m.*) language, 3

iglesia church, 6

Igualmente. Likewise. 1

impaciente impatient, 2

impermeable (*m.*) raincoat, 8

importar to be important to someone; to mind, 4

impresionante impressive

impresora printer, 4

imprimir to print, 3

impulsivo(a) impulsive, 2

incendio forestal forest fire

increíble incredible

indefinido(a) indefinite, 1

índice (*m.*) index

indio(a) Indian, 2

indígena indigenous

influencia influence

influir (y) to influence

informática computer science, 3

informe (*m.*) report

ingeniería engineering, 3

ingeniero(a) engineer, 5

inglés (inglesa) English, 2

inglés (*m.*) English language, 3

ingrediente (*m.*) ingredient, 9

ingreso revenue

inmigración (*f.*) immigration

insistir to insist, 10

instalar to install, 4

instructor(a) instructor, P

inteligente intelligent, 2

intentar to attempt

intercambiar to exchange

interesante interesting, 2

interesar to interest, to be interesting, 4

Internet (*m.* or *f.*) Internet

intérprete (*m., f.*) interpreter

íntimo(a) intimate

introvertido(a) introverted, 2

invertir to invest

invierno winter, 7

ir (*irreg.*) to go, 3; **~ a** (+ *inf.*) to be going to (*do something*), 3; **~ de compras** to go shopping, 8; **irse** to leave, to go away, 5

irresponsable irresponsible, 2

italiano(a) Italian, 2

italiano (*m.*) Italian language

izquierda: a la ~ to the left, 6

J

jabón (*m.*) soap, 5

jamás never, 6

jamón (*m.*) ham, 6

japonés (japonesa) Japanese, 2

japonés (*m.*) Japanese language, 3

jardín (*m.*) garden, 10

jeans (*m. pl.*) jeans, 8

jornada laboral workday

joven young, 2

joyas (*f. pl.*) jewelry, 8

joyería jewelry store, 6

juego interactivo interactive game, 4

jueves (*m.*) Thursday, 3

jugar (ue) (gu) to play, 4; **~ tenis (béisbol, etc.)** to play tennis (baseball, etc.), 7

jugo de fruta fruit juice, 9

juguete (*m.*) toy, 10

juguetón (juguetona) playful

julio July, 1

junio June, 1

juntar to group

juntarse to join

juventud (*f.*) youth

K

kilo kilo, 9; **medio ~** half a kilo, 9

L

la (*f.*) the, 1

labio lip

lado side; **al ~ de** next to, on the side of, 6

ladrillo brick

lago lake, 7

lámpara lamp, 10

lana wool, 8

langosta lobster, 9

lanzarse (c) to throw oneself

lápiz (*m.*) pencil, P

lavadora washer, 10

lavandería laundry room, 10

lavaplatos (*m. s.*) dishwasher, 10

lavar to wash, 5; **~ los platos (la ropa)** to wash the dishes (the clothes), 10

lavarse to wash oneself, 5; **~ el pelo** to wash one's hair, 5; **~ los dientes** to brush one's teeth, 5

le to / for you (*form. s.*), to / for him, to / for her, 8

lección (*f.*) lesson, P

leche (*f.*) milk, 6

lector (*m.*) **de CD-ROM / DVD** DVD / CD-ROM drive, 4

leer (y) to read, 3; **Lean el Capítulo 1.** Read Chapter 1. P

lejos de far from, 6

lema (*m.*) slogan

lentes (*m. pl.*) eyeglasses

lento(a) slow, 4

les to / for you (*form. pl.*), to / for them, 8

letrero sign

levantar to raise, to lift, 5; **~ pesas** to lift weights, 2

levantarse to get up, 5

libra pound, 9

libre free

librería bookstore, 3

libro book, P; **~ electrónico** e-book, P

licencia de manejar driver's license

licuado de fruta fruit shake, smoothie

licuadora blender, 10

ligero(a) light, lightweight, 9

limonada lemonade, 9

limpiar el baño to clean the bathroom, 10

lindo(a) pretty, 2

línea: en ~ online, 4

lingüístico(a) linguistic

lino linen, 8

literatura literature, 3

litro liter, 9

llamar to call, 2; **llamarse** to name, 2; **Me llamo . . .** My name is . . . , 1

llano(a) flat

llanura plain

llegar (gu) to arrive, 2

llenar to fill

llevar to take, to carry **llover** to rain; **Está lloviendo. (Llueve.)** It's raining. 7

lobo wolf

lodo mud

lograr to achieve

lomo de res prime rib, 9

los (las) (*pl.*) the, 1

luego later, 5

lugar (*m.*) place; **~ de nacimiento** birthplace

lujoso(a) luxurious

lunares: de ~ polka-dotted, 8

lunes (*m.*) Monday, 3

luz (*f.*) light; **~ solar** sunlight

M

madera wood

madrastra stepmother, 5

madre (*f.*) mother, 5

maestro(a) teacher, 5

maíz (*m.*) corn

mal badly, 4

malo(a) bad, 2

mamá mother, 5

mañana morning, 3; tomorrow, 3; **de la ~** in the morning (*with precise time*), 3; **por la ~** during the morning, 3

mandar to send; to order, 8

mandato command

manejar to drive, 5

mantel (*m.*) tablecloth, 9

mantener (*irreg.*) to keep, maintain

mantequilla butter, 9

manzana apple, 9

maquillaje (*m.*) makeup, 5

maquillarse to put on makeup, 5

máquina de afeitar electric razor, 5

maravilla wonder

marcar (qu) to mark; to point out

marisco shellfish, 9

marrón brown, 4

martes (*m.*) Tuesday, 3

marzo March, 1

más more; **~ que** more than, 8

masculino(a) masculine

matemáticas (*f. pl.*) mathematics, 3

mayo May, 1

mayonesa mayonnaise, 9

mayor older, greater, 8

mayoría majority

mayúsculo(a) capital (letter)

me to / for me, 8

mecánico(a) mechanic, 5

medio(a) hermano(a) half-brother (half-sister), 5

medianoche (*f.*) midnight, 3

medicina medicine, 3

médico(a) doctor, 5

medida measurement, 9

medio ambiente (*m.*) environment

mediodía (*m.*) noon, 3

medios de transporte means of transportation, 6

medir (i, i) to measure

meditación (*f.*) meditation

mejilla cheek

mejor better, 8

melón (*m.*) melon, 9

memoria flash flash drive, 4

menor younger; less, 8

menos: ~ que less than, 8; **por lo ~** at least, 10

mensajero(a) messenger

mentiroso(a) dishonest, lying, 2

menú (*m.*) menu, 9

mercadeo marketing, 3

mercado market, 6; **~ al aire libre** open-air market, farmer's market, 6

merecer (zc) to deserve

merienda snack

mes (*m.*) month, 3; **~ pasado** last month, 7

mesa table, P; **poner la ~** to set the table, 9; **quitar la ~** to clear the table, 10

mesita de noche night table, 10

meta goal

metro: en ~ on the subway, 6

mexicano(a) Mexican, 2

mezcla mix

mezclar to mix, 9

mezclilla denim, 8

mi (*adj.*) my, 3

mí (*pron.*) me, 8

micro bus (*Chile*)

micrófono microphone, 4

microondas (*m. s.*) microwave, 10

miedo: tener (*irreg.*) **~ (a, de)** to be afraid (of), 7

mientras while, during

miércoles (*m.*) Wednesday, 3

mil (*m.*) one thousand, 8

miles (*pl.*) thousands

millón (*m.*): **un ~** one million, 8; **dos millones** two million, 8

mío(a) (*adj.*) my, 10; (*pron.*) mine, 10

mirar televisión to watch television, 2

misionero(a) missionary

mismo(a) same; **lo mismo** the same (thing)

mitad (*f.*) half

mixto(a) mixed

mochila backpack, P; knapsack

moda fashion, 8; **(no) estar de ~** (not) to be fashionable, 8; **pasado(a) de ~** out of style, 8

modales (*m. pl.*) manners

modas: de ~ (*adj.*) fashion

módem (*m.*) **externo / interno** external / internal modem, 4

molestar to bother, 4

molido(a) crushed, ground, 9
monitor (*m.*) monitor, 4
mono monkey
montañoso(a) mountainous
montar to ride; **~ a caballo** to ride horseback, 7; **~ en bicicleta** to ride a bike, 7
monte (*m.*) mountain
morado(a) purple, 4
morirse (ue, u) to die, 8
mortalidad (*f.*) mortality
mostaza mustard, 9
mostrar (ue) to show
MP3 portátil portable MP3 player, P
muchacho(a) boy (girl), P
muchedumbre (*f.*) crowd
mucho a lot, 4; **~ que hacer** a lot to do; **No ~.** Not much. 1
mudarse to move (*change residence*)
muebles (*m. pl.*) furniture, 10
mujer (*f.*) woman, P; **~ de negocios** businesswoman, 5
mundo world
muñeca doll
museo museum, 6
música music, 3
muy very, 2

N

nacer (zc) to be born
nacionalidad (*f.*) nationality, 2
nada nothing, 1; **De ~.** You're welcome. 1
nadar to swim, 7
nadie no one, nobody, 6
naranja orange (*fruit*), 9
narrador(a) narrator
natación (*f.*) swimming, 7
naturaleza nature; **~ muerta** still life
navegación (*f.*) navigation; **~ en rápidos** whitewater rafting, 7
navegar (gu): ~ en rápidos to go whitewater rafting, 7; **~ por Internet** to browse the Internet, 2
necesitar to need, 2
negocio business, 3; (*pl.*) business
negro(a) black, 4
nervioso(a) nervous, 4
nevar to snow, 7; **Está nevando. (Nieva.)** It's snowing. 7

ni... ni neither . . . nor, 6
nicaragüense (*m., f.*) Nicaraguan, 2
nieto(a) grandson (granddaughter), 5
niñero(a) baby-sitter
ningún, ninguno(a) none, no, not any, 6
niño(a) boy (girl), P
nivel (*m.*) level
noche (*f.*) night, 3; **de la ~** in the evening (*with precise time*), 3; **por la ~** during the evening, 3
nombre (*m.*) name; **Mi ~ es...** My name is . . . , 1; **~ completo** full name
normal normal, 4
Norteamérica North America
norteamericano(a) North American
nos to / for us, 8; **¿~ vemos donde siempre?** See you at the usual place? 1
nosotros(as) we, 1; us, 8
nota grade, P
novato(a) newbie, novice
novecientos(as) nine hundred, 8
novedoso(a) novel, new
novelista (*m., f.*) novelist
noveno(a) ninth, 10
noventa ninety, P
noviembre November, 1
novio(a) boyfriend (girlfriend)
nublado: Está ~. It's cloudy. 7
nuera daughter-in-law, 5
nuestro(a) (*adj.*) our, 3; (*pron.*) ours, 10
nueve nine, P
número number, 8; **~ ordinal** ordinal number, 10
nunca never, 5

O

o... o either . . . or, 6
ochenta eighty, P
ocho eight, P
ochocientos(as) eight hundred, 8
octavo(a) eighth, 10
octubre October, 1
ocupado(a) busy, 4
ocupar to live in
odio hatred
oferta especial special offer, 8

oficina office, 6; **~ de correos** post office, 6
oír (*irreg.*) to hear, 5
ojear to scan
ola wave
ómnibus (*m.*) bus
once eleven, P
onda: en ~ in style
oprimir to push
opuesto(a) opposite
oración (*f.*) sentence
ordenar to order, 9
organización (*f.*) **benéfica** charity
orgulloso(a) proud
originar to originate
orilla shore
oro gold, 8
ortografía spelling
os to / for you (*fam. pl.*), 8
otoño fall, autumn, 7

P

paciente (*m., f.*) patient, 2
padrastro stepfather, 5
padre (*m.*) father, 5; **padres** (*m. pl.*) parents, 5
pagar (gu) to pay, 9
página page, P; **~ web** web page, 4
pago: método de ~ form of payment, 8**país** (*m.*) country
paisaje (*m.*) scenery
pájaro bird
pan (*m.*) bread, 6; **~ tostado** toast, 9
panameño(a) Panamanian, 2
pandilla gang
pantalla screen, 4
pantalones (*m. pl.*) pants, 8; **~ cortos** shorts, 8
pañuelo handkerchief
papá (*m.*) father, 5
papas fritas (*f. pl.*) French fries, 9
papel role; paper; **hoja de ~** sheet of paper, P
papelería stationery store, 6
papitas fritas (*f. pl.*) potato chips, 6
paquete (*m.*) package, 9
para for, toward, in the direction of, in order to (+ *inf.*), 10
paracaídas (*m.*) parachute
parada stop

paraguayo(a) Paraguayan, 2
parar to stop
parecer (zc) to seem
pared (*f.*) wall, P
pariente (*m.*, *f.*) family member, relative, 5
parque (*m.*) park, 6
párrafo paragraph
parrilla: a la ~ grilled, 9
partido game, match, 7
pasar to pass (by), 2; **~ la aspiradora** to vacuum, 10
pasear: sacar a ~ al perro to take the dog for a walk, 10
pasillo hallway, 10
pasta de dientes toothpaste, 5
pastel (*m.*) cake, 9
patinar to skate, 2; **~ en línea** to inline skate (rollerblade), 7; **~ sobre hielo** to ice skate, 7
patio patio, 10
patrocinador(a) sponsor
pavo turkey, 6
paz (*f.*) peace
pedazo piece, slice, 9
pedir (i, i) to ask for (*something*), 1; to request, 10; **~ la hora** to ask for the time, 3
peinarse to brush / comb one's hair, 5
peine (*m.*) comb, 5
pelar to peel, 9
pelearse to have a fight, 5
peligro danger, 7
peligroso(a) dangerous, 7
pelirrojo(a) redheaded , 2
pelo hair; **~ castaño / rubio** brown / blond hair, 2
pelota ball, 7
peluquero(a) barber / hairdresser, 5
pendiente (*m.*) earring, 8
pendrive (*m.*) flash drive, 4
pensar (ie) to think, 4; **~ de** to have an opinion about, 4; **~ en (de)** to think about, to consider, 4
penúltimo(a) next-to-last
peor worse, 8
pequeño(a) small, 2
perder (ie) to lose, 4; **perderse (ie)** to lose oneself, to get lost
Perdón. Excuse me. 4
perejil (*m.*) parsley
perezoso(a) lazy, 2

periódico newspaper
periodismo journalism, 3
periodista (*m.*, *f.*) journalist, 5
permiso: Con ~. Pardon me. 4
permitir to permit, to allow, 10
pero but, 2
perro(a) dog, 2; **perro caliente** hot dog, 9
persiana Venetian blind, 10
personalidad (*f.*) personality
peruano(a) Peruvian, 2
pesar: a ~ de in spite of
pesas: levantar ~ to lift weights, 2
pescado fish (*caught*), 9
pescar (qu) to fish, 7
pez (*m.*) fish (*alive*)
piano piano, 2
picante spicy, 9
picar (qu) to chop, to mince, 9
pie (*m.*): **a ~** on foot, walking, 6
piel (*f.*) leather, 8
pimienta pepper, 9
pingüino penguin
pintar to paint, 2
pintoresco(a) picturesque
pintura painting, 3
pirata (*m.*) pirate
pisar to step on
piscina swimming pool, 6
piso floor; **primer (segundo, etc.) ~** first (second, etc.) floor, 10
pista de atletismo athletics track, 6
pizarra interactiva interactive whiteboard, P
pizzería pizzeria, 6
placer: Un ~. My pleasure. 1
plancha iron, 10
planchar to iron, 10
plata silver, 8
plátano banana, 9
plato plate, 9; **~ hondo** bowl, 9; **~ principal** main dish, 9
plaza plaza, 6
plomero(a) plumber, 5
poblar (ue) to populate
pobre poor
poco little, small amount, 4; **muy ~** very little
poder (*m.*) power; (*irreg.*) to be able to, 4
poderoso(a) powerful
poesía poetry
poeta (poetisa) poet

policía (*m.*, *f.*) policeman (policewoman), 5
político(a) political
pollo chicken, 6; **~ asado** roasted chicken, 9; **~ frito** fried chicken, 9
polvo dust
poner (*irreg.*) to put, 5; **~ en equilibro** to balance; **~ la mesa** to set the table, 9; **~ mis juguetes en su lugar** to put my toys where they belong, 10 to put on (clothing), 5
por for, during, in, through, along, on behalf of, by, 10; **~ avión** by plane, 6; **~ ejemplo** for example, 10; **~ eso** so, that's why, 10; **~ favor** please, 1; **~ fin** finally, 9; **~ lo menos** at least, 10; **~ supuesto** of course, 10
¿por qué? why? 3
porcentaje (*m.*) percentage
porque because, 3
portarse to behave
portátil: MP3 ~ portable MP3 player, P; **computadora ~** laptop computer, P
portugués (portuguesa) Portuguese, 2
postre (*m.*) dessert, 9
pozo well; hole
practicar (qu) to practice; **~ alpi-nismo** to hike, to (mountain) climb, 7; **~ deportes** to play sports, 2; **~ surfing** to surf, 7
precio: Está a muy buen ~. It's a very good price. 8
preferencia preference
preferir (ie, i) to prefer, 4
pregunta: hacer preguntas to ask questions, 3
premio prize
prenda de ropa article of clothing, 8
preocupado(a) worried, 4
preocuparse to worry, 5
preparación (*f.*) preparation, 9
preparar to prepare, 2; **~ la comida** to prepare the food, 10; **prepararse** to get ready, 5
preposición (*f.*) preposition, 6
presa dam
presentar a alguien to introduce someone, 1
préstamo loan, 8

prestar to loan, 8

primavera spring, 7

primer(o)(a) first, 10; **primer piso** first floor, 10

primo(a) cousin, 5

principiante(a) beginner

prisa haste, hurry; **tener** (*irreg.*) ~ to be in a hurry, 7

probarse (ue): Voy a probármelo / la(los / las). I'm going to try it (them) on. 8

procesador de comida food processor, 10

producto electrónico electronic product, 4

profesión (*f.*) profession, 5

profesor(a) professor, P

programa (*m.*) program; ~ **antivirus** anti-virus program, 4; ~ **de procesamiento de textos** word-processing program, 4

programador(a) programmer, 5

prohibir to forbid, 10

promover (ue) to promote

pronombre (*m.*) pronoun, 1

propina tip, 9

propósito purpose

proveedor (*m.*) **de acceso** Internet service provider, 4

provocador(a) provocative

próximo(a) next

proyector projector, P

psicología psychology, 3

publicidad (*f.*) public relations, 3

publicitario(a) (*adj.*) pertaining to advertising

pueblo town, 6

puerta door, P

puerto de USB USB port, 4

puertorriqueño(a) Puerto Rican, 2

pulgada inch

pulsera bracelet, 8

punto de vista viewpoint

punto period

Q

¿qué? what? which? 3; **¿~ hay denuevo?** What's new? 1; **¿~ hora es?** What time is it? 3; **¿~ significa…?** What does . . . mean? P; **¿~ tal?** How are things going? 1; **¿~ te gusta hacer?** What do you like to do? 2

quedar to fit; **Me queda bien / mal.** It fits nicely / badly. 8; **Me queda grande / apretado.** It's too big / too tight. 8; **quedar(se)** to remain; to be

quehacer (*m.*) **doméstico** housechore, 10

quejarse to complain, 5

querer (*irreg.*) to want, to love, 4; to wish, 10

queso cheese, 6

¿quién(es)? who? 3; **¿De ~ es?** Whose is this? 3; **¿De ~ son?** Whose are these? 3

química chemistry, 3

quince fifteen, P

quinientos(as) five hundred, 8

quinto(a) fifth, 10

quisiera (+ *inf.*) I'd like (+ *inf.*), 6

quitar to take off, to remove 5; ~ **la mesa** to clear the table, 10; **quitarse (la ropa)** to take off (one's clothing), 5

quizás perhaps

R

raíz (*f.*) root

rango rank

rápido(a) fast, 4

rasgado torn up

rasgar (gu) to tear up

rasuradora razor, 5

ratón (*m.*) mouse, 4

rayado(a) striped, 8

rayas: a ~ striped, 8

razón (*f.*) reason; **tener** (*irreg.*) ~ to be right, 7

realidad: en ~ actually

realizarse (c) to take place

rebajado(a): estar ~ to be reduced (in price) / on sale, 8

recámara bedroom, 10

recibir to receive, 3

reciclaje (*m.*) recycling, 10

recomendar (ie) to recommend, 10

reconocer (zc) to recognize

recordar (ue) to remember

recorte (*m.*) cutting

recuerdo souvenir

recurrir to fall back on, to resort to

red (*f.*) web, Internet; ~ **mundial** World Wide Web, 4; ~ **social** social networking site, 4

redactar to edit

reflejar to reflect

reflexión (*f.*) reflection

refresco soft drink, 6; beverage, 9; **tomar un ~** to have a soft drink, 2

refrigerador (*m.*) refrigerator, 10

regalar to give (as a gift), 8

regalo present, gift, 8

regar (ie) (gu) las plantas to water the plants, 10

regla rule

regresar to return, 2

regular so-so, 1

reina queen

reírse (*irreg.*) to laugh, 5

relajarse to relax, 5

reloj (*m.*) watch, 8

remar to row, 7

remero(a) rower

renombre (*m.*) renown

renovar (ue) to renovate

repente: de ~ suddenly, 9

repetir (i, i) to repeat, 4; **Repitan.** Repeat. P

reproductor (*m.*) **de discos compactos / DVD** CD / DVD recorder, 4

requerir (ie, i) to require, 10

residencia estudiantil dorm, 3

respirar to breathe

responder to respond, 1

responsable responsible, 2

restaurante (*m.*) restaurant, 6

resumen: en ~ in short, to sum up

reto challenge

reunión (*f.*) meeting

reunirse to meet, to get together, 5

revista magazine; ~ **de moda** fashion magazine

rey (*m.*) king

riesgo risk

rima rhyme

río river, 7

riqueza wealth

rodeado(a) surrounded

rojo(a) red, 4

ropa clothing, 5

rosa rose, 4

rosado(a) pink, 4

rubio(a) blond(e), 2
rueda wheel
ruta route

S

sábado Saturday, 2
saber (*irreg.*) to know (*a fact, information*), 5; **~** (+ *inf.*) to know how (*to do something*), 5
sabor (*m.*) flavor
sacar (**qu**) to take out; **~ a pasear al perro** to take the dog for a walk, 10; **~ fotos** to take photos, 2; **~ la basura** to take out the garbage, 10
sacerdote (*m.*) priest
saco jacket, sports coat, 8
sacudir los muebles to dust the furniture, 10
sal (*f.*) salt, 9
sala living room, 10
salchicha sausage, 6
salir (*irreg.*) to leave, to go out, 5
salmón (*m.*) salmon, 9
salón (*m.*) **de clase** classroom, P
salud (*f.*) health, 3
saludable healthy
saludar to greet, 1
saludo greeting
salvadoreño(a) Salvadoran, 2
salvaje wild, untamed
salvavidas (*m. s.*) lifejacket
sandalia sandal, 8
sandwich (*m.*) sandwich, 9; **~ de jamón y queso con aguacate** ham and cheese sandwich with avocado, 9
secadora dryer, 10
secar (**qu**) to dry (*something*), 5; **secarse** (**qu**) **el pelo** to dry one's hair, 5
secretario(a) secretary, 5
secreto secret
sed (*f.*) thirst; **tener** (*irreg.*) **~** to be thirsty, 7
seda silk, 8
seguido(a) continued
seguir (**i, i**) to continue, 6; **~ derecho** to go straight ahead
según according to
segundo(a) second, 10
seguro(a) sure, 4; safe, 7
seis six, P
seiscientos(as) six hundred, 8

semana week, 3; **~ pasada** last week, 7; **fin** (*m.*) **de ~** weekend, 2; **todas las semanas** every week, 5
semejanza similarity
sencillo(a) simple; single (*room*)
sentarse (**ie**) to sit down, 5
sentir (**ie, i**) to feel, 4; **Lo siento.** I'm sorry. 4
señalar to point out
señor (*abbrev.* **Sr.**) Mr., Sir, 1
señora (*abbrev.* **Sra.**) Mrs., Ms., Madam, 1
señorita (*abbrev.* **Srta.**) Miss, Ms., 1
separarse to get separated, 5
septiembre September, 1
séptimo(a) seventh, 10
ser (*irreg.*) to be, 1
serio(a) serious, 2
servicio service **servilleta** napkin, 9
servir (**i, i**) to serve, 4; **¿En qué puedo servirle?** How can I help you? 8
sesenta sixty, P
setecientos(as) seven hundred, 8
setenta seventy, P
sexto(a) sixth, 10
sí yes, 1
siempre always, 5
siete seven, P
siglo century
significar (**qu**): **Significa...** It means . . . , P
significado meaning
siguiente following, next
silla chair, P
sillón (*m.*) armchair, 10
símbolo symbol
simpático(a) nice, 2
sin without; **~ control** uncontrolled
sincero(a) sincere, 2
sino but instead
sistemático(a) systematic
sitio place; **~ web** website, 4
smartphone smartphone, 4
snowboarding snowboarding, 7
soberanía sovereignty
sobre on, above, 6
sobrepasar to surpass
sobresaliente outstanding
sobrino(a) nephew (niece), 5
sofá (*m.*) sofa, 10

software (*m.*) software, 4
sol (*m.*) sun; **Hace ~.** It's sunny. 7
soltero(a) single (unmarried)
sombrero hat, 8
sonar (**ue**) to ring, to go off (*phone, alarm clock, etc.*), 4
sonido sound
sonreír (*irreg.*) to smile, 8
sonrisa smile
soñar (**ue**) **con** to dream about, 4
sopa soup, 9; **~ de fideos** noodle soup, 9
sorpresa surprise
sorteo raffle; evasion
sortija ring
sótano basement, cellar, 10
su (*adj.*) your (*s. form., pl.*), his, her, their, 3
suave soft
subir to go up, to get on, 6; to upload, 4
suburbio suburb, 10
sucio(a) dirty
sudadera sweatsuit, track suit, 8
Sudamérica South America
suegro(a) father-in-law (mother-in-law), 5
sueño dream; **tener** (*irreg.*) **~** to be sleepy, 7
suéter (*m.*) sweater, 8
sugerencia suggestion
sugerir (**ie, i**) to suggest, 8
superación (*f.*) overcoming
supermercado supermarket, 6
supuesto: por ~ of course, 10
surfing: hacer / practicar (**qu**) **~** to surf, 7
sustantivo noun
sustituir (**y**) to substitute
suyo(a) (*adj.*) your (*form. s., pl.*), his, her, its, their, 10; (*pron.*) yours (*form. s., pl.*), his, hers, its, theirs, 10

T

tabla de snowboard snowboard, 7
tableta tablet computer, 4
tal vez perhaps
talla size, 8
taller (*m.*) workshop
también also, 2
tampoco neither, not either, 2
tan... como as . . . as, 8
tanto(a)(s)... como as much (many) . . . as, 8

tarde (*f.*) afternoon, 3; **de la ~** in the afternoon (*with precise time*), 3; **por la ~** during the afternoon, 3; (*adv.*) late, 3

tarea homework, P

tarjeta ~ de crédito credit card, 8; **~ de débito** (bank) debit card, 8

te to / for you (*fam. s.*), 8

té hot tea, 9; **~ helado** iced tea, 9

teatro theater, 6

tecnología technology, 4

techo roof, 10

tecla key (*on a keyboard*), 4

teclado keyboard, 4

tejer to weave

tejido weaving

tela fabric, 8

teléfono inteligente smartphone, 4

televisor (*m.*) television set, 10

temperatura temperature, 7; **La ~ está a 20 grados Celsio(s) (Fahrenheit).** It's 20 degrees Celsius (Fahrenheit). 7

temporada: ~ de lluvias rainy season; **~ de secas** dry season

temprano early, 3

tender to tend (to)

tenedor (*m.*) fork, 9

tener (*irreg.*) to have, 1; **~ ... años** to be . . . years old, 1; **~ calor** to be hot, 7; **~ cuidado** to be careful, 7; **~ frío** to be cold, 7; **~ ganas de** to have the urge to, to feel like (doing), 7; **~ hambre** to be hungry, 7; **~ miedo (a, de)** to be afraid (of), 7; **~ prisa** to be in a hurry, 7; **~ que** (+ *inf.*) to have to (+ *verb*), 1; **~ razón** to be right, 7; **~ sed** to be thirsty, 7; **~ sueño** to be sleepy, 7; **~ vergüenza** to be embarrassed, ashamed, 7

tenis (*m.*) tennis, 7

teoría theory

tercer(o, a) third, 10

término term

terrible terrible, awful, 1

tesoro treasure

texto text

tez (*f.*) skin, complexion

ti you (*fam. s.*), 8

tiburón (*m.*) shark

tiempo weather, 7; **¿Qué ~ hace?** What's the weather like? 7

tienda store, 6; **~ de equipo deportivo** sporting goods store, 6; **~ de juegos electrónicos** electronic games store, 6; **~ de ropa** clothing store, 6

tierra earth, ground

tímido(a) shy, 2

tinto: vino ~ red wine, 9

tío(a) uncle (aunt), 5

típico(a) typical, 9

tira cómica comic strip

tiroteo shooting

titular to title

título title, 1

tiza chalk, P

toalla towel, 5; **~ de mano** handtowel, 5

tocador (*m.*) dresser, 10

tocar (qu) un instrumento musical to play a musical instrument, 2

todavía still

todo everything

todo(a) all, every; **todas las semanas** every week, 5; **todos los días (años)** every day (year), 9

tomar to take; **~ un refresco** to have a soft drink, 2; **~ el sol** to sunbathe, 2

tonto(a) silly, stupid, 2

tormenta thunderstorm

torpe awkward

tostadora toaster, 10

trabajador(a) (*adj.*) hard-working, 2; (*noun*) worker, 5

trabajar to work, 2

traducir (zc) to translate, 5

traer (*irreg.*) to bring, 5

traje (*m.*) suit, 8; **~ de baño** bathing suit, 8

trama plot

tramos sections

transmitir to broadcast, 3

trapear el piso to mop the floor, 10

tratar de to try

tratarse de to be a matter of; to be

través: a ~ de across, throughout

trece thirteen, P

trecho distance, period

treinta thirty, P

tren: en ~ by train, 6

tres three, P

trescientos(as) three hundred, 8

trigo wheat

tripulación (*f.*) crew

triste sad, 4

triunfar to triumph

trompeta trumpet, 2

trozo chunk, 9

trucha trout, 9

truco trick

tu your (*fam.*), 3

tú you (*fam.*), 1

tuyo(a) (*adj.*) your (*fam.*), 10; (*pron.*) yours (*fam.*), 10

U

ubicado(a) located

Ud. (*abbrev. of* **usted**) you (*form. s.*), 8

Uds. (*abbrev. of* **ustedes**) you (*fam. or form. pl.*), 8

último: lo ~ the latest (thing)

un(a) a, 1

único(a) only, unique

unido(a) united

unir to mix together, to incorporate, 9

universidad (*f.*) university, 6

uno one, P

unos(as) some, 1

uruguayo(a) Uruguayan, 2

usar to use, 2

usted you (*s. form.*), 1

ustedes you (*fam. or form. pl.*), 1

usuario(a) user, 4

útil useful

uva grape, 9

V

vacío(a) empty

valer (*irreg.*) **la pena** to be worthwhile

valioso(a) valuable

valle (*m.*) valley

valor (*m.*) value

vanidoso(a) vain

vapor: al ~ steamed, 9

vaquero cowboy

variedad (*f.*) variety

varios(as) various, several

varonil   manly

vaso   glass, 9

veces (*f. pl.*)   times; **a ~** sometimes, 5; **(dos) ~ al día / por semana**   (two) times a day / per week, 5

vecino(a)   neighbor, 6

vegano: algo ~   something vegan, 9

vegetal (*m.*)   vegetable, 6

vegetariano(a)   vegetarian; **~ estricto**   vegan, 9

vehículo   vehicle

veinte   twenty, P

veintiuno   twenty-one, P

vender   to sell, 3

venezolano(a)   Venezuelan, 2

venir (*irreg.*)   to come, 5

venta: estar en ~   to be on sale, 8

ventana   window, P

ver (*irreg.*)   to see, 5; **Nos vemos.**   See you later. 1

verano   summer, 7

veras: de ~   truly, really

verbo   verb, 3

verdad   true; **~** (*f.*)   truth

verde   green, 4

vergüenza shame; **tener** (*irreg.*) **~** to be embarrassed, ashamed, 7

verso libre   blank verse

vestido   dress, 8

vestir (i, i)   to dress (*someone*), 5; **vestirse (i, i)**   to get dressed, 5

veterinario(a)   veterinarian, 5

vez (*f.*)   time; **de ~ en cuando**   sometimes; **en ~ de**   instead of; **rara ~**   hardly ever; **tal ~** perhaps; **una ~**   once, 9

viajar   to travel, 2

vida   life

videocámara   videocamera, 4

viejo(a)   old, 2

viento   wind; **Hace ~.**   It's windy. 7

viernes (*m.*)   Friday, 2

vinagre (*m.*)   vinegar, 9

vino: ~ blanco   white wine, 9; **~ tinto**   red wine, 9

violín (*m.*)   violin, 2

viraje (*m.*)   turn

visitante (*m., f.*)   visitor

visitar a amigos   to visit friends, 2

vivienda   housing

vivir   to live, 3

volibol (*m.*)   volleyball, 7

volver (ue)   to return, 4

vosotros(as)   you (*fam. pl.*), 1

voz (*f.*)   voice

vuestro(a) (*adj.*)   your (*fam. pl.*), 3; (*pron.*)   yours (*fam. pl.*), 3

W

wifi (*m.*)   wifi, wireless connection, 4

Y

yerno   son-in-law, 5

yo   I, 1

yogur (*m.*)   yogurt, 6

Z

zanahoria   carrot, 9

zapato   shoe, 8; **~ de tacón alto**   high-heeled shoe, 8; **~ de tenis**   tennis shoe, 8

English–Spanish Glossary

A

a un(a), 1
à la carte a la carta, 9
above sobre, 6
abundance abundancia
academic académico(a)
access acceder, 4
accessory accesorio, 8
according to según
accountant contador(a), 5
accounting contabilidad (f.), 3
achieve alcanzar (c), lograr
acquisition adquisición (f.)
across a través de
action acción (f.), 5
active activo(a), 2
activity actividad (f.), P
actor actor (m.), 5
actress actriz (f.), 5
actually en realidad
ad: personal ~ anuncio personal
add agregar, añadir, 9
address dirección (f.)
advertising (adj.) publicitario(a)
advise aconsejar, 10
affection cariño
afternoon tarde (f.), 3;
 during the ~ por la tarde, 3;
 Good ~. Buenas tardes. 1;
 in the ~ (with precise time)
 de la tarde, 3;
 late ~ atardecer (m.)
age edad (f.)
agreement concordancia
agricultural agrícola (m., f.)
ahead adelante
airport aeropuerto, 6
all todo(a)
alligator aligátor (m.), caimán
 (m.)
along por, 10
alphabet alfabeto
also también, 2
altitude altitud (f.)
always siempre, 5
ambassador embajador(a)
ambiguity ambigüedad (f.)
amusement diversión (f.)
ancestor antecesor(a),
 antepasado(a)
anger cólera

angry enojado(a), 4
anonymous anónimo(a)
answer contestar;
 Answer. Contesten. P
Antarctica Antártida
antiquated anticuado(a)
any algún, alguno(a) 6
apartment apartamento, 6
appear aparecer (zc)
apple manzana, 9
appliance electrodoméstico, 10
application aplicación (f.), 4
appreciate apreciar
appropriate apropiado(a)
April abril, 1
apt apto(a)
architect arquitecto(a), 5
architecture arquitectura, 3
Argentinian argentino(a), 2
armchair sillón (m.), 10
around alrededor de
arrive llegar, 2
arrogant altivo(a)
art arte (m.), 3
article artículo, 1
artist artista (m., f.), 5
as como; **~ . . . ~** tan... como, 8;
 ~ many . . . ~ tantos(as)...
 como, 8; **~ much . . . ~**
 tanto(a)(s)... como, 8
ask: ~ questions hacer
 (irreg.) preguntas, 3; **~ for
 something** pedir (i, i), 1; **~ for
 the time** pedir (i, i) la hora, 3
asparagus espárragos (m. pl.), 9
at en; **~ least** por lo menos, 10;
 ~ low heat a fuego suave /
 lento, 9
athletics track pista de
 atletismo, 6
atmosphere ambiente (m.)
attachment anexo
attack ataque (m.)
attempt intentar
attend acudir; asistir a, 3
attractive guapo(a), 2
audio audio, P
audiotape cinta, P
auditorium auditorio, 6
August agosto, 1
aunt tía, 5
Australian australiano(a), 2

**automated bank teller
 (ATM)** cajero automático, 6
autumn otoño, 7
availability disponibilidad (f.)
avenue avenida, 1
avoid evitar
awful fatal, terrible, 1
awkward torpe

B

baby-sitter niñero(a)
background fondo
backpack mochila, P
bad malo(a), 2
badly mal, 4
balance poner (irreg.) en
 equilibro
ball pelota, 7
ballpoint pen bolígrafo, P
banana plátano, 9
bank (commercial) banco, 6
barber peluquero(a), 5
barefooted descalzo(a)
baseball béisbol (m.), 7
basement sótano, 10
basket canasta
basketball básquetbol (m.), 7
bather bañador(a)
bathing suit traje (m.) de baño, 8
bathroom baño, 10
be estar (irreg.), ser (irreg.), 1;
 ~ . . . years old tener (irreg.)...
 años, 1; **~ a matter of** tratarse
 de; **~ able to** poder (irreg.),
 4; **~ afraid (of)** tener
 (irreg.) miedo (a, de), 7;
 ~ ashamed tener (irreg.)
 vergüenza, 7; **~ born** nacer
 (zc); **~ careful** tener (irreg.)
 cuidado, 7; **~ certain of** contar
 (ue) con; **~ cold** tener (irreg.)
 frío, 7; **~ embarrassed** tener
 (irreg.) vergüenza, 7; **~ familiar
 with** conocer (zc), 5; **~ going
 to** ir a, 3; **~ hot** tener (irreg.)
 calor, 7; **~ hungry** tener
 (irreg.) hambre, 7;
 ~ important importar, 4; **~ in
 a hurry** tener (irreg.) prisa,
 7; **~ interesting** interesar, 4;
 ~ jealous tener (irreg.) celos;

~ right tener (*irreg.*) razón, 7; **~ sleepy** tener (*irreg.*) sueño, 7; **~ thirsty** tener (*irreg.*) sed, 7; **~ worthwhile** valer (*irreg.*) la pena

bean haba (*f. but* el haba); **(green) ~** habichuela, 9; **refried beans** frijoles refritos, 9

beat batir

beautiful bello(a), hermoso(a)

beauty belleza

because porque, 3

bed cama, 10

bedroom cuarto, dormitorio, habitación (*f.*), recámara, 10

beef stew guisado, 9

beer cerveza, 9

before antes, 5

begin comenzar (ie) (c), empezar (ie) (c), 4

beginner principiante

behave portarse

behavior comportamiento

behind detrás de, 6

believe (in) creer (en), 3

below debajo de, 6

belt cinturón (*m.*), 8

besides además

better mejor, 8

between entre, 6

beverage bebida, refresco, 9

bicycle: on ~ en bicicleta, 6

big grande, 2

bilingual bilingüe

bill cuenta, 9

biology biología, 3

bird pájaro

birthplace lugar (*m.*) de nacimiento

black negro(a), 4

blank verse verso libre

blender licuadora, 10

blind ciego(a); **~ date** cita a ciegas

block cuadra, 6

blog blog, 4

blond(e) rubio(a), 2

blouse blusa, 8

blue azul, 4

boat barco, bote (*m.*)

boil hervir (ie, i), 9

boiled hervido(a), 9

Bolivian boliviano(a), 2

book libro, P

bookstore librería, 3

boot bota, 8

border frontera

boredom aburrimiento

bored aburrido(a), 4

boring aburrido(a), 2

both ambos(as)

bother molestar, 4

bowl plato hondo, 9

box: large ~ cajón (*m.*)

boxing boxeo, 7

boy chico, P; muchacho, P; niño, P

boyfriend novio

bracelet brazalete (*m.*), pulsera, 8

bread pan (*m.*), 6

break (a record) batir

breakfast desayuno, 9

breathe respirar

brick ladrillo

brief breve

bring traer (*irreg.*), 5

broadcast transmitir, 3

broccoli bróculi (*m.*), 9

brother (younger, older) hermano (menor, mayor), 5

brother-in-law cuñado, 5

brown castaño, 2; café, marrón, 4

browse: the Internet navegar por Internet, 2

brush cepillo, 5; **~ one's hair** cepillarse el pelo, peinarse, 5; **~ one's teeth** lavarse los dientes, 5

buddy cuate(a)

building edificio, 6

burn arder

burning encendida

bus ómnibus (*m.*), colectivo, guagua (*Cuba, Puerto Rico*), micro (*Chile*)

business negocio, 3; **~ administration** administración (*f.*) de empresas, 3; **~ district** centro comercial, 10

businessman hombre (*m.*) de negocios, 5

businesswoman mujer (*f.*) de negocios, 5

busy ocupado(a), 4

but pero, 2; **~ instead** sino

butcher shop carnicería, 6

butter mantequilla, 9

buy comprar, 2

by por, 10; **~ bus** en autobús, 6; **~ car** en carro / coche / automóvil, 6; **~ check** con cheque, 8; **~ plane** por avión, 6; **~ train** en tren, 6

Bye. Chau. 1

C

cable cable (*m.*), 4

cafeteria cafetería, 3

cake pastel (*m.*), 9

calculator calculadora, P

calculus cálculo, 3

call llamar, 2

can opener (electric) abrelatas (*m.*) (eléctrico), 10

Canadian canadiense (*m., f.*), 2

cap gorra, 8

capital (letter) mayúsculo(a)

card tarjeta; **credit ~** tarjeta de crédito, 8; **debit ~** tarjeta de débito, 8

cardboard cartón (*m.*)

career carrera, 5

Careful! ¡Cuidado!

Caribbean (Sea) Caribe (*m., f.*)

carpenter carpintero(a), 5

carpet alfombra, 10

carrot zanahoria, 9

carry llevar

cash: in ~ en efectivo, al contado, 8

cashmere cachemira

cat gato(a), 2

cattle ganado, ganadería

cattle-raising industry industria ganadera

cautious cuidadoso(a), 2

CD: CD / DVD recorder grabador (*m.*) de discos compactos / DVD, reproductor (*m.*) de discos compactos / DVD, 4

celebration celebración (*f.*)

cellar sótano, 10

Celsius degree grado Celsio(s), 7

census censo

cent centavo

center centro

Central America Centroamérica

century siglo

cereal cereal (*m.*), 9

certain cierto(a)

chain cadena, 8

chair silla, P

chalk tiza, P

challenge reto

change cambio; convertir (ie, i);

chapter capítulo, P

charity organización (f.) benéfica

chat chatear (online), 4; **~ room** grupo de conversación, 4

check cheque (m.); (restaurant check) cuenta, 9

cheek mejilla

cheese queso, 6

cheeseburger hamburguesa con queso, 9

chef cocinero(a), 5

chemistry química, 3

chess ajedrez (m.)

chicken pollo, 6; **~ soup** caldo de pollo, 9; **~ with rice** arroz (m.) con pollo, 9; **fried ~** pollo frito, 9; **roasted ~** pollo asado, 9;

Chilean chileno(a), 2

Chinese chino(a), 2; **~ language** chino, 3

chocolate cacao

choose escoger (j)

chronology cronología

chunk trozo, 9

church iglesia, 6

cinema cine (m.), 6

cinnamon canela

city ciudad (f.), 6

clam almeja, 9

clarity claridad (f.)

class clase (f.), P; **lower ~** clase baja

classroom salón (m.) de clase, P

clean the bathroom limpiar el baño, 10

clear the table quitar la mesa, 10

click hacer (irreg.) clic, 4; **double ~** hacer (irreg.) doble clic, 4

close cerrar (ie), 4; **~ your books.** Cierren los libros. P

close to cerca de, 6

closet clóset (m.), 10

clothing ropa, 5; **article of ~** prenda de ropa, 8; **~ store** tienda de ropa, 6

cloudburst chaparrón (m.)

cloudy: It's ~. Está nublado. 7

coat abrigo, 8

code código

codfish bacalao, 9

coffee café (m.), 9

cold (adj.) frío(a); **It's ~.** Hace frío. 7

Colombian colombiano(a), 2

color color (m.), 4; **solid ~** de un solo color, 8

comb peine (m.), 5; **~ one's hair** peinarse, 5

come venir (irreg.), 5

comic strip tira cómica

comma coma

command mandato

compact disc CD, disco compacto (m.)

comparison comparación (f.), 8

compete competir (i, i)

competition competencia, 7

complain quejarse, 5

complexion tez (f.)

complicity complicidad (f.)

computer computadora, P; **~ center** centro de computación, 3; **~ functions** funciones (f. pl.) de la computadora, 4; **~ science** computación (f.), informática, 3

conduct conducir (zc), 5

confection confección (f.)

connect conectar, 4

connection conexión (f.), 4

consider pensar (ie) en (de), 4

contest concurso

continue seguir (i, i), 6

continued seguido(a)

contraction contracción (f.), 3

contrary: on the ~ al contrario

conversation conversación (f.)

cook cocinar, 2; cocer (-z) (ue), 9; cocinero(a), 5

cookie galleta, 9

cool, chévere; **It's cool.** Hace fresco. 7

copper cobre (m.)

corn maíz (m.)

corner esquina, 6

correct corregir (i, i) (j)

Costa Rican costarricense (m., f.), 2

cotton algodón (m.), 8

country país (m.)

courage coraje (m.)

course: basic ~ curso básico, 3

courtesy cortesía, 4

cousin primo(a), 5

cowboy vaquero

cradle cuna

create crear

creative creativo(a)

crew tripulación (f.)

crowd muchedumbre (f.)

cruise ship crucero

crushed molido(a), 9

Cuban cubano(a), 2

culinary culinario(a)

culture cultura

cumin comino, 9

cup taza, 9

curtain cortina, 10

custard flan (m.), 9

customer cliente (m., f.), 8

cutting recorte (m.)

cyberspace ciberespacio, 4

cycling ciclismo, 7

D

daily cotidiano(a)

dam presa

dance bailar, 2; baile (m.), 3

danger peligro, 7

dangerous peligroso(a), 7

date fecha, 3; **blind ~** cita a ciegas

daughter hija, 5

daughter-in-law nuera, 5

dawn amanecer (zc)

day día (m.), 3; **~ before yesterday** anteayer, 7; **~ of the week** día de la semana, 3; **every ~** todos los días, 3

December diciembre, 1

decoration decoración (f.), 10

definite definido(a), 1

degree grado

Delighted to meet you. Encantado(a). 1

demand exigir (j)

demonstrate demostrar (ue)

demonstrative demostrativo(a), 6

denim mezclilla, 8

dentist dentista (m., f.), 5

deodorant desodorante (m.), 5

describe describir, 2

deserve merecer (zc)

design diseño; **graphic ~** diseño gráfico, 3

designer: graphic ~ diseñador(a) gráfico(a), 5

desire afán (m.); anhelo

desk escritorio, P

dessert postre (*m.*), 9
detail detalle (*m.*)
determined resuelto (*p.p. of* resolver)
develop desarrollar
dialect dialecto
dictionary diccionario, P
die morirse (ue, u), 8
difference diferencia
difficult difícil, 4
digital camera cámara digital, 4
dining room comedor (*m.*), 10
dinner cena
dirty sucio(a)
disappointment desilusión (*f.*)
disaster desastre (*m.*)
discount descuento, 8
discover descubrir, 3
disgusting asco
dish: main ~ plato principal, 9
dishonest mentiroso(a), 2
dishwasher lavaplatos (*m. s.*), 10
disillusionment desengaño
dispatch despachar
disqualify descalificar (qu)
distance trecho
diversity diversidad (*f.*)
divide dividir
do hacer (*irreg.*), 5; **a lot to ~** mucho que hacer; **~ the homework for tomorrow.** Hagan la tarea para mañana. P; **~ the recycling** hacer el reciclaje, 10
doctor doctor(a); médico(a), 5
dog perro(a), 2
doll muñeca
dollar dólar (*m.*)
Dominican dominicano(a), 2
door puerta, P
dorm residencia estudiantil, 3; dormitorio estudiantil, 6
download descargar, bajar, 4
downpour chaparrón (*m.*)
downtown centro de la ciudad, 10
dozen docena, 9
drawing dibujo, P
dream sueño; **~ (about)** soñar (ue) con, 4
drenched empapado(a)
dress vestido, 8; **~ (someone)** vestir (i, i), 5; **get dressed** vestirse (i, i), 5
dresser cómoda, tocador (*m.*), 10
drink beber, 3
drive manejar, conducir (zc), 5

driver's license licencia de manejar
dry (something) secar (qu), 5; **~ one's hair** secarse (qu) el pelo, 5
dryer secadora, 10
during mientras, por, 10
dust polvo; **~ the furniture** sacudir los muebles, 10
DVD / CD-ROM drive lector (*m.*) de CD-ROM / DVD, 4

E

early temprano, 3
earphones audífonos (*m. pl.*), 4
earring arete (*m.*), pendiente (*m.*), 8
earth tierra
easy fácil, 4
eat comer, 3; **~ dinner** cenar, 2
e-book libro electrónico, P
economics economía, 3
Ecuadoran ecuatoriano(a), 2
edit redactar
education educación (*f.*), 3
egg huevo, 6; **~ sunny-side up** huevo estrellado, 9; **scrambled ~** huevo revuelto, 9
egotistic egoísta, 2
eight ocho, P; **~ hundred** ochocientos(as), 8
eighteen dieciocho, P
eighth octavo(a), 10
eighty ochenta, P
either . . . or o... o, 6
electricity electricidad (*f.*)
electronic electrónico(a); **~ games store** tienda de juegos electrónicos, 6; **~ mailbox** buzón (*m.*) electrónico, 4; **~ notebook** asistente (*m.*) electrónico, 4; **electronics** aparatos electrónicos, 4
elephant elefante (*m.*)
eleven once, P
e-mail correo electrónico, e-mail (*m.*), P
embarrass avergonzar (ue) (c)
embarrassed avergonzado(a)
embroidered bordado(a), 8
emotion emoción (*f.*), 4

emphasize destacar (qu), enfatizar (c)
empty vacío(a)
encounter encuentro
end cabo; fin (*m.*)
engineer ingeniero(a), 5
engineering ingeniería, 3
English inglés (inglesa), 2; **~ language** inglés (*m.*), 3
enjoy gozar (c); **~ (life)** disfrutar (la vida)
enough: it is ~ basta
enroll alistar
entertain entretener (*like* tener)
entertaining divertido(a), 2
environment medio ambiente (*m.*)
equator ecuador (*m.*)
era etapa
essay ensayo
Europe Europa
evaluation calificación (*f.*)
evasion sorteo
even aun
evening noche (*f.*); **during the ~** por la noche, 3; **Good ~.** Buenas noches. 1; **in the ~** (*with precise time*) de la noche, 3
everything todo
everywhere por dondequiera
example ejemplo, 10
exchange intercambiar; **in ~ for** a cambio de; **~ rate** cambio
Excuse me. Disculpe. Perdón. 4
exercise hacer (*irreg.*) ejercicio, 7
exhibit exhibir
exotic exótico(a)
expensive: It's (too) ~. Es (demasiado) caro(a). 8
express preferences expresar preferencias, 2
expression expresión (*f.*), 1
extroverted extrovertido(a), 2
eyeglasses lentes (*m. pl.*), anteojos (*m. pl.*)

F

fabric tela, 8
fact dato, hecho
Fahrenheit degree grado Fahrenheit, 7
fairy tale cuento de hadas

fall caer (*irreg.*);
(**autumn**) otoño, 7;
~ **asleep** dormirse (ue, u), 5;
~ **back on** recurrir; ~ **in love** enamorarse, 5
false falso(a)
family familia;
~ **member** pariente (*m., f.*), 5;
nuclear ~ familia nuclear, 5;
~ **tree** árbol (*m.*) genealógico
fantasy fantasía
far from lejos de, 6
fascinate fascinar, 4
fashion (*adj.*) de modas
fashion moda, 8;
~ **magazine** revista de moda
fashionable: (not) to be ~ (no) estar de moda, 8
fast rápido(a), 4
fat gordo(a), 2
father padre (*m.*), papá (*m.*), 5
father-in-law suegro, 5
fax: external / internal ~ fax (*m.*) externo / interno, 4
February febrero, 1
feed the dog darle de comer al perro, 10
feel sentir (ie, i), 4; ~ **like (doing)** tener (*irreg.*) ganas de, 7
feminine femenino(a)
field of study campo de estudio, 3
fifteen quince, P
fifth quinto(a), 10
fifty cincuenta, P
file archivar, 4; archivo, 4
fill llenar
final final
finally por fin, 9
financial financiero(a)
find encontrar (ue), 4
find out averiguar (gü)
Fine, thank you. Bien, gracias. 1
fire fuego; ~ **fighter** bombero(a), 5
fired despedido(a)
fireplace chimenea, 10
first primer(o)(a), 10;
~ **floor** primer piso, 10
fish pescar (qu), 7; pez (*m.*) (*alive*); pescado (*caught*), 9
fit apto(a); **It fits nicely / badly.** Me queda bien / mal. 8
five cinco, P;
~ **hundred** quinientos(as), 8;
~ **thousand** cinco mil, 8

flash drive la memoria flash, el pendrive, 4
flat llano(a)
flavor sabor (*m.*)
floating flotador(a)
floor piso; **first ~** primer piso, 10
flour harina, 9
flourish florecer (zc)
flower florecer (zc); flor (*f.*)
fold doblar, 6

following siguiente
fondness cariño
food comida, 6
food processor procesador (*m.*) de comida, 10
fool engañar
foot: on ~ a pie, 6
football fútbol americano, 7
footprint huella
for para, por, 10; ~ **example** por ejemplo, 10
forbid prohibir, 10

fork tenedor (*m.*), 9
fortress fortaleza
forty cuarenta, P
forum foro, 4
founder fundador(a)
four cuatro, P; ~ **hundred** cuatrocientos(as), 8
fourteen catorce, P
fourth cuarto(a), 10
free libre
freezer congelador (*m.*), 10
French francés (francesa), 2;
~ **fries** papas fritas, 9;
~ **language** francés (*m.*), 3
frequently frecuentemente, 4
fresh fresco(a), 9
Friday viernes (*m.*), 2
fried frito(a), 9
friend amigo(a), P; cuate(a)
from the del (de + el), 3
front: in ~ of delante de, frente a, enfrente de, 6
frozen congelado(a), 9
fruit fruta, 6; ~ **juice** jugo de fruta, 9; ~ **salad** ensalada de fruta, 9; ~ **shake** licuado de fruta
fry freír (i, i), 9
fun divertido(a), 2
function funcionar, 4
funny cómico(a), 2

furious furioso(a), 4
furniture muebles (*m. pl.*), 10

G

gallon galón (*m.*), 9
game partido, 7; **interactive ~** juego interactivo, 4
gang pandilla
garage garaje (*m.*), 10
garbage basura, 10
garden jardín (*m.*), 10
garlic ajo, 9
generally por lo general, 9
generous generoso(a), 2
genre género
gentle apacible
geography geografía, 3
German alemán (alemana), 2;
~ **language** alemán (*m.*), 3
get conseguir (i, i), 8;
~ **ahead** adelantar;
~ **cold** enfriarse, 9;
~ **divorced** divorciarse, 5;
~ **down from** bajar, 6;
~ **dressed** vestirse (i, i), 5;
~ **engaged** comprometerse, 5;
~ **married** casarse, 5;
~ **off of** (*a bus, etc.*) bajar, 6;
~ **on** subir, 6;
~ **ready** prepararse, 5;
~ **separated** separarse, 5;
~ **sick** enfermarse, 5;
~ **together** reunirse, 5;
~ **up** levantarse, 5
gift regalo
girl chica, P; muchacha, P; niña, P
girlfriend novia
give dar (*irreg.*), 5;
~ **as a gift** regalar, 8;
~ **directions** decir (*irreg.*) cómo llegar, 6; ~ **personal information** dar (*irreg.*) información personal, 1;
~ **preference** anteponer;
~ **someone a bath** bañar, 5;
~ **the time** dar (*irreg.*) la hora, 3
glass vaso, 9
glove guante (*m.*), 8
go acudir; ir (*irreg.*), 3;
~ **away** irse (*irreg.*), 5;
~ **off** (*alarm clock, etc.*) sonar (ue), 4; ~ **offline** cortar la conexión, 4; ~ **online** hacer (*irreg.*) una conexión, 4;

~ out salir (*irreg.*), 5; **~ shopping** hacer (*irreg.*) las compras, 6; ir de compras, 8; **~ straight** seguir (i, i) (g) derecho; **~ to bed** acostarse (ue), 5; **~ up** subir, 6

goal meta

gold oro, 8

golden dorado(a), 9

golf golf (*m.*), 7

good bueno(a), 2; bondadoso(a)

goodbye adiós, 1

gossip chisme (*m.*)

gossiping chismoso(a)

governor gobernador(a)

grade nota, P

granddaughter nieta, 5

grandfather abuelo, 5

grandmother abuela, 5

grandson nieto, 5

grape uva, 9

graph gráfica

gray gris, 4

great chévere (*Cuba, Puerto Rico*); grande, 2

greater mayor, 8

green verde, 4

greet saludar, 1

greeting saludo

grilled asado(a); a la parrilla, 9

ground molido(a), 9; tierra

group (*m.*) conjunto; **group** (*v.*) juntar

growth crecimiento

Guatemalan guatemalteco(a), 2

guess adivinar; **Guess.** Adivina. P

guinea pig cuy (*m.*)

guitar guitarra, 2

gymnasium gimnasio, 3

H

hair: blond ~ pelo rubio, 2; **brown ~** pelo castaño, 2

hairdresser peluquero(a), 5

half mitad (*f.*)

half-brother medio hermano, 5

half-sister media hermana, 5

hallway pasillo, 10

ham jamón (*m.*), 6

hamburger hamburguesa, 9

handicrafts artesanía

handkerchief pañuelo

handsome hermoso(a); guapo(a), 2

handtowel toalla de mano, 5

happiness dicha; felicidad (*f.*)

happy contento(a), 4

hard duro(a); **~ drive** disco duro, 4

hardly ever rara vez

hardware hardware (*m.*), 4

hard-working trabajador(a), 2

haste prisa

hat sombrero, 8

hatred odio

have tener (*irreg.*), 1; **~ a fight** pelearse, 5; **~ a soft drink** tomar un refresco, 2; **~ fun** divertirse (ie, i), 5; **~ the urge to** tener (*irreg.*) ganas de, 7; **~ to** (+ *inf.*) tener (*irreg.*) que (+ *inf.*), 1

he él, 1

health salud (*f.*), 3

healthy saludable

hear oír (*irreg.*), 5

heat calentar (ie), 9

heavy fuerte, 9

height altitud (*f.*), altura; (*of a person*) estatura

hello hola, ¿Aló? (*on the phone*), 1

helmet casco

help ayudar; ayuda

her (*pron.*) ella, 8; (*adj.*) su, 3; suyo(a), 10; **to / for ~** le, 8

here aquí, 6

heritage herencia

hers (*pron.*) suyo(a), 10

hide esconder

hike hacer (*irreg.*) alpinismo, practicar (qu) alpinismo, 7

him (*pron.*) él, 8; **to / for ~** le, 8

his (*adj.*) su, 3; (*adj., pron.*) suyo(a), 10

Hispanic hispano(a)

history historia, 3

hoax engaño

hockey: field ~ hockey (*m.*) sobre hierba, 7; **ice ~** hockey (*m.*) sobre hielo, 7

hole pozo

home hogar (*m.*)

homeless sin hogar

homemade casero(a)

homework tarea, P

Honduran hondureño(a), 2

honest honesto(a)

hope esperanza; esperar, 10

hospital hospital (*m.*), 6

hot: be ~ tener (*irreg.*) calor, 7; **~ dog** perro caliente, 9; **It's ~.** Hace calor. 7

hour hora

house casa, 6; **the ~ special** la especialidad de la casa, 9

housechore quehacer (*m.*) doméstico, 10

housing vivienda

how? ¿cómo? 3; **~ are things going?** ¿Qué tal? 1; **~ are you?** (*form. s.*) ¿Cómo está (usted)? / (*form. pl.*) ¿Cómo están (ustedes)? / (*s. fam.*) ¿Cómo estás (tú)? 1; **~ can I help you?** ¿En qué puedo servirle? 8; **~ do you say . . . ?** ¿Cómo se dice...? P; **~ do you wish to pay?** ¿Cómo desea pagar?, 8; **~ many?** ¿cuántos(as)? 3; **~ much?** ¿cuánto(a)? 3; **~ much does it cost?** ¿Cuánto cuesta? 8; **How's it going with you?** ¿Cómo te / le(s) va? 1

humanities humanidades (*f. pl.*), 3

humble humilde

humid húmedo(a)

hunger hambre (*f. but* el hambre)

hurry prisa; **be in a ~** tener (*irreg.*) prisa, 7

husband esposo, 5

hymn himno

I

I yo, 1

ice: (vanilla / chocolate) ~ cream helado (de vainilla / de chocolate), 9; **~ hockey** hockey (*m.*) sobre hielo, 7; **~ skate** patinar sobre hielo, 7

identity identidad (*f.*)

immigration inmigración (*f.*)

impatient impaciente, 2

impressive impresionante

impulsive impulsivo(a), 2

in en; por, 10; **~ charge of** encargado de; **~ order to** (+ *inf.*) para, 10; **~ relation to** en cuanto a; **~ short** en resumen; **~ spite of** a pesar de; **~ the direction of** para, 10; **the "in" place** "antro"

inch pulgada
increase acrecentar (ie), aumentar
incredible increíble
indefinite indefinido(a), 1
index índice (m.)
Indian indio(a), 2
indigenous indígena
influence influir (y); influencia
ingredient ingrediente (m.), 9
inhabitant habitante (m., f.)
in-laws familia política, 5
inline skate (rollerblade) patinar en línea, 7
inside of dentro de, 6; ~ **the house** dentro de la casa, 10
insist insistir, 10
install instalar, 4
instead of en vez de
instructor instructor(a), P
intelligent inteligente, 2
intention fin (m.)
interactive whiteboard pizarra interactiva, P
interest interesar, 4
interesting interesante, 2
Internet Internet (m. or f.), red (f.); ~ **provider** proveedor (m.) de acceso, 4
interpreter intérprete (m., f.)
intimate íntimo(a)
introduce someone presentar a alguien, 1
introverted introvertido(a), 2
invest invertir
iron planchar, 10; (metal) hierro; (appliance) plancha, 10
irresponsible irresponsable, 2
Italian italiano(a), 2; ~ **language** italiano, 3
its (adj.) su, 3; (pron.) suyo(a), 10

J

jacket (*suit jacket, blazer*) saco; (*outdoor, non-suit coat*) chaqueta 8
January enero, 1
Japanese japonés (japonesa), 2; ~ **language** japonés (m.), 3
jealous celoso(a); **be** ~ tener (irreg.) celos
jealously celosamente
jeans jeans (m. pl.), 8
jewelry store joyería, 6
jewelry joyas (f. pl.), 8

join juntarse
joke broma
journalism periodismo, 3
journalist periodista (m., f.), 5
July julio, 1
June junio, 1

K

keep: (oneself) separate mantenerse apartado
key (on a keyboard) tecla, 4
keyboard teclado, 4
kilo kilo, 9; **half a** ~ medio kilo, 9
kind bondadoso(a)
king rey (m.)
kiss besar
kitchen cocina, 10
knapsack mochila, P
knife cuchillo, 9
know: ~ **a person** conocer (zc), 5; ~ **a fact,** ~ **how to** saber (irreg.), 5
Korean coreano(a), 2

L

lake lago, 7
lamp lámpara, 10
language idioma (m.), lengua, 3
laptop computer computadora portátil, P
late tarde, 3
later luego, 5
latest: the ~ lo último
laugh reírse (irreg.), 5
laundry room lavandería, 10
lawn césped (m.), 10; **mow the** ~ cortar el césped, 10
lawyer abogado(a), 5
lazy perezoso(a), 2
learn aprender, 3
learning aprendizaje (m.)
leather piel (f.), cuero, 8
leave dejar, 2; salir (irreg.), irse (irreg.), 5
left: to the ~ a la izquierda, 6
lemonade limonada, 9
less menor, 8; ~ **than** menos que, 8
lesson lección (f.), P
level nivel (m.)
life vida
lifejacket salvavidas (m. s.)

lift levantar, 5; ~ **weights** levantar pesas, 2
light luz (f.); (adj.) ligero(a), 9
like gustar; ~ **a lot** encantar, 4; (**They / You** [pl.]) ~ . . . A... les gusta... 2; **He / She likes** . . . A... le gusta... 2; **I / You** ~ . . . A mí / ti me / te gusta... 2; **I'd** ~ (+ inf.) quisiera (+ inf.), 6; Me gustaría (+ inf.) 6
Likewise. Igualmente. 1
linen lino, 8
linguistic lingüístico(a)
link enlace (m.), 4
lip labio
listen escuchar; ~ **to music** escuchar música, 2; ~ **to the audio** Escuchen el audio. P
liter litro, 9
literature literatura, 3
little poco, 4
live vivir, 3, ocupar
livestock ganadería
living room sala, 10
loan préstamo, 8; (v.) prestar, 8
lobster langosta, 9
located ubicado(a); **is** ~ queda
long for apetecer (zc)
look: ~ **for** buscar (qu), 2
lose perder (ie), 4; ~ **oneself** perderse (ie)
love querer (irreg.), 4; amar; amor (m.), cariño
lover amante (m., f.)
lunch almuerzo, 9
luxurious lujoso(a)
lying mentiroso(a), 2

M

made: It's ~ out of . . . Está hecho(a) de... 8; **They're** ~ **out of** . . . Están hechos(as) de... 8
magazine revista
mailbox buzón (m.)
majority mayoría
make hacer (irreg.), 5; ~ **sure** asegurarse; ~ **the bed** hacer la cama, 10
makeup maquillaje (m.), 5
mall centro comercial, 6
man hombre (m.), P
manager gerente (m., f.), 5
manly varonil

manners modales (*m. pl.*)
March marzo, 1
marital status estado civil
mark marcar (qu)
market mercado, 6; **open-air ~ ,
farmer's ~** mercado al aire
libre, 6
marketing mercadeo, 3
masculine masculino(a)
match emparejar; (*sports*)
partido, 7
mathematics matemáticas
(*f. pl.*), 3
matter (to someone) importar, 4
May mayo, 1
mayonnaise mayonesa, 9
mayor alcalde (alcaldesa)
me mí, 8; **to / for ~** me, 8;
with ~ conmigo, 8
mean: It means . . . Significa… P
meaning significado
means of transportation medios
de transporte, 6
measure medir (i, i)
measurement medida, 9
meat carne (*f.*), 9
meatball albóndiga
mechanic mecánico(a), 5
media center centro de
comunicaciones, 3
medicine medicina, 3
meditation meditación (*f.*)
meet conocer (zc), reunirse, 5
meeting encuentro, reunión (*f.*)
melon melón (*m.*), 9
menu menú (*m.*), 9
messenger mensajero(a)
Mexican mexicano(a), 2
microphone micrófono, 4
microwave microondas (*m. s.*), 10
midnight medianoche (*f.*), 3
mild apacible
milk leche (*f.*), 6
mine (*pron.*) mío, 10
mirror espejo, 10
Miss señorita (*abbrev.* Srta.), 1
missionary misionero(a)
mix mezclar, 9; mezcla
mixed mixto(a)
modem: external / internal ~
módem (*m.*) externo /
interno, 4
Monday lunes (*m.*), 3
money dinero
monitor monitor (*m.*), 4
monkey mono

month mes (*m.*), 3; **last ~** mes
pasado, 7
mop the floor trapear el piso, 10
more más; **~ than** más que, 8
morning mañana, 3; **during the ~**
por la mañana, 3; **Good ~.**
Buenos días. 1; **in the ~**
(*with precise time*) de la
mañana, 3
mortality mortalidad (*f.*)
mother madre (*f.*), mamá, 5;
Mother's Day día (*m.*) de las
Madres, 3
mother-in-law suegra, 5
mountain monte (*m.*);
~ range cordillera
mountainous montañoso(a)
mouse ratón (*m.*), 4
move (*change residence*)
mudarse
mow the lawn cortar el
césped, 10
Mr. señor (*abbrev.* Sr.), 1
Mrs. señora (*abbrev.* Sra.), 1
Ms. señorita (*abbrev.* Srta.), 1
much mucho, 4
mud lodo
museum museo, 6
music música, 3
mustard mostaza, 9
my (*adj.*) mi, 3; (*pron.*) mío(a), 10;
~ pleasure. Mucho gusto. Un
placer. 1

N

name llamar, 2; nombre (*m.*);
full ~ nombre (*m.*) completo;
My ~ is . . . Me llamo…, Mi
nombre es…, 1
napkin servilleta, 9
narrator narrador(a)
nationality nacionalidad (*f.*), 2
nature naturaleza
navigation navegación (*f.*)
necklace collar (*m.*), 8
need necesitar, 2
neighbor vecino(a), 6
neighborhood barrio, colonia, 1
neither tampoco, 2; **~ . . .
nor** ni… ni, 6
nephew sobrino, 5
nervous nervioso(a), 4
never nunca, 5; jamás, 6
nevertheless sin embargo
new novedoso(a)

news: ~ group grupo de
noticias, 4
newspaper periódico
next próximo(a); **~ to** al lado
de, 6; **~ to last** penúltimo(a)
Nicaraguan nicaragüense
(*m., f.*), 2
nice simpático(a), 2
nickname apodo
niece sobrina, 5
night noche (*f.*), 3; **Good ~.**
Buenas noches. 1; **last ~**
anoche, 7
nine hundred novecientos(as), 8
nine nueve, P
nineteen diecinueve, P
ninety noventa, P
ninth noveno(a), 10
no one nadie, 6
nobody nadie, 6
none ningún, ninguno(a), 6
noodle soup sopa de fideos, 9
noon mediodía (*m.*), 3
normal normal, 4
North America Norteamérica
not: ~ any ningún, ninguno(a),
6; **~ either** tampoco, 2;
~ much no mucho, 1
notebook cuaderno, P
notes apuntes (*m. pl.*), P
nothing nada, 1
noun sustantivo
novel novedoso(a)
novelist novelista (*m., f.*)
November noviembre, 1
novice novato(a)
number número, 8
nurse enfermero(a), 5

O

obey hacer (*irreg.*) caso
obtain conseguir (i, i), 8
October octubre, 1
of: ~ course cómo no, 6; por
supuesto, 10; **~ the** del
(de + el), 3
offer: special ~ oferta
especial, 8
office oficina, 6
old viejo(a), 2
old-fashioned anticuado(a)
olive oil aceite (*m.*) de oliva, 9
on en, sobre, encima de, 6;
~ behalf of por, 10
once una vez, 9

one uno, P; **~ hundred** cien, P; **~ hundred and ~** ciento uno, 8; **~ hundred thousand** cien mil, 8; **~ million** millón (*m.*), un millón, 8; **~ thousand** mil (*m.*), 8

onion cebolla, 9

online en línea, 4

only único(a)

open abrir, 3; **~ your books.** Abran los libros. P

opposite enfrente de, frente a, 6; opuesto(a)

orange (*color*) anaranjado(a), 4; (*fruit*) naranja, 9

order ordenar, 9; mandar, 10

ordinal number número ordinal, 10

originate originar

ought deber (+ *inf.*), 3

our (*adj.*) nuestro(a)(s), 3

ours (*pron.*) nuestro(a)(s), 10

outline bosquejo

outside of fuera de, 6; **~ the house** fuera de la casa, 10

outskirts afueras (*f. pl.*), 10

outstanding sobresaliente

oven horno

overcoming superación (*f.*)

owner dueño(a), 5

P

package paquete (*m.*), 9

page página, P

paint pintar, 2

painting pintura, 3; cuadro, 10

Panamanian panameño(a), 2

pants pantalones (*m. pl.*), 8

paper papel (*m.*), P

parachute paracaídas (*m. s.*)

paragraph párrafo

Paraguayan paraguayo(a), 2

Pardon me. Con permiso. 4

parents padres (*m. pl.*), 5

park parque (*m.*), 6

parking lot estacionamiento, 6

parsley perejil (*m.*)

pass (by) pasar, 2

password contraseña, 4

patient paciente (*m., f.*), 2

patio patio, 10

paving stone baldosa

pay pagar (gu), 9; **~ attention** hacer (*irreg.*) caso

payment: form of ~ método de pago, 8

PDF file archivo PDF, 4

pea guisante (*m.*), 9

peace paz (*f.*)

peel pelar, 9

pencil lápiz (*m.*), P

penguin pingüino

people gente (*f.*)

pepper pimienta, 9

percentage porcentaje (*m.*)

perhaps quizás, tal vez

period (*punctuation*) punto; trecho

permit permitir, 10

personality personalidad (*f.*); **~ trait** característica de la personalidad, 2

Peruvian peruano(a), 2

pharmacy farmacia, 6

philanthropic filantrópico(a)

philosophy filosofía, 3

photo foto (*f.*), P

physical físico(a), 5; **~ appearance** apariencia física; **~ trait** característica física, 2

physics física, 3

piano piano, 2

picturesque pintoresco(a)

piece pedazo, 9

pillow almohada

pink rosado(a), 4

pirate pirata (*m.*)

pizzeria pizzería, 6

place lugar (*m.*), sitio

plaid a cuadros, 8

plain llanura

plate plato, 9

play jugar (ue) (gu), 4; **~ a musical instrument** tocar (qu) un instrumento musical, 2; **~ sports** practicar (qu) deportes, 2; **~ tennis (baseball, etc.)** jugar tenis (béisbol, etc), 7

playful juguetón (juguetona)

plaza plaza, 6

please por favor, 1

pleasure: A ~ to meet you. Mucho gusto en conocerte. 1

plot trama

plumber plomero(a), 5

poet poeta (poetisa)

poetry poesía

point: ~ out marcar (qu), señalar; **to the ~** al grano

policeman (policewoman) policía (*m., f.*), 5

political político(a); **~ science** ciencias políticas (*f. pl.*), 3

polka-dotted de lunares, 8

poor pobre

populate poblar (ue)

pork chop chuleta de puerco, 6

portable CD / MP3 player CD portátil / MP3, P

Portuguese portugués (portuguesa), 2

post office oficina de correos, 6

potato: ~ chips papitas fritas, 6; **~ salad** ensalada de papa

pound libra, 9

power poder (*m.*)

powerful poderoso(a)

practice practicar (qu)

prefer preferir (ie, i), 4

preference preferencia

prenuptial agreement contrato prenupcial

preparation preparación (*f.*), 9

prepare preparar, 2; **~ the food** preparar la comida, 10

preposition preposición (*f.*), 6

present (*gift*) regalo; **at the ~ time** en la actualidad

pretty bonito(a); lindo(a), 2

price: It's a very good ~. Está a muy buen precio. 8

priest sacerdote (*m.*)

prime rib lomo de res, 9

print imprimir, 3; (*patterned fabric*) estampado(a), 8; (*art*) cuadro, 10

printer impresora, 4

prize premio

profession profesión (*f.*), 5

professor profesor(a), P

program programa (*m.*); **anti-virus ~** programa antivirus, 4; **~ icon** ícono del programa, 4

programmer programador(a), 5

projector proyector, P

promote adelantar, promover (ue)

pronoun pronombre (*m.*), 1

proud orgulloso(a)

provocative provocador(a)

psychology psicología, 3

public: ~ communications comunicación (*f.*) pública, 3; **~ relations** publicidad (*f.*), 3

Puerto Rican puertorriqueño(a), 2

purple morado(a), 4

purpose propósito
purse bolsa, 8
push oprimir
put poner (*irreg.*), 5; **~ away the clothes** guardar la ropa, 10; **~ my toys where they belong** poner mis juguetes en su lugar, 10; **~ on (clothing)** ponerse (la ropa), 5; **~ on makeup** maquillarse, 5

Q

quality calidad (*f.*); **of good (high) ~** de buena (alta) calidad, 8
queen reina
questionnaire cuestionario
quotation cita

R

raffle sorteo
railroad ferrocarril (*m.*)
rain llover (ue); **~ forest** bosque (*m.*) tropical, bosque (*m.*) pluvial; **It's raining.** Está lloviendo. (Llueve.), 7
raincoat impermeable (*m.*), 8
raise levantar, 5
ranch estancia
rank rango
rather bastante, 4
raw crudo(a), 9
razor rasuradora, 5; **electric ~** máquina de afeitar, 5
read leer (y), 3; **~ Chapter 1.** Lean el Capítulo 1. P
really de veras
reason razón (*f.*)
receive recibir, 3
recipe receta, 9
recognize reconocer (zc)
recommend recomendar (ie), 10
record grabar, 4
recruit alistar
recycling reciclaje (*m.*), 10
red rojo(a), 4
redheaded pelirrojo(a), 2
reduced: It's ~. Está rebajado(a). 8
reflect reflejar
reflection reflexión (*f.*)
refrigerator refrigerador (*m.*), 10
relate contar (ue), 4
relative pariente (*m., f.*), 5

relax relajarse, 5
remain quedar(se)
remember recordar (ue)
renovate renovar (ue)
renown renombre (*m.*)
rent alquiler (*m.*); **~ videos** alquilar videos, 2; **~ movies** alquilar películas, 2
repeat repetir (i, i), 4; **~.** Repitan. P
report informe (*m.*)
request pedir (i, i), 10
require requerir (ie, i), 10
residential neighborhood barrio residencial, 10
resort to recurrir
respond responder, 1
responsible responsable, 2
rest descansar, 2
restaurant restaurante (*m.*), 6
return regresar, 2; volver (ue), 4
revenue ingreso
rhyme rima
rich adinerado(a)
ride montar; **~ a bike** montar en bicicleta, 7; **~ horseback** montar a caballo, 7
right: to the ~ a la derecha, 6
ring sonar (ue), 4; anillo, 8; sortija
ripped rasgado
risk riesgo
river río, 7
roasted (in the oven) al horno, 9
role papel (*m.*)
roof techo, 10
room cuarto, P **roommate** compañero(a) de cuarto, P
root raíz (*f.*)
rose rosa, 4
rough draft borrador (*m.*)
route ruta
row remar, 7
rower remero(a)
rude descortés
rug alfombra, 10
rule regla
run correr, 3
rural campestre

S

sad triste, 4
safe seguro(a), 7

said: It's said . . . Se dice..., P
salad ensalada, 9; **lettuce and tomato ~** ensalada de lechuga y tomate, 9; **tossed ~** ensalada mixta, 9
sale: It's on ~. Está en venta. 8
salesclerk dependiente (*m., f.*), 5
salmon salmón (*m.*), 9
salt sal (*f.*), 9
Salvadoran salvadoreño(a), 2
same mismo(a); **~ (thing)** lo mismo
sandal sandalia, 8
sandwich bocadillo, sandwich (*m.*), 9; **ham and cheese ~ with avocado** sandwich de jamón y queso con aguacate, 9
Saturday sábado, 2
sausage salchicha, 6
save guardar, 4
say decir (*irreg.*), 5; **~ good-bye** despedirse (i, i), 1
saying dicho
scan ojear
scarcely apenas
scarf bufanda, 8
scenery paisaje (*m.*)
schedule horario
school escuela, 3
science ciencia, 3
scientific científico(a)
scream gritar; grito
screen pantalla, 4
script guión (*m.*); **~ writer** guionista (*m., f.*)
search engine buscador (*m.*), 4
season estación (*f.*), 7; **dry ~** temporada de secas; **rainy ~** temporada de lluvias
second segundo(a), 10
secret secreto
secretary secretario(a), 5
sections tramos
see ver (*irreg.*), 5; **~ you at the usual place?** ¿Nos vemos donde siempre? 1; **~ you later.** Hasta luego. Nos vemos. 1; **~ you soon.** Hasta pronto. 1; **~ you tomorrow.** Hasta mañana. 1
seem parecer (zc)
selfish egoísta, 2
sell vender, 3
send enviar, 4; mandar, 8
sentence oración (*f.*)
separate apartado

September septiembre, 1
serious serio(a), 2
serve servir (i, i), 4
set the table poner (*irreg.*) la mesa, 9
seven siete, P; **~ hundred** setecientos(as), 8
seventeen diecisiete, P
seventh séptimo(a), 10
seventy setenta, P
several varios(as)
shame vergüenza
shampoo champú (*m.*), 5
share compartir, 3
shark tiburón (*m.*)
shave oneself afeitarse, 5
she ella, 1
sheet of paper hoja de papel, P
shellfish marisco, 9
shelter albergar (gu)
shirt camisa, 8
shoe zapato, 8; **high-heeled ~** zapato de tacón alto, 8; **tennis ~** zapato de tenis, 8
shooting tiroteo
shore orilla
short (*in length*) corto(a); (*in height*) bajo(a), 2
shorts pantalones (*m. pl.*) cortos, 8
should deber (+ *inf.*), 3
shout gritar
show demostrar (ue), mostrar (ue)
shred picar (qu), 9
shrimp camarón (*m.*), 9
shy tímido(a), 2
sick enfermo(a), 4
side lado; **on the ~ of** al lado de, 6
sign letrero
silk seda, 8
silly tonto(a), 2
silver plata, 8
similarity semejanza
simple sencillo(a)
sincere sincero(a), 2
sing cantar, 2
singer cantante (*m., f.*)
single soltero(a)
sister (younger, older) hermana (menor, mayor), 5
sister-in-law cuñada, 5
sit down sentarse (ie), 5
six seis, P; **~ hundred** seiscientos(as), 8

sixteen dieciséis, P
sixth sexto(a), 10
sixty sesenta, P
size talla, 8
skate patinar, 2
ski esquiar, 7; esquí (*m.*)
skiing esquí (*m.*); **downhill ~** esquí alpino, 7; **water ~** esquí acuático, 7
skin tez (*f.*)
skirt falda, 8
slave esclavo(a)
sleep dormir (ue, u), 4
slice pedazo, 9
slogan lema (*m.*)
slow lento(a), 4
slowly despacio
small pequeño(a), 2; **a ~ amount** un poco, 4
smartphone teléfono inteligente, smartphone, 4
smile sonreír (*irreg.*), 8; sonrisa
snack merienda
snow nevar (ie); **It's snowing.** Está nevando. (Nieva.), 7
snowboard tabla de snowboard, 7
snowboarding snowboarding, 7
so por eso, 10
soap jabón (*m.*), 5
soccer fútbol (*m.*), 7; **~ field** cancha, campo de fútbol, 6
social: media director director(a) de social media, 5; **~ networking site** red social, 4
sock calcetín (*m.*), 8
sofa sofá (*m.*), 10
soft suave; **~ drink** refresco, 6
software software (*m.*), 4
solved resuelto
some unos(as), 1; algún, alguno(a), 6
someone alguien, 6
something algo, 6; **~ vegan** algo vegano, 9
sometimes de vez en cuando; a veces, 5
somewhat bastante, 4
son hijo, 5
son-in-law yerno, 5
sorry: I'm sorry. Lo siento. 4
So-so. Regular. 1
soul alma (*f.*) (*but* el alma)
sound sonido
soup sopa, 9; **cold ~** gazpacho (*Spain*), 9

source fuente (*f.*)
South America Sudamérica
souvenir recuerdo
sovereignty soberanía
spa balneario
Spain España
Spanish español (a), 2; **~ language** español (*m.*), 3
Spanish-speaking hispanohablante
speaker conferencista (*m., f.*); altoparlante (*m., f.*), 4
species especie (*f.*)
spelling ortografía
spicy picante, 9
sponsor patrocinador(a)
spoon cuchara, 9
sport deporte (*m.*), 7; **~ activity** actividad (*f.*) deportiva, 7
sporting goods store tienda de equipo deportivo, 6
sports coat saco, 8
spring primavera, 7
stadium estadio, 6
stairs escaleras (*f. pl.*), 10
state estado, 5
station estación (*f.*); **train / bus ~** estación de trenes / autobuses, 6
stationery store papelería, 6
statistics estadística, 3
steak bistec (*m.*), 6
steamed al vapor, 9
steel acero
step on pisar
stepbrother hermanastro, 5
stepfather padrastro, 5
stepmother madrastra, 5
stepsister hermanastra, 5
still todavía; **~ life** naturaleza muerta
stop (*e.g., bus stop*) parada; **~ (doing something)** dejar de (+ *inf.*), 2; parar (de), 3
store guardar; almacén (*m.*), tienda, 6; **music (clothing, video) ~** tienda de música (ropa, videos), 6
stove estufa, 10
straight ahead todo derecho, 6
straighten out the bedroom arreglar el dormitorio, 10
strategy estrategia
strawberry fresa, 9

street calle (*f.*), 1
strengthen acrecentar (ie)
stringed al hilo, 9
striped rayado(a), a rayas, 8
strong fuerte
student estudiante (*m.*, *f.*), P;
~ **center** centro estudiantil, 6
studio estudio, 3
study estudiar; ~ **at the library
(at home)** estudiar en la
biblioteca (en casa), 2;
~ **pages . . . to . . .**
Estudien las páginas . . .
a . . ., P
stupid tonto(a), 2
style estilo; **in** ~ en onda; **out
of** ~ pasado(a) de moda, 8
substitute sustituir (y)
suburb barrio residencial,
suburbio, 10
subway: on the ~ en metro, 6
success éxito
suddenly de repente, 9
sugar azúcar (*m.*, *f.*), 9;
~ **cane** caña de azúcar
suggest sugerir (ie, i), 8
suggestion sugerencia
suit traje (*m.*), 8; **bathing** ~
traje (*m.*) de baño, 8
summer verano, 7
sun sol (*m.*)
sunbathe tomar el sol, 2
Sunday domingo, 2
sunglasses gafas (*f. pl.*)
de sol, 8
sunlight luz (*f.*) solar
sunny: It's ~. Hace sol. 7
supermarket supermercado, 6
support apoyar
sure seguro(a), 4
surf hacer (*irreg.*) surfing,
practicar (qu) surfing, 7
surpass sobrepasar
surprise sorpresa
surrounded rodeado(a)
survey encuesta
sweater suéter (*m.*), 8;
chompa
sweatsuit sudadera, 8
sweep the floor barrer el suelo /
el piso, 10
sweet dulce (*m.*); (*adj.*)
dulce
swim bañar, 5; nadar, 7
swimming natación (*f.*), 7;
~ **pool** piscina, 6

symbol símbolo
systematic sistemático(a)

T

table mesa, P; **night** ~ mesita
de noche, 10; **set the** ~ poner
(*irreg.*) la mesa, 9
tablecloth mantel (*m.*), 9
tablespoon cucharada, 9
tablet: ~ **computer** tableta, 4
take tomar, llevar; ~ **a
bath** bañarse, 5; ~ **a
shower** ducharse, 5; ~ **off
clothing** quitarse la ropa, 5;
~ **out the garbage** sacar (qu)
la basura, 10; ~ **photos** sacar
(qu) fotos, 2; ~ **place** realizarse
(c); ~ **the dog for a walk**
sacar (qu) a pasear al
perro, 10
talk hablar; ~ **on the telephone**
hablar por teléfono, 2
tall alto(a), 2
tamed domesticado(a)
taste gusto; **to individual** ~ al
gusto, 9
tavern bodegón (*m.*)
tea: hot ~ té (*m.*), 9; **iced** ~ té
(*m.*) helado, 9
teach enseñar
teacher maestro(a), 5
team equipo, 7
tear up rasgar (gu)
teaspoon cucharadita, 9
technology tecnología, 4
television; ~ **set** televisor
(*m.*), 10;
tell contar (ue), 4; decir (*irreg.*),
5; ~ **the time** decir la hora, 3
temperature temperatura, 7
ten diez, P; ~ **thousand** diez
mil, 8
tend tender
tennis tenis (*m.*), 7;
~ **court** cancha de tenis, 6;
~ **shoes** zapatos (*m. pl.*) de
tenis, 8
tenth décimo(a), 10
term término
terrible fatal, terrible, 1
terrific chévere (*Cuba, Puerto
Rico*)
text texto
Thank you very much. Muchas
gracias. 1

that (*adj.*) ese(a), 6; (*pron.*)
ése(a), 6; ~ **over there** (*adj.*)
aquel (aquella), 6; (*pron.*) aquél
(aquélla), 6
that's why por eso, 10
the el, la, los, las, 1
theater teatro, 6
their su, 3; suyo(a), 10
theirs (*pron.*) suyo(a), 10
them ellos(as), 8; **to / for** ~ les, 8
then entonces
theory teoría
there allí, 6; **over** ~ allá, 6; ~ **is /
~ are** hay, 1
these (*adj.*) estos(as), 6; (*pron.*)
éstos(as), 6
they ellos(as), 1
thin delgado(a), 2
think (about) pensar (ie)
(en, de), 4
third tercer(o, a), 10
thirst sed (*f.*)
thirsty: be ~ tener (*irreg.*) sed, 7
thirteen trece, P
thirty treinta, P
this (*adj.*) este(a), 6; (*pron.*)
éste(a), 6
those (*adj.*) esos, 6; (*pron.*)
ésos(as), 6; ~ **(over there)**
(adj.) aquellos(as), 6; (*pron.*)
aquéllos(as), 6
thousands miles
threat amenaza
three tres, P; ~ **hundred**
trescientos(as), 8
through por, 10
throughout a través de
throw: ~ **oneself** lanzarse (c);
~ **out** botar
thunderstorm tormenta
Thursday jueves (*m.*), 3
time hora; vez (*f.*)
times veces (*f. pl.*); **(two, three,
etc.)** ~ **a day / per week** (dos,
tres, etc.) veces al día / por
semana, 5
tip propina, 9
tired cansado(a), 4
title titular; título, 1
to a; **to the** al (a + el), 3
toast pan (*m.*) tostado, 9
toaster tostadora, 10
today hoy, 3; ~ **is Tuesday the
30th.** Hoy es martes treinta. 3
tomorrow mañana, 3
too much demasiado, 4

toothbrush cepillo de dientes, 5
toothpaste pasta de dientes, 5
top: on ~ of encima de, 6
toward para, 10
towel toalla, 5
town pueblo, 6
toy juguete (*m.*), 10
track suit sudadera, 8
train (*for sports*) entrenarse, 7; tren, 6
trainer entrenador(a) (*m.*)
trait característica
translate traducir (zc), 5
traveler's check cheque (*m.*) de viajero, 8
treasure tesoro
tree árbol (*m.*)
trick truco
triumph triunfar
trout trucha, 9
true verdad
truly de veras
trumpet trompeta, 2
try intentar, tratar de; **I'm going to ~ it on.** Voy a probármelo(la). 8
t-shirt camiseta, 8
Tuesday martes (*m.*), 3
tuna atún (*m.*), 9
turkey pavo, 6
turn cruzar (c), doblar, 6; viraje (*m.*); **~ in** entregar; **~ in your homework.** Entreguen la tarea. P; **~ off** apagar (gu), 2
twelve doce, P
twenty veinte, P
twenty-one veintiuno, P
twice dos veces, 9
two dos, P; **~ hundred** doscientos(as), 8; **~ million** dos millones, 8; **~ thousand** dos mil, 8
typical típico(a), 9

U

U.S. citizen estadounidense (*m., f.*), 2
ugly feo(a), 2
uncle tío, 5
underneath debajo de, 6
understand comprender, 3; entender (ie), 4
understanding comprensión (*f.*)
unique único(a)

unite unir, 9
united unido(a); **~ States** Estados Unidos
university universidad (*f.*), 6
unpleasant antipático(a), 2
untamed salvaje
upload subir, cargar, 4
Uruguayan uruguayo(a), 2
us nosotros(as), 8; **to / for ~** nos, 8
use usar, 2
useful útil
user usuario(a), 4

V

vacuum (*verb*) pasar la aspiradora, 10; **~ cleaner** aspiradora, 10
vain vanidoso(a)
valley valle (*m.*)
valuable valioso(a)
value valor (*m.*)
variety variedad (*f.*)
various varios(as)
vegan vegetariano(a) estricto(a), 9
vegetable vegetal (*m.*), 6
vegetarian vegetariano(a)
vehicle vehículo
Venetian blind persiana, 10
Venezuelan venezolano(a), 2
verb verbo, 3
very muy, 2; **~ little** muy poco
vest chaleco, 8
veterinarian veterinario(a), 5
videocamera videocámara, 4
videotape (*noun*) video
viewpoint punto de vista
vinegar vinagre (*m.*), 9
violin violín (*m.*), 2
visit friends visitar a amigos, 2
visitor visitante (*m., f.*)
voice voz (*f.*)
volcanic eruption erupción (*f.*) volcánica
volleyball volibol (*m.*), 7

W

waiter camarero, 5
waitress camarera, 5
wake up despertarse (ie), 5; **wake someone up** despertar (ie), 5
walk caminar, 2; andar (*irreg.*), 8

walking a pie, 6
wall pared (*f.*), P
wallet cartera, 8
want desear, querer (*irreg.*), 10
warm caluroso(a)
warning aviso
wash lavar, 5; **~ one's hair** lavarse el pelo, 5; **~ oneself** lavarse, 5; **~ the dishes (the clothes)** lavar los platos (la ropa), 10
washer lavadora, 10
wastebasket basurero
watch reloj (*m.*), 8; **~ television** mirar televisión, 2
water agua (*f.*) (*but:* el agua); **fresh ~** agua dulce; **sparkling ~** agua mineral, 9; **~ skiing** esquí acuático, 7; **~ the plants** regar (ie) las plantas, 10
watercress berro
waterfall catarata
wave ola
we nosotros(as), 1
wealth riqueza
wealthy adinerado(a)
weather tiempo, 7; **It's nice / bad ~.** Hace buen / mal tiempo. 7
weave tejer
weaving tejido
web red (*f.*); **~ page** página web, 4
webcam cámara web, 4
website sitio web, 4
wedding boda
Wednesday miércoles (*m.*), 3
week semana, 3; **during the ~** entresemana, 3; **every ~** todas las semanas, 5; **last ~** semana pasada, 7
weekend fin (*m.*) de semana, 2
welcome bienvenido(a); **You're ~.** De nada. 1
well bien, 4; **(Not) Very ~.** (No) Muy bien. 1; **Quite ~.** Bastante bien. 1; (*for drawing water*) pozo
well-being bienestar (*m.*)
what? ¿cuál(es)? ¿qué? 3; **~ day is today?** ¿Qué día es hoy? 3; **~ do you like to do?** ¿Qué te gusta hacer? 2; **~ does . . . mean?** ¿Qué significa…? P; **~ is today's date?** ¿A qué

fecha estamos? 3; **~ is your phone number?** ¿Cuál es tu / su número de teléfono? (*s. fam. / form.*), 1; **~ time is it?** ¿Qué hora es? 3; **~'s he / she / it like?** ¿Cómo es? 2; **~'s the weather like?** ¿Qué tiempo hace? 7; **~'s your (e-mail) address?** ¿Cuál es tu / su dirección (electrónica)? (*s. fam. / form.*), 1; **~'s your name?** ¿Cómo se llama (*s. form.*) / te llamas (*s. fam.*)? 1; **~ 's new?** ¿Qué hay de nuevo? 1

whatever cualquier

which? ¿qué? 3; **~ one(s)?** ¿cuál(es)? 3

wheat trigo

wheel rueda

when? ¿cuándo? 3; **~ is your birthday?** ¿Cuándo es tu cumpleaños? 1

where? ¿dónde? 3; **~ (to)?** ¿adónde?; **~ do you live?** ¿Dónde vives / vive? (*s. fam. / form.*), 1; **~ does your . . . class meet?** ¿Dónde tienes la clase de… ? 3

while mientras

white blanco(a), 4

whitewater rafting: go ~ navegar en rápidos, 7

who? ¿quién(es)? 3

whose cuyo(a)(s); **~ are these?** ¿De quiénes son? 3; **~ is this?** ¿De quién es? 3

why? ¿por qué? 3

wife esposa, 5

wifi wifi, 4

wild salvaje

willing dispuesto(a)

win ganar, 7

wind viento

window ventana, P

windy: It's ~. Hace viento. 7

wine: red ~ vino tinto, 9; **white ~** vino blanco, 9

wineglass copa, 9

winter invierno, 7

wireless connection wifi, 4

wish desear, querer (*irreg.*), 10; esperanza

with con

wolf lobo

woman mujer (*f.*), P

wonder maravilla

wood madera

wooden cart carreta

wool lana, 8

word-processing program programa (*m.*) de procesamiento de textos, 4

work trabajar, 2

workday jornada laboral

worker trabajador(a), 5

workshop taller (*m.*)

world mundo; **~ Wide Web** red (*f.*) mundial, 4; **~wide** a nivel mundial

worried preocupado(a), 4

worry preocuparse, 5

worse peor, 8

wrinkled arrugado(a)

write escribir, 3; **~ in your notebooks.** Escriban en sus cuadernos. P

Y

year año, 3; **every ~** todos los años, 9; **last ~** año pasado, 7

yellow amarillo(a), 4

yes sí, 1

yesterday ayer, 3

yogurt yogur (*m.*), 6

you vosotros(as) (*fam. pl.*), tú (*fam. s.*), usted (Ud.) (*form. s.*), ustedes (Uds.) (*fam. or form. pl.*), 1; ti (*fam. s.*), Ud(s). (*form.*), 8; **to / for ~** os (*fam. pl.*), te (*fam. s.*), le (*form. s.*), les (*form, pl.*), 8; **with ~** contigo (*fam.*), 8

young joven, 2

younger menor, 8

your (*adj.*) tu (*fam.*), su (*s. form. pl.*), vuestro(a) (*fam.*), 3; suyo(a) (*form. s., pl.*), tuyo(a) (*fam.*), 10

yours (*pron.*) vuestro(a) (*fam. pl.*), suyo(a) (*form. s., pl.*), tuyo(a) (*fam. s.*), 10

youth juventud (*f.*)

Z

zero cero, P

Index